More Praise for *Present Beyond Measure*

"Lea writes that we should 'present data by design, not by default,' a principle I've taught for years. This book will show you how in a practical and fun way."
—Alberto Cairo, Knight Chair at the University of Miami and author of *The Art of Insight: How Great Visualization Designers Think*

"So you've got your dataset and you have a room full of people to impress with it. What now? This is the starting point of Lea's amazing book. Her inimitable style, uncompromising approach to teaching, and unmatched experience conspire to create THE handbook for today's data practitioners."
—Simo Ahava, Analytics Developer and Co-founder of Simmer and 8-bit-sheep

"*Present Beyond Measure* is written from the trenches by someone who has been there and done that, made the mistakes, and learned the hard way, and is now sharing insider wisdom to all who would read this book. Plus, it's a delight to read because Lea Pica knows how to tell a story."
—Jim Sterne, Author of *Artificial Intelligence for Marketing*

"I've seen Lea Pica capture and engage her audiences with data like no one else. She knows what to do and why it works. This is the book to read if you want to be seen, heard, and valued by your stakeholders too."
—Allison Hartsoe, CEO of Ambition Data

"I've spent years applying the concepts and techniques from Lea's presentations and blog posts both to my own work as an analyst and as a resource and reference as I've coached and guided other analysts. This book packs those ideas and more into a fun and digestible guide for anyone who realizes that an analysis is only as good as the effectiveness with which it is delivered."
—Tim Wilson, Analytics Industry Leader and Co-Host of the Analytics Power Hour Podcast

Present Beyond Measure

Design, Visualize, and Deliver Data Stories That Inspire Action

Lea Pica

WILEY

This book is dedicated to my colleagues, mentors, and dear friends Tim Wilson, the Grumpy Cat of Analytics, and Jim Sterne, the Godfather of Analytics.

Tim's selfless encouragement, mentorship, and dedication to upgrading the analytics community set my fantastic journey as a facilitator into motion.

"You know, you could like, do this for a living," are words that will live on in infamy and gratitude. Thank you for the push, old friend.

Jim, your support at the genesis of my training and speaking career was vital to becoming an engine to serve tens of thousands of practitioners worldwide.

Thank you both for being proponents of the humble mission of this deeply grateful Woman in Analytics.

Contents

Prologue

"Storytelling is the most powerful way to put ideas into the world today."

—Robert McAfee Brown

On January 9, 2007, the CEO of a well-known electronics manufacturer stepped onto the stage of his annual customer conference. Per tradition, he broke the news of products his company was releasing that year. This was always a frantically exciting moment for their customer fan base.

But this year was different.

He announced three new products that he predicted would change the way the world communicates forever. It was a bold statement, which this man was no stranger to making.

He hinted that these three new products were an MP3 player, a touchscreen phone, and a breakthrough communications device. These were all products his company had released before, so nothing was new or notable there.

Then, he delivered the punchline.

He began repeating the three new products in an accelerating sequence that seemed odd at first. But after several repetitions, one could hear the flash of awareness dawning upon the audience. In his famous words:

"These are not three separate devices. They are *one* device."

The audience broke out into thunderous applause as this god of technology unveiled his magical new toy in blazing color on the giant screen. His masterful storytelling was complete, and history was made in announcing a product that would go on to enrapture millions, disrupt and make entire industries obsolete, and, as promised, forever change the way we communicate.

By now, you may have guessed that the presenter was Steve Jobs, the event was Macworld, and the product announcement was for the very first iPhone.

In addition to the hundreds of millions of views this keynote has amassed on YouTube, experts in the field of public speaking cite this as one of the most incredible acts of business storytelling of all time.[1]

---

[1]Gallo, Carmine. "5 Reasons Why Steve Jobs's iPhone Keynote Is Still the Best Presentation of All Time." Inc.com. Inc., June 29, 2017. www.inc.com/carmine-gallo/5-reasons-why-steve-jobs-iphone-keynote-is-still-the-best-presentation-of-all-ti.html.

With that stage set, I present a more personal experience that may sound all too familiar to you.

In my former life working in the advertising agency of a Fortune 500 finance firm, I watched a colleague stand in front of a conference room packed with our most senior stakeholders, including the department president.

It was a quarterly media campaign presentation (or "readout" as they're known in the data field), and the audience was eagerly waiting to hear the results of their significant investment in digital advertising.

What I'd hoped to see was my colleague confidently stepping into the room, warmly greeting the audience, and engaging everyone with an insightful dive into the data story.

Instead, they nervously stumbled through a series of jumbled, visually over-whelming slides; spoke in complex technical terms; and couldn't remember why certain slides were in there! The audience quickly became confused and impatient and began frequently checking their watches and BlackBerry devices (yikes, I'm old).

It was painful to witness, and it was at that moment I realized something was going very wrong with business presentations.

The experience was representative of the data presentations I was both attending and delivering, and as you can see, these two scenarios show a stark contrast. And perhaps, since you're here reading this right now, this scenario feels uncomfortably familiar. Maybe this one does as well:

Data and information play a crucial role in your job.

You either crunch data for a living and feed it to people or have people who crunch data feed it to you. And, you're routinely mandated to show up in a live or virtual conference room to present your crunched data to a bunch of important-looking people called *stakeholders*.

Not only do you have to stand there and calmly deliver your data, but you also need to make them understand it, care about it, and get them to act on it.

Oh, and wouldn't it be *so* nice if they recognized you for your hard work, too?

You may enjoy this essential part of your role immensely. But you also may loathe it, wishing you could be a chameleon and blend into the walls of your cubicle every time your boss asks you to present at the next quarterly business review.

You may loathe it because it proves to be, time and time again, the least rewarding part of your job. Instead of being showered with appreciation, insightful questions, and action. . .

. . .people look more confused leaving the conference room than entering it. Worse yet, your audience has visibly transformed into something much more terrifying.

Glazed eyeballs, vacant expressions, a dribble of drool, and the telltale "browser tab eye dart." It isn't pretty. Your stakeholders are now the unwitting victims of an affliction affecting billions of business meetings worldwide.

I call it *data presentation zombification.*

By the end of that meeting, you're not exactly sure what all that hard work has amounted to other than spawning a zombie infestation. You know how valuable your skills and insights are. You see the value your agency team has contributed to your clients' successes.

The ultimate question is, do *they* see it?

So, you spend day after day wondering if your contribution mattered. No visible progress in improving business strategies, no tangible action taken on optimization test results. You begin to wonder if all that hard work has flown into what I call the dreaded *data black hole.*

And it's only gotten worse. As the world plunged into disorganized chaos due to the coronavirus pandemic, practitioners and companies worldwide scrambled to continue the vital process of sharing critical business data by taking all presentations online. With that effort came a deluge of virtual presentation problems for which the global workforce was utterly unprepared. As a result, staying visible became more critical than ever as we go into a new normal of blended office locations.

Right now, it might all feel like too much. You may be wondering what's in it for you other than a steady paycheck, which may not feel so steady if your organization doesn't recognize your contribution.

Why Are You Here?

I'm guessing you're here because you're ready and able to join the Marketing or data and analytics A-Team, the elite special forces who are brought in at the start of every project and asked for their sage advice. You want to become an invaluable asset whom managers, teams, and even companies fight over. But you have no idea how to get there.

Am I close?

If so, this is the right book for exactly where you are right now.

It was written specifically for data practitioners, marketing professionals, and leaders just like you, as you embark upon your journey to go from crunching numbers in a back room to an invaluable team player and influential thought leader. It means you are willing to throw everything you know about PowerPoint and slides and charts into the fire and start from scratch with a beginner's mind.

If you follow these steps, it will get you there.

In the pages that follow, I teach you everything you need to know, soup to nuts, about how to create, design, and deliver in-person and virtual data presentations. You hold in your hands the bible of data presentation that I wish I'd had when I began my career, and you will use these tools to engage your audiences, get them to understand your insights, and act on your recommendations.

The Way Out Is Through

I have a disclaimer. There is some friendly advice yet tough love ahead. The mission of this book is to create awareness of the habits that are holding you back, show you why, and empower you to build more effective practices.

Note that I use PowerPoint as my chosen tool for presenting information in a linear format. For most techniques, you can use Google Slides and Keynote interchangeably (except when noted). I have not geared the design process toward Prezi, which requires an entirely different approach. So whenever you see "PowerPoint," mentally replace it with your presentation tool of choice.

Prepare to Reimagine What's Possible for You

Let's say you read this book, follow all the principles, rigorously apply them to your presentations, overcome your fear of presenting, and start delivering like a boss to your boss. What can you expect to happen when you unleash your fabulous new data presentations?

You'll notice higher engagement, enthusiasm, and interest in your insights. Your audience will excitedly discuss your recommendations, maybe engaging in a healthy debate.

Your measures finally matter, and now your stakeholders and clients know why. You start getting emails and calls from decision-makers who want to discuss your work in more detail.

You've gained membership to the A-Team. Your contributions are becoming known throughout the team, the department, and maybe even the company.

You're rapidly ascending the ranks from cog in the machine to change agent.

As such, you're gaining access to the professional benefits you've only dreamt of: higher pay, stable job security, promotions, a bigger team. But hold up, why stop there?

You get so passionate about the changes you've inspired that you start a blog. Word gets out about your communication prowess. Maybe you get invited to speak at an industry conference or two to wild acclaim.

You're asked to appear on industry podcasts, contribute guest blog articles, collaborate with other industry influencers, and even consider publishing a book.

You realize you're capable of making a difference in any role you choose to take on. Now, it truly is *your* choice.

Sound far-fetched? Sure, I get it. Except, it's precisely what happened to me and others I've observed on this journey. It's not typical, but it is *possible*. You just have to follow the instructions in this book. It's not an easy path, and it requires commitment and tenacity. But it's ready for you.

Why Listen to Me?

I've been transforming walls of data into compelling and memorable data stories and communicating them for more than two decades. I am a digital analyst turned data storytelling advocate, workshop facilitator, and international speaker having delivered hundreds of corporate and conference presentations and spoken to tens of thousands of audience members worldwide.

I'm also the host of the *Present Beyond Measure Show* podcast, garnering hundreds of thousands of downloads and a place on 15 industry "Best Of" lists.

The practitioners I've trained have gone from almost quitting their jobs to extending client contracts, reducing client and employee churn, becoming renowned industry experts and board members of professional associations, and carving a path toward lucrative paid speaking careers.

If everything I've just shared hits home for you and if these are the skills you want to learn because you know they'll let you write your career ticket, then look no further. It's time to stop turning your boardrooms into bored rooms and start making your measures matter.

I can't promise you a Macworld keynote, but I can promise you that big, beautiful change is around the corner.

And, ACTION!

How to Get the Most Out of This Book

It's important to set proper expectations when engaging in an immersive learning experience. In this section, I level-set the anticipated outcome for your time investment.

This book teaches you how to do the following:

- Eliminate data overwhelm and find the right insights to present
- Speak the language of different stakeholders' personality types
- Weave a persuasive, easy-to-understand data narrative
- Leverage cinematic storytelling techniques to hold your audience's attention
- Position your strategic and tactical recommendations for action
- Quickly design crisp, simple, and beautiful slides
- Create sequenced "slide builds" that walk your audience through your story
- Choose the most effective charts for your data scenarios
- Design charts that are simple and easy to comprehend
- Prepare and deliver your presentation with confidence

- Navigate challenging questions and comments
- Efficiently craft presentation handouts and leave-behinds
- Finally, reprogram the limiting beliefs that tend to steer practitioners away from achieving their true presenting potential

You'll also hear sage words of wisdom from several brilliant expert guests I've interviewed on my podcast. Now, here's the real talk.

This book does *not* teach you any of this:

- An easy, shortcut to data presentation stardom. This approach isn't for the casual passerby; it's for those who are ready to make big moves *now*.
- How to analyze your data. This book assumes you're already a data exploration and analysis ace. However, I do offer prompts to identify what data and ideas to present.
- A dissertation of neuroscience and data visualization history, theory, and abstract concepts. There already are excellent books where you can dive deep into the underpinnings of information communication. This book encompasses the entire data presentation ecosystem, with essential techniques that will help you in every step of this process.
- How to build dashboards. These data visualization techniques will undoubtedly improve your dashboards, but they are a fundamentally different vehicle for communicating data than the live presentation.
- How to code in R, Python, or other programming languages (but you will learn to tell more compelling stories with charts created in any platform).
- How to get paid speaking engagements or TED Talks (but you can develop skills to speak at that level).

Learn by Doing

The cone of learning and experience, created by Edgar Dale, visually displays the effectiveness of different learning modalities (see Figure P.1). It distinguishes between active learning methods (discussing, presenting) and passive methods (watching, hearing, and reading).

FIGURE P.1 Funnel chart adaptation of Edgar Dale's cone of learning
Originally created by Edgar Dale

As you can see, reading is the most passive way to learn, as we retain only 10 percent of what we read after two weeks. The most effective way to learn a new skill at a 90 percent retention rate is by doing the real thing.

Sandbox Assessments

That's why this book will help you actively integrate these principles and practices into your own data scenario! I've created self-practice "sandbox" assignments, where you get to play with your new tools risk-free. These exercises are marked in a box like this one.

To participate, you need to go through your bank of data presentations and select one to use as your "sandbox." Keep your sandbox at the forefront of your mind and apply each step to it as you go along so that you're *doing* as you're *reading*.

The ideal sandbox data presentation includes the following:

- Analytical insights, facts, and figures
- A variety of charts and graphs
- An executive summary and agenda
- Recommendations or suggestions for action

Every time I refer to the sandbox, it will be this presentation.

> To make learning even easier, I've created a robust Resource Center (see https://LeaPica.com/pbm-resource-center) with downloadable companion worksheets and tools. They will assist you along the way.
>
> As a "hearing" bonus, I've also sampled some of the best advice I've heard as "Sound Bytes" from my podcast. You'll recognize some of your favorite industry leaders and can take the learning even deeper.

Set Regular Practice Dates

The best way to break through old habits is to stay consistent with your commitment. Schedule a recurring meeting on your calendar for each week for the next six weeks or so to work through the book with your sandbox scenario. Go ahead. . .the book will be waiting for you.

It's important to move at the pace that works best for you, as long as you don't let this blueprint fall by the wayside and gather dust!

Got all that? Great. Grab your sandbox pail and shovels, and I'll see you inside!

Act I: Conceptualize

Presentation Planning, Story, Structure, and Brainstorming

Understand Why Effective Data Presentation Is Critical to Good Business

1

"If you had to identify, in one word, the reason why the human race has not achieved, and never will achieve, its full potential, that word would be meetings."

—Dave Barry

In 2014, an up-and-coming digital agency invited me to speak at their annual client summit. It was only my third event gig, so I was riddled with "newbie" nerves. It didn't help that I was sharing the stage with one of the most well-known analytics experts *in the world.*

To calm my nerves, I settled in the audience for the session before mine to observe the attendees. I spied an intelligent-looking data practitioner taking the stage, his slides lighting up the theater backdrop behind him. And then, I can't remember a whole lot after that.

I vaguely recall his droning, monotone voice, unintelligible visuals, and lots of claiming to be an expert in this and that without providing any actionable information.

But there is one thing I will never forget during his conclusion. Amidst the tepid applause, I overheard an audience member turn to his companion and whisper something that made my blood run ice cold:

"That was, like, the worst presentation I've *ever* seen."

These words, in this order, are the kiss of death to a presenter's confidence. I felt my stomach drop out, knowing that the stage had already been set for such harsh criticism.The truth was, I agreed with the critic. Clearly, the presenter's content, slides, or delivery weren't designed to connect with the most important person in the room: the audience member. Still, I felt compassionate because, well, I was once that guy, and I simply didn't know the tools.

Unfortunately, this story is representative of the state of business presentations and meetings in general. To get to the root cause, we must first unpack what a meeting is and where we're missing the mark with them.

Bad Meetings Cost Money

The Wikipedia definition of a meeting is "a gathering of two or more people that has been convened for the purpose of achieving a common goal through verbal interaction, such as sharing information or reaching an agreement."[1]

Did you catch that? "For the purpose of achieving a common goal." As in, a *specific* purpose. Yet, based on the following research and anecdotal experience from most practitioners and leaders I've worked with, the majority of meetings are not even close to fulfilling that definition. The consensus around the usefulness of business meetings is perhaps best articulated by Joseph Stillwell: "A meeting is an event at which the minutes are kept and the hours are lost."

Every year, online scheduling service `Doodle.com` conducts a research study into the effectiveness of business meetings in the United States and the United Kingdom. In assessing more than 19 million meetings in its 2019 State of Meetings report, Doodle estimated that between just these two nations, the cost of poorly organized and ineffective meetings amounts to more than half a trillion dollars per year.[2] More precisely (and mind-bogglingly), that's $541,000,000,000. No, my cat did not just walk all over my keyboard.

Take a moment to let that sink in. Imagine if you spent $1 million every single day. At that rate, it would take you almost *1,500 years* to burn through the cash our meetings are wasting every year in just two countries.

"CEO Whisperer" Cameron Herold has written an entire book about ineffective meetings, appropriately titled *Meetings Suck*. Herold has a refreshing take on the real root cause of this issue, which isn't the meeting itself:

> *"We aren't training or equipping our people with the right skills and tools to run effective meetings. It's like sending your kid into a Little League game without ever giving him a glove and playing catch in the backyard or teaching him how to swing a bat.*
>
> *And yet, that's essentially what we do with our employees when we send them into meetings without training them. It's like a parent blaming the game of baseball for why their child hates Little League. It's not the game of baseball that's to blame, it's the parent."[3]*

[1]Wikipedia contributors. (2023, February 6). Meeting. In *Wikipedia, The Free Encyclopedia*. Retrieved 18:12, June 23, 2023, from `https://en.wikipedia.org/w/index.php?title=Meeting&oldid=1137757429`

[2]`en.blog.doodle.com/2019/01/10/pointless-meetings-will-cost-companies-530bn-in-2019`

[3]*Meetings Suck*. Cameron Herold

I believe the skills gap Herold refers to affects not just how we run meetings but the entire process of data presentation before, during, and after meetings. Data can be dry and soulless without being told through skillful storytelling strategies. It's why I believe that there are no bad presenters; there are just presenters who've gained the skills and ones who haven't. . .yet.

Winning Over the Audience

But I have good news. This book will help your presentation meetings avoid joining that statistic in a way that leverages your most unexpected ally in the room.

Who is this ally, you ask?

It's your audience member's brain.

That's right. This massive collection of neurons, synapses, and glial cells all bundle up to be your best friend or your worst enemy during your data presentations. Every single person sitting at that conference table has a brain, and despite different preferences and personalities, they all function in a similar way in how they absorb, recall, and react to information. Knowing what makes the brain tick is your key to conference room conquest.

That means knowing things like, from the moment you begin speaking to them, you are in a race of *seconds* to maintain the audience's ever-shrinking attention spans. With "mobile everywhere always" and multiple browser tabs competing for attention, that mission is getting harder and harder.

It means knowing things like repetition is a mechanism that commits your information to their long-term memory, which leads to post-meeting action-taking.

These two bits are just scratching the surface; the inner workings of the human mind are vast. Because I didn't know this information, my data presentations were failing two fundamental goals:

- To maintain the attention of the audience during the meeting
- To be memorable enough to make them want to act after the meeting

Thankfully, you're going to learn a comprehensive blueprint for everything you'll need to achieve those two goals.

Even better, none of this is overwhelmingly complex or hard to do. Effective data storytelling is surprisingly simple. Contrary to common belief, you don't need a PhD in psychology or a master's degree in design to tell powerful visual data stories. You also don't need a certification in R or Python, and you certainly don't need to have a TED Talk under your belt (although it certainly helps!).

You need to leverage neuroscience principles and storytelling techniques that most of the corporate workforce doesn't know about.

When I was tired of my hard-earned insights flying into the Data Black Hole, I embarked upon a philosophical journey to answer a deep, metaphysical question:

Why do bad things happen to good data?

Am I right? It's perfectly good data! I've rechecked it three times! My statistical significance calculator says okey dokey! What is going on here?!

My quest to create inspiring and brain-friendly data presentations led me to all sorts of answers, the biggest one being about my audience's brain. That's when I came to understand this:

This is where I was going critically wrong. Time and time again, I dumped cluttered, jam-packed report slides into my audience's head and expected them to make sense of it. That's why you aren't going to learn to build reports and rattle them off to live humans. You are going to learn to build and present *presentations and stories.*

NOTE

There is a difference between reading from a report and delivering a presentation.

The Two Pillars of Successful Data Presentations

If I could give you two magical cornerstones to uphold your new presentation, it would be these: **simplicity and intentionality.**

Simplicity

Simplicity means presenting nothing more and nothing less than what is needed. One of the most common complaints about presenting data from presenters and consumers is that there's too much information. But what is presentation simplicity? It means simple insights, simple language, simple slide design, simple charts, and simple recommendations.

But what does the word *simple* even mean? Simple is defined as "easily understood or done; presenting no difficulty." Here is that last part again: presenting no difficulty is the essence of simple data presentation. Your job, from this moment forward, is to create data presentations with this tenet: make them do less work.

This must be your driving force. As you explore the mechanics of the human brain, you'll understand why the less work you make your audience do, the more they're able to pay attention to you, and the less likely they'll be zombies by the Q&A.

Intentionality

Intentionality is the conscious and aware application of data presentation practices. Presenting data with intention means that every step you take in planning, brainstorming, designing, charting, and delivering your insights was a thoughtfully deliberate choice. So, your second tenet is this:

Present data by design, not by default.

When you make an intentional choice about every aspect of your data presentations, your audience will see, hear, and feel the difference.

Throw Down the Gauntlet

Making a change to any way of doing something requires resolve and commitment. You must prepare to unlearn everything you know about presenting data.

For this first chapter, I have two vitally important action steps. They will crystallize your commitment to learning and integrating this process into your work.

The first thing I want you to do right now is to stop, take a deep breath, and ask yourself: **what is my big why?** Why is this important to me? Why am I ready to make this change? What's waiting for me on the other side of my fear and doubt?

On the surface, your big why might sound like any of these:

- I'm ready to score that promotion or top year-end bonus.
- I'm ready to hire a team to help me elevate to more visible projects.
- I'm ready to feel confident in my job security and sleep better at night.
- I'm ready to sell more of my software solution to potential customers who don't know they need it yet.

These are all good starting points. But I want you to go deeper than that. I'm talking about driving-force-behind-life whys.

Are you ready for the next big step in your career? Are you ready to lead a bigger team so you can have a more measurable impact on your organization? Are you bored out of your mind at work because you never grow? Are you drowning in bills or debt and are ready to achieve financial stability and abundance?

Go ahead and close your eyes and ask yourself again. Really *feel* it.

Got your big why? Excellent. Now for the second step: it's easy to declare your why to yourself with the best of intentions. And, life can get in the way. Schedules are jam-packed, deadlines creep up, and that newfound commitment gets put on a shelf to gather dust. **What you also need is accountability.**

That's why I want to be your accountability buddy. I want you to commit. . .to me.

YOUR MISSION

Email me at Lea@LeaPica.com (yup, that's my direct address) with the subject line, "I'm committing!" That way, I can easily pick it out among my deluge of messages. Then in the email message, let me know what led you here and how you're ready to go big. Something like this:

"Starting today, I commit to presenting data by design and creating an impact with my insights!" Include your reasons, your rationale, and your big why.

Making a pact with someone else is a powerful way to instill new habits and accomplish your goals. I read every response and will respond (albeit glacially slowly at times).

That's my commitment back to you, and I will be rooting for you through the finish line and beyond!

Chapter Recap

- The two primary goals of presenting data are to maintain the audience's attention and be memorable enough to inspire them to take action afterward.
- The two pillars of presentation success are simplicity and intentionality.
- The two keys to successful habit change are committing and holding yourself accountable to that commitment.

Sandbox Assignment

(Sandbox doesn't sound familiar? Return to the "Learn by Doing" section of the prologue for full instructions on how to implement these tools and techniques in your own work example.)

■ Begin to contemplate your sandbox data presentation.

Be Your Audience   2

"Make it about them, not about you."

—Simon Sinek

"Lea, these numbers are. . .interesting. . .but what I really wanted to know was why our test ad creative didn't outperform the control as we'd hoped. Why isn't that in here?"

I stared at my client for a moment, a well of frustration bubbling up inside of me. I was presenting my insights during a high-profile campaign readout that included my client, boss, and teammates. My first thought was, *where is the nearest open window*? Watching helplessly as he publicly poked holes in my work was so embarrassing!

But the more frustrating aspect of that moment was that I'd presented exactly what he'd asked me for before the meeting. I simply didn't understand his confusion. I gave him what he wanted yet still missed the mark.

When I share this story with data practitioners, it usually strikes a deep chord. **I call this the dreaded "stakeholder switcheroo."** Stakeholders often seem to tell us one thing they want and then later say they wanted something else. They also often make vague requests for "campaign updates," "the latest," or, my personal favorite, "give me all the numbers." This may be hard to believe, but they're likely not intentionally trying to grind your gears; rather, it's more likely that what they are receiving doesn't meet their needs, and they don't know how else to ask.

The Most Important Person in the Conference Room Is. . .Not You

The general goal of presenting data in a corporate setting is to make decisions that benefit the customer (if you're with the right company) and the company. So just present everything about what *you* want to happen, what *you* think is important, or what *you* think is best for the company or the customer, right?

Think again. Here's an important truth in corporate presentation:

The presentation audience is king (or queen, ahem).

Now, I ask you to pause and repeat that last sentence out loud at 0.5x speed. That's how important that truth is. I am telling you with 100 percent certainty that if you go into any presentation, in any context, without putting your audience front and center, you will not win with them. End of data story.

This chapter teaches you how to be your audience. Something truly magical happens when you stop and place yourself in the shoes and perspectives of the stakeholders, clients, and colleagues you're speaking to. Why is this so important?

Because decision-makers are *not* you and because they call the shots.

Many presenters focus on what's essential to the business. That's a great starting point. But shockingly, I've discovered that all businesses are run by an animal species called *homo sapiens*, otherwise known as humans. Humans are organisms with the power of both rational logic and irrational emotions, desires, biases, and fears. Therefore, humans make decisions with a blend of logic and emotion.

You are presenting to humans. If you want them to do what's best for your customer and the business, you'll have to do something you may have never done before.

When I say needs, I mean needs, wants, desires, goals, fears, or any motivating factor that will lead them toward or away from a decision. The secret is, they often don't know how to explicitly tell you what those needs are.

> **TIP**
>
> You must present your insights and recommendations in the language of your stakeholder's needs.

There Is No "Stakeholder School"

Just like we weren't taught the fundamentals of data communication in nonexistent "data practitioner school," our stakeholders weren't taught how to consume data in "stakeholder school."

In the book *Data Fluency*, my friends Chris and Zach Gemignani of Juice Analytics share a perspective on this that I've found helpful:

> *"Many of the audiences we design for—are unfamiliar and inexperienced with getting value from the data even in small doses. Presenters of data need to meet their audiences where they are in ways that their audience can comfortably engage with content."*

Did you read that right? We presenters need to meet our audiences where *they* are at so they can get the most value from our content. While it may seem frustrating to feel like we're shouldering all the burden, a service mindset is useful here.

Think of the task of presenting data not as a necessary evil but as an opportunity to facilitate a transformation for your customers, business, stakeholders, and yourself.

What I do wish someone had told me was that this is what stakeholders are really thinking:

> "Hey there, you. Look, uh, I've got a lot on my plate right now. I know you want to tell me how complicated your analysis was, how long it took you, or the exact P-value range of your landing page T-test, but that's not what I actually *need*.
>
> I need you to tell me how to move my business *forward*.
>
> I need you to tell me in a way I understand *quickly* and *easily*.
>
> And. . .this is the key. . .in a way that makes me want to *take action*. Capisce?"

Yikes. That's a tall order for us number nerds who just want to roll around in paid search pivot tables all day. But the reality is that if you are responsible for managing the flow of data in your organization, you're most likely responsible for communicating the state of data to your organization. But how do you convince them that what you're presenting is important to them, if they don't know it yet?

You must stop *hearing the words* they say and start *listening to the needs* they're not saying. Get in their heads; be like their therapist. Understand them from the inside and learn how to connect the dots between your insights and their goals.

The most powerful way to approach is to think about the two most motivating factors driving stakeholder decisions: **aspirations and obstacles**. Learn how to address both with your insights and they'll become your fan club president.

If you can't intuit these answers yourself, then pick up this ancient, mythical communication device called the telephone and ask them! As a bonus, this simple action can earn a lot of relationship equity when you take the time to reach out and make their needs feel important to you.

And their needs *are* important to you now, yes? Here are some prompts to get started:

Questions for revealing stakeholder aspirations:
- What's at the top of their to-do lists?
- What are their biggest aspirations?
- What are their goals for this month, this quarter, this year?
- What criteria are used to earn their performance bonuses?
- How can you and your data make their lives better?

Questions for unpacking stakeholder obstacles:
- What's keeping them up at night?
- What are their biggest professional fears?
- What are the most stubborn obstacles interfering with their chance at completing a project, meeting their quota, scoring a promotion, or locking in a budget increase?
- How can your data help them overcome these obstacles?

Now, there's something important to keep in mind. Your stakeholders are not the only ones affected by the decisions they make; you must remember that there is another human on the receiving end of these decisions:

The customer.

All the questions you ask here should always keep the customer as the ultimate benefactor of your data presentation. It's well-understood that customer-centric organizations enjoy the greatest sustainability and competitive advantage.

So, as you are contemplating your presentation theme and content, make these the final questions you ask during this process:

- Who stands to benefit from your insights and recommendations?
- How can you help your customers achieve their goals?

- What information, if given to your stakeholder, will benefit your customers the most?
- What are your customer's greatest obstacles to feeling confident about their relationship with you?

More Essential Questions to Get Started on Your Data Presentation

As I began to create customer and stakeholder-centric data presentations, I was often stumped. Where should I begin? What should I be thinking about? How can I feel prepared for this? Sitting in front of vast oceans of data with no compass, I began to go a little loco.

One day, I sat down and thought about the most common areas where my presentations fell short or didn't get the job done. Then I generated a list of questions that would plug those gaps right at the beginning—a road map to starting on the right foot.

I've used this exact list to interview key meeting decision-makers well before dumping charts onto slides and always enjoyed better outcomes.

What Is the Purpose/Objective/Theme of the Meeting?

Ideally, there is a purpose. I don't mean to sound facetious, but I used to receive tidal waves of meeting invitations with vague titles like "Campaign Overview" and "Report Readout." One of my workshop students received an invitation to a meeting called "Data." "Data" does not qualify as a purpose or objective. A presentation meeting without a clear goal is like getting in a boat without a destination or compass. In contrast, effective meeting objectives lead to effective meetings.

Effective meeting objectives start with verbs that indicate action and prevent ambiguity. Here are examples of practical meeting objectives:

- **Decide** on our display ad optimization plan for Q3
- **Launch** new paid search campaign
- **Collaborate** on market research survey implementation
- **Establish** a plan for new marketing warehouse deployment

When your meeting objectives become more concrete, you'll have much more clarity on your analysis starting point. The next question can help clarify that objective if it's not already evident.

What Decisions Are at Stake, and How Will You Measure Their Success?

Finding the right data to include is much easier when you have decisions to point toward, even if there isn't any one insight that stands out yet. These are examples of specific decisions:

- Whether to shut down a marketing campaign
- How to proceed with the next phase of an optimization test
- Which areas of the website to refine during a redesign

If you're not sure, it's time to dial up your boss or your stakeholder who can give you direction and context! And if they get stuck, steer the conversation toward what decisions would most benefit your customers.

Once you've determined the decisions, you must identify the metrics you'll use to measure their success (or not). I ask these questions:

- What are the measures that will best inform on your progress?
- What are the most reliable and accessible metrics you have at your disposal?

Whether it's conversion rate, cost per lead, or customer satisfaction score, assigning measurement ensures accountability for the decision.

Who Is Attending the Meeting? At What Savviness Level Are They?

This answer will guide you toward the appropriate tone and complexity of your content. It's important to avoid talking over anyone's head, so you want to speak to the lowest common denominator in the room in terms of technical savvy, which tends to be your highest-ranking executives. In Chapter 3, I give you a framework for decoding the language you should speak with different stakeholder types.

What Are Three to Five Key Questions You'd Like to "Ask" the Data?

This is my favorite question in this list of questions because. . .it asks questions! Curiosity is the most potent weapon in your analysis arsenal, and it can empower your stakeholder to get to the heart of what they need in *their* language.

I ask my stakeholders to imagine sitting down to coffee (or tea or kombucha) with the data as if it is a person and "catching up" with it in human language.

For example, I've heard, "I'm interested to know if the new creative we launched last month is outperforming our old one" or "I'm curious if our customer satisfaction has improved after we fixed the site search bug."

Human language questions are more accessible for less tech-savvy executives to identify their needs and desires. That's because it's highly likely that humans and their behavior generated the numbers in your data sets. So use human questions to probe into your human data.

I hope you can already see how the answers to these questions will serve as your runway. Are these the only questions you can ask? No, of course not. Are they a fine starting point that minimizes wasted effort and reduces the chances of ye olde "stakeholder switcheroo"? Yes indeed!

Logistics Questions

Now, there are two more questions regarding logistics that are crucial to get answers to early on. I wouldn't necessarily ask my stakeholders these unless they were running the meeting themselves. So, hunt down the meeting coordinator to find out the answers.

Q: Is this part of a team meeting, and if so, how much time do I have?

I once brought a 45-minute block of content to a 15-minute time slot during a team presentation. Don't be like me. Also, make sure your findings and recommendations align with your team's content to avoid contradicting ideas and appearing out of step.

Q: Is the meeting in-person, virtual, or a mix of both?

This question became particularly important because 100 percent of meetings went online during the COVID-19 lockdown. This prompted a surge of technical demons to emerge and plague virtual conference rooms. Despite the world's return to work, I believe hybrid models and online meetings are here to stay, and planning for them is essential.

Starting to conceptualize a new data presentation can feel daunting, but it doesn't have to be. With the right set of Qs, you'll have all your I's dotted and T's crossed and meeting your stakeholders' insight needs with ease.

Chapter Recap

- An effective data presentation frames what's happening in the data and what would benefit the customer in the language of your stakeholders' needs.
- Your stakeholders were not trained to articulate what they need from you, so help them by being their translator.
- The key to understanding your stakeholders' needs are twofold: their aspirations and obstacles and how your data can help achieve and overcome them.

Sandbox Assignment

- Answer the essential questions with your sandbox presentation and audience in mind.

Learn to Speak Different Audience Languages

3

> "One language sets you in a corridor for life. Two languages open every door along the way."
>
> —Frank Smith

Don't you just love presenting insights to a room full of like-minded, rational people who "speak geek" with you?

Don't you love it when they get it all right away, showering you with glowing accolades and thoughtful questions that show that they totally get it?

Don't you love it when they all have the same interpretations of your data, pleasantly praising each other's perspectives and amicably agreeing to the same courses of action?

Don't you love subtle sarcasm? [subtle sarcasm]

I wish I could say that the previous scenarios are the norm for data presentations. . .but alas, I cannot. One reason is that audiences are comprised of individual human beings who have a diverse array of needs, desires, challenges, and biases.

But another reason that flies under the radar is that, depending on each stakeholder's role, experience, and personality type, they speak different communication languages.

I'm going to give you a mighty lens through which to examine your stakeholders. It was inspired by wisdom dropped by e-commerce marketing legend and podcast guest Kevin Hillstrom of *Mine That Data*.

I call it the Stakeholder-Savvy Quadrant, and it's helping practitioners all over the world effectively tailor what they say to whom.

What Is the Stakeholder-Savvy Quadrant?

The framework for the Stakeholder-Savvy Quadrant plots stakeholders into four main personality types based on their "savviness" in two areas: business-side expertise and technical/data competence. You can see the quadrants created by these two spectrums in Figure 3.1.

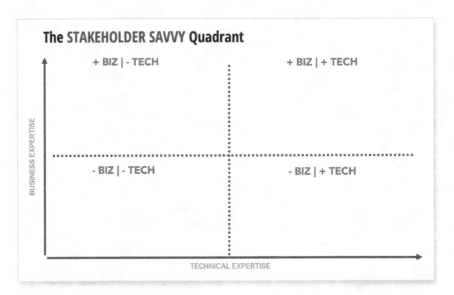

FIGURE 3.1 Blank Stakeholder-Savvy Quadrant

I'll dive into each type's unique personality quirks and strategies for working with them.

Quadrant 1: High Business Expertise, Low Technical Savvy

This is your heavy-hitter team. Typical roles include the C-suite and VPs of marketing, technology, e-commerce, and finance. If you work at an agency, they are your client decision-makers who call the shots on strategy and budget. This group is your prime target for enabling the decisions you need to move forward. As such, you must focus on exactly what they need to make those decisions and little else.

When delivering insights to a blended group of quadrants, this is the one to cater to. They generally don't care about the "how" behind your analysis but, rather, the "what" and "what next" part.

Your insights should precisely align with the specific goals of the business, the department, and the stakeholders as individuals. The questions we asked in Chapter 2 will be your allies with this crowd.

In this quadrant, you must avoid getting bogged down in explaining the technical details of your analyses. As soon as you start speaking over their heads, they tune you out and unconsciously wander to other thoughts like their Sunday to-do list.

One effective strategy is to use simple and straightforward language to explain complex concepts. It's commonly thought that the more advanced vocabulary we use to communicate, the more intelligent and impressive we sound. While it may seem like demonstrating your verbal acumen by dropping tech jargon and statistical slang will increase your credibility, this actually confuses the audience.

In his book *The Scribe Method*, four-time *New York Times*–bestselling author Tucker Max asserts that while lofty language is expected in certain arenas like academia, it can backfire anywhere outside that arena including reading and speaking.

Tucker's advice? Speak to your audience at the level of a curious, intelligent 7th grader. Yes, that means explaining your latest paid search test results to a *brainy 12-year-old*. One of my favorite strategies to go simpler is using relatable, real-world analogies that connect the visual dots between your concept and the audience's brain. I explore analogies in Chapter 6.

With this group, it's important to mind the usage of acronyms in presentations. Acronyms are useful for saving time by abbreviating long-winded names of products and processes. Yet, they run the risk of baffling a presentation audience who isn't familiar with SEO, CLV, and OWBL. This is especially true for those in this less-savvy yet highly influential quadrant. Don't assume they already know your data and marketing acronyms if it's not their wheelhouse.

If you must use acronyms in your presentation, spell them out in full the first time you use them, followed by the abbreviation. For example, if I were presenting about GDPR to a non-technical client, I would say, "What is General Data Protection Regulation (GDPR)?"

The important thing to remember about this quadrant is to keep it as simple as possible for them and don't talk over their heads.

Quadrant 2: Low Business Expertise, Low Technical Savvy

The roles that fall into this quadrant are typically in enablement areas like human resources and quality control. While they aren't revenue centers, this doesn't mean they aren't savvy or important; quite the contrary. These roles are system supports and your allies in implementing your recommendations.

This quadrant doesn't care about the complexities of the analysis, but they do want to know where they will play a part in execution. The less you focus on the nitty-gritty and more on how they can help you, the better chance you have at getting it done. Focus on the "what now" of your findings, rather than the "what" and "why."

Quadrant 3: Low Business Expertise, High Technical Savvy

We're moving toward the side of the spectrum that will be more interested in the "how" side of your analysis. These folks are more comfortable with the numbers and technical nuances. That can be a good or a bad thing from your perspective.

In this quadrant, you'll find mid-level folks from the IT and finance departments, who are often the gatekeepers of the technical systems and the financial backing you'll need to deploy your business initiatives.

These are the professional "hole-pokers" of the org chart, meaning they have the expertise and appetite for dissecting the numbers. They'll put your findings under the microscope, ask for the raw data, and question your conclusions and recommendations. These folks are interested in understanding your work while also tending to be more risk-averse and not accepting things at face value.

There's a lot of pressure on them to ensure all systems are a go.

The best thing you can do to prepare is to have your analysis buttoned up to the very top button and then one button higher. Triple-check your calculations, keep your data refreshed, and run it past one or two knowledgeable colleagues who can boost your confidence in the numbers. Be prepared for a questioning match during the meeting and a plan for communicating your way through any conflict.

Quadrant 4: High Business Expertise, High Technical Savvy

This quadrant will test your business and analytical mettle. Hillstrom deems these roles "superhumans": unicorns who master business, marketing, and technology. They are surprisingly common in the higher ranks of organizations like digital marketing and analytics agencies.

This quadrant represents your toughest customers because their sharp intellect predisposes them to being biased against any fact or opinion that contradicts what they believe. They're naturally competitive and unreceptive to ideas they didn't think of first.

Here, the ultimate goal is the joint adoption of your idea. They are possibly in a decision-making role, so getting in alignment without getting mired in muddy technical details is crucial to getting buy-in for your recommendations.

Facilitating dialogues with a collaborative spirit is the key here. However, if you get embroiled in a debate, take the high road by agreeing to disagree when necessary. If that still doesn't work, be prepared before the meeting to call in a tie-breaker from the leadership team.

So many personalities and eccentricities, yes? You've possibly recognized different types of stakeholders in the people you currently work with and how to work collaboratively with them. Perhaps you even recognized yourself and how you can shift to make meetings more collaborative as well!

Figure 3.2 shows a graphic of the full Stakeholder-Savvy Quadrant, which you'll also find in the Resource Center (see `https://LeaPica.com/pbm-resource-center`). Keep it handy as you proceed with developing your message and content.

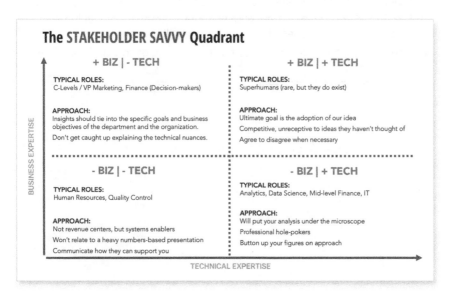

FIGURE 3.2 Complete Stakeholder-Savvy Quadrant

EXTRA CREDIT
Explore your stakeholders' psychological terrain with my podcast episode "Six Core Human Needs," an idea from Tony Robbins, and Gary Chapman's book, *The 5 Languages of Appreciation in the Workplace.*

I'll close this chapter with questions I was asked during a conference panel: "Why do I have to learn their language? Do I have to understand the business, or can I just do my analytics work?"

My answer appeared to surprise the group: "It depends on you and what you want out of your career. If you are proficient only at analysis, how far can you truly go? **How far could you go if you always tie your insights to the needs of your customer, stakeholders, and the greater mission of the company?"**

The distance you go in your data career is up to you, and connecting your data to the audience's needs and languages is vital to go that distance.

Chapter Recap

- Your stakeholders weren't trained to effectively consume data and extract the value needed for informed decision-making.
- Your role as presenter is to meet them where they are by speaking their language with your content and tone.

Sandbox Assignment

- Download the Stakeholder-Savvy Quadrant from the Resource Center (see `https://LeaPica.com/pbm-resource-center`) and fill in each quadrant with the types of stakeholders you'll present to.
- Consider the approach you'll use for the meeting overall and specifically to each group.

Transmit a Clear Message

4

"Um, can you repeat the part of the stuff where you said all about the things?"

—Homer Simpson

How often do you get a presentation meeting invitation with a title along the lines of "Campaign Overview," "Test Results," or "Report Review"?

When this happens, do you:

A. Jump out of your seat shouting, "Yahtzee!" with excitement and enthusiasm?

B. Scratch your head and reluctantly accept the invite out of obligation?

C. Dramatically fake your disappearance?

When I used to get those invites, my typical reaction was B or C (C only worked the first time, go figure). I rarely understood what the purpose of the meeting was, what decisions were at stake, and what was expected of me.

The trouble was, I was asked to present insights at these meetings with minimal context or direction. So, I learned by watching what everyone else was doing. I would create a terrifying document that I now call the "kitchen sink presentation."

I would scrape every metric from every dimension from every available reporting platform, throw my digits in a bunch of charts on a bunch of slides, and present them all hoping *something* would stick.

Then I would be mystified as to why my room was transformed into *Zombieland: Corporate Edition*.

Data overwhelm is one of the chief complaints I hear about from the organizational leaders who enlist me to train their practitioner teams, and the result is confused clients and frustrated executives. While the solution is simple, its execution is not instinctual.

A message says something specific. It communicates information. Your message is the most important thing your audience should know about your presentation topic.

"Campaign Overview" is not a presentation message. Neither is "Q1 Readout," "Test Results," or "Data." None of these titles actually *communicates* anything.

NOTE

Every effective presentation has one clear message at its core.

One Tool to Rule Them All

The question is, what should your message be? I discovered a tool that transformed the focus of my presentations and "stickiness" of my insights. It's sourced directly from a little-known but growing upstart named TED (Technology, Education, Design).

OK, TED not a little-known upstart; it is an organization renowned for hosting the world's most captivating speakers in the world transmitting the most innovative ideas. And not a single TED speaker can take the stage without having one of these in their talks:

It's called the *throughline*.

The throughline was coined by Chris Anderson, the genius who took a chance and bought the tiny TED conference years ago, transforming it into a global juggernaut of innovation and awe. Not surprisingly, Chris has learned a lot about the elements that make or break a compelling presentation.

In his book *TED Talks*, Chris defines the throughline as "a connecting theme that ties together each narrative element. You can think of a throughline as a strong cord or rope, onto which you will attach all the elements that are part of the idea you're building."[1]

TIP

Think of the throughline as a movie trailer for your presentation.

More simply put, it is the entire theme of your presentation summarized in a single sentence. Think about that for a moment. When is the last time you gave a presentation that could be summed up in one, two, or even ten sentences? Presentations with that level of simplicity are about as common as a white peacock in a county petting zoo.

A trailer gives away just enough to get a sense of where a story is going yet creates enough anticipation that one simply must stick around to learn more. An effective throughline empowers your stakeholder to understand the presentation purpose so well that if they leave the meeting early, they can clearly and accurately relay it to their boss. It opens what's called a *story loop*, where a storyline is opened like a door and triggers the human urge to "close" it by staying to hear the conclusion.

Isn't that the kind of appetite you want to create with your presentations? Can you imagine your audience strapping themselves into their seats and giving you their rapt attention? How rewarding would that feel?

---

[1] Anderson, Chris. *TED Talks: The Official TED Guide to Public Speaking.*

Anderson cites these examples of intriguing throughlines from popular TED talks:

- "Terrible city flags can reveal surprising design secrets."
- "The combination of three simple technologies creates a mind-blowing sixth sense."
- "Online videos can humanize the classroom and revolutionize education."

Do you see how, in just one sentence, the idea is crystal clear and enticing enough to learn more? It's not just stating a topic like "extra-sensory perception technology" or "online classroom videos." Throughlines draw you into learning about the subject because they show how the topic matters and open an irresistible story loop. And they're certainly a far cry from "Test Results."

Now, I've studied quite a few TED Talk throughlines in my journey, and as wildly intriguing as they are, they're a little impractical for a business meeting. That's why I developed and tested my own throughline formula! It goes like this:

1. Explain the subject +
2. Hint at what you found (and whether it surprised you) +
3. Hint that you have a solution or plan at the ready

So, a fill-in-the-blank template would sound like "[Something happened] in the area of [meeting topic]; we found [number of] reasons why this happened and [number of] potential solutions to it."

Here are several effective throughlines I've used in the past:

Our search marketing program efficiency surprisingly declined during May; we've found three reasons for why this may have happened and four potential solutions for it.

Our January A/B landing page test netted a positive gain of 16 percent conversion rate, which could continue to grow another 10 percent in Q4 with our two next test recommendations.

Our web satisfaction score unexpectedly dropped after our web redesign; we've found four potential contributing factors and several options to remediate it.

Now, analytics and data are not the only kind of presentations where you can use a throughline. Maybe you're trying to whip up excitement for a new platform or marketing strategy. If so, this throughline could work:

We'll show you how the capabilities of our new email marketing platform could dramatically increase our subscriber engagement rates and the three most important features to use right away.

Notice how these all follow the throughline formula: the topic, what happened, why it happened, and a solution.

This single sentence should act as your North Star for the entire session. Later in the chapters on brainstorming, I show you how to corral your ideas using the throughline. It will save you hours of headache and prevent audience confusion.

Make the Title Slide Your Presentation Trailer

NOTE

Curiosity is the fuel for attention and anticipation, and the more you inspire, the more engaged your audience will be.

A properly constructed throughline has the power to elicit the one emotion that ensures people are glued to you: curiosity.

I like to evoke curiosity by pulling some of the mystery from my throughline into the title of the presentation. Let's say you're preparing to present landing page results and your throughline is "Our landing page test results revealed several wins and lessons; we've found three main drivers behind this and have two new test ideas for optimization."

Figure 4.1 shows what the title slide of this readout might typically say.

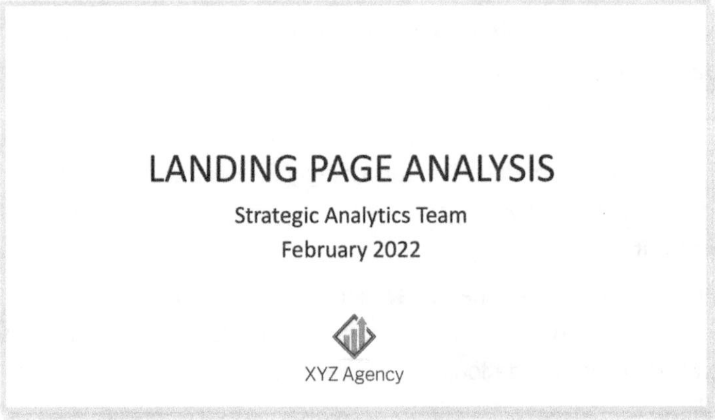

LANDING PAGE ANALYSIS
Strategic Analytics Team
February 2022
XYZ Agency

FIGURE 4.1 Typical uninspiring and unintriguing title slide

What a snooze fest! Instead, I distill my throughline format into what's commonly used as a book title format: a simple, catchy main title with a longer, more explanatory subtitle.

Watch what happens (see Figure 4.2) when you draw inspiration from your throughline into the title.

FIGURE 4.2 Impactful and optimized title slide

Can you immediately feel how differently each of these titles land? Which one might you want to "stick" around for? This was an outstanding example from a workshop student who took the theme of gymnastics and cleverly applied it to a well-known digital marketing term.

Notice that I took the old main title of the previous incarnation but demoted it to a subtitle. That way, the contents are still clear. Soon, you will learn how to leverage this title technique on your interior slides as well. I want to plant the seed early of rethinking your entire approach to titles.

Something to note is that the throughline is different from the meeting objective.

- The objective declares what the predetermined desired outcome is for the meeting, ideally framed with an action verb.
- The throughline summarizes and teases at the journey you'll take the audience on.

You are now in possession of a tool used by the most influential presenters in the world. Soon you'll learn to use it as the North Star for your presentation content.

Chapter Recap

- A presentation throughline can give your data presentation focused simplicity and a centralized theme your audience can understand.
- The throughline should summarize your presentation in a single sentence.

Sandbox Assignment

■ Use the throughline formula or access the Throughline Generator in the Resource Center (see https://LeaPica.com/pbm-resource -center).

■ Use your throughline as the North Star of your presentation content.

■ Send me bouquets of exotic and expensive flowers; trust me, you'll want to after trying this!

Tell an Actual Story 5

"No guts, no story."

—Chris Brady

What's the difference between an average campaign readout and *Game of Thrones*? Give up?

Answer: One is data. The other is a story.

During my training workshops and conference sessions, I ask my audience to stop and think about the most memorable stories of our time: the stories that moved them, changed them, and transformed them. I'll ask you to do the same now: what movies, books, myths, and fables come to mind?

Perhaps you think of *The Odyssey*, *Romeo and Juliet*, *The Wizard of Oz*, *The Shawshank Redemption*, *Forrest Gump*, or *Breaking Bad*. Next, I ask the audience to call out the common elements they can think of in those stories. I usually end up with a list that looks like this:

- Relatable and endearing characters
- Charismatic and despicable villains
- An intriguing plot
- Surprising twists and turns
- A dramatic climax
- A satisfying conclusion

Finally, I ask the audience to think about how they relate those elements to the real presentation slides you see in Figure 5.1.

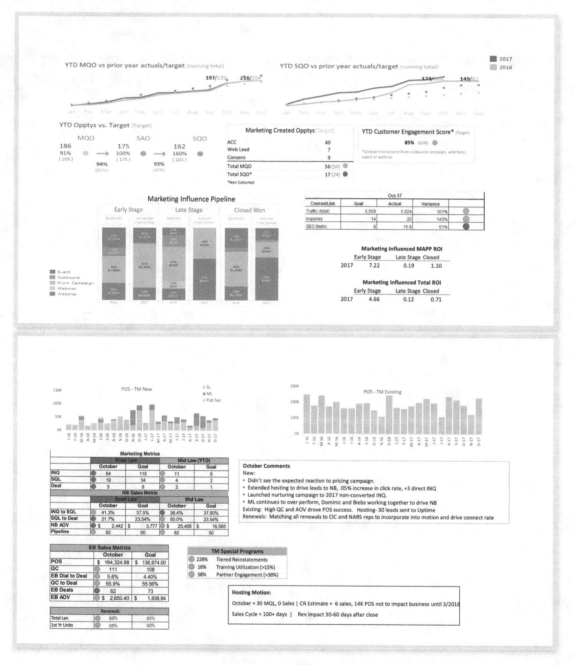

FIGURE 5.1 Examples of typical business data presentation slides

At this point, the crowd predictably goes silent, with some nervous twittering. I continue with, "So there's some data. And lots of other stuff. But do you see any of the actual story elements we just talked about? No? Well, that's because this is *not* a story. There's a story in there somewhere, but it's kinda hard to find, right?"

The audience uncomfortably nods. I empathize: they now see the stark contrast between a great story and the cluttered, nonsensical slides before them. Slides that look very familiar to them. The number-one element I see missing from most data stories is the *story* part. That's why if there's one chapter to infuse into your presentation DNA, it's this one. This is where your big shift will happen.

Data Storytelling: It's Not What You Think It Is

Despite the rise of *data storytelling* as the business buzzword du jour, it's still a mystery to most practitioners. Let's start with my favorite definition of a story.

A *story* is a compilation of characters, circumstances, and sequence of events with a beginning, a middle, and an end, which all lead to a transformation.

If your data presentation were a movie, the *message* would be the tagline, and the *story* would be the film itself. The story is the meat and potatoes of your session (or beans, if you're veggie), and it supports and reinforces the overarching theme. Unfortunately, the only thing most current data presentations have in common with that definition is a beginning and an end, signaled by our notification alarms for our next meeting.

This is a huge missed opportunity, as illustrated by a research exercise made famous by Chip Heath, Stanford professor and coauthor of *Made to Stick*. In the book, Heath describes how he tests his students to see whether facts supercede story. He instructs them to give one-minute speeches to persuade their class about a societal issue. Within 10 minutes of hearing the speeches, the students document every idea they can recall.

The results are consistent and illuminating: "When students are asked to recall the speeches, 63 percent remember the stories. Only 5 percent remember any individual statistic."[1] That is a considerable difference and incredibly important!

---

[1] Heath, Chip and Dan. *Made to Stick: Why Some Ideas Survive and Others Die*. Random House, 2010. ISBN # 978-0812982008

This corroborates a key neuroscientific finding: facts and data, often the backbone of our business presentations, can stimulate only two areas of the left hemisphere of our brain, which are responsible for language and analysis. A well-told story, on the other hand, activates seven distinct regions on both left and right hemispheres![2] No other element of presentation can accomplish this feat.

In fact, you may remember this fact in the future because now you know the story behind it! That's why story is so powerful: it helps you meet your first goal of maintaining audience attention by firing their brains on all cylinders. **This begs the question, are the decisions we make during meetings truly data-driven, or perhaps. . .*story-driven*?**

Ryan Levesque, the mastermind behind a popular business framework called the Ask Method, has the answer. He says that "people buy with emotions and then justify with logic." Think about that for a moment.

Was it data like iPhone storage capacity and processing power that whipped Apple customers into a frenzy at the Macworld keynote? Of course not! It was the emotions Steve Jobs triggered by painting a clear picture of how the iPhone would *change their lives.*

We humans can't just shut off our emotions to make purely "data-driven decisions." While the data we provide should be free from subjective bias and manipulation, the storytelling part is more pivotal than we realize. The reality is that story and emotions drive decisions, and data substantiates them.

Story is also powerful because it elicits empathy in our audience. Researcher Paul J. Zak runs the neuroscience lab that discovered the relationship between oxytocin release and the feeling of safety in the world. His research led him to an exciting discovery that has implications for using story to create influence.

"Oxytocin is produced when we are trusted or shown a kindness, and it motivates cooperation with others. It does this by enhancing the sense of empathy, our ability to experience others' emotions."[3]

In a subsequent experiment, his team found that character-driven narratives "consistently cause oxytocin synthesis. Further, the amount of oxytocin released by the brain predicted how much people were willing to help others."

---

[2]ethos3.com/2015/02/the-science-of-storytelling-for-presentations-infographicthe-neuroscience-of-storytelling-infographic/1
[3]hbr.org/2014/10/why-your-brain-loves-good-storytelling

Did you catch that? **Telling compelling, character-driven stories inspires audiences to help people.** Can you think of a people whom you're trying to inspire your audience to help? [cough-customer people-cough)]

Now you know why story is critical in communicating data; let's zoom in on a keystone of story: **the narrative arc**.

The Narrative Arc in Storytelling

Narrative arc (used interchangeably with story arc) refers to the shape and structure of a story. Think of it like the matrix: it is all around us and invisible, yet it organizes the components of story in a way where they flow to create drama, relief, and transformation throughout the journey.

Two of the more familiar story structures you may have heard of are the three-act play (beginning, middle, and end) and Joseph Campbell's hero's journey. I've already described the three-act play: it's the one with a beginning, middle, and end. The hero's journey is more intricate: it breaks down the passage of the hero through three main phases of Departure, Initiation, and Return (plus a multitude of subphases with esoteric names like Apotheosis, Woman as the Temptress, and Belly of the Whale). Intriguing, yet not terribly practical for business purposes.

I find the three-act structure too simplistic and the hero's journey too complex for presenting data in a business meeting. Luckily, as would delight our beloved nursery heroine Goldilocks, there is a structure in the middle that feels *just* right.

The Five-Step Narrative Arc Structure

Gustav Freytag, German novelist and playwright, is best known for his analysis of the three-act play. He more granularly defines that structure with a bell-curve shape demarcated by five distinct plot points.[4] I'll explain each of those plot points in the context of both traditional cinema (film and TV) and presentation. Speaking of *The Matrix*, I use it as a comparative template, as it exemplifies the Freytag structure and the hero's journey as well.

---

[4]en.wikipedia.org/wiki/Dramatic_structure

Step 1: Exposition

Exposition sets the stage. Here, you weave a tapestry of the time and place, current events, and characters (including identifying the hero); see Figure 5.2.

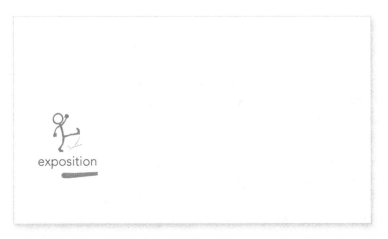

FIGURE 5.2 Narrative arc step: exposition

You meet Neo, the reluctant anti-hero, and see his bland cityscape in the current timeline.

For a data presentation, this is where you'd review the backdrop of your topic: the marketing campaign, the ad creative, the A/B test parameters, or whatever information is needed to understand what's to come.

Step 2: Rising Action (The Conflict)

Our hero encounters their first obstacles and villain. This stage is dubbed "rising" because it elevates tension and, when done well, the audience's blood pressure. A tense state puts the audience on high alert, which draws them in. Without it, there's no reason to pay attention. An easy way to remember this turning point is this: no tension, no attention. (See Figure 5.3.)

FIGURE 5.3 Narrative arc step: rising action

The challenges are ominous, the villain is dastardly. Neo is extracted from the Matrix by Trinity and team after being targeted by the computer "program" Agent Smith and joins the Resistance against the machines.

For you, this is where you begin to reveal your insights and expose the conflict, which is either a problem or opportunity in the data. A conflict can be negative or positive because it is simply something standing in the way of what the hero wants.

You might open with the expected key performance indicators or show an insight everyone anticipated. But to raise the action, you show them something they didn't expect. Perhaps you dug deeper into a customer segment and found an anomaly, or the predicted test winner didn't pull through. This is where you want to build suspense so that they're primed for the big shoe drop during. . .

Step 3: The Climax

The hero is now in the most treacherous territory, and the stakes are at their highest. Here, decisions mean epic victory or epic failure. Smith and his agents engage Neo in an epic death match, and we're not sure if our hero is going to make it out of the Matrix alive. (See Figure 5.4.)

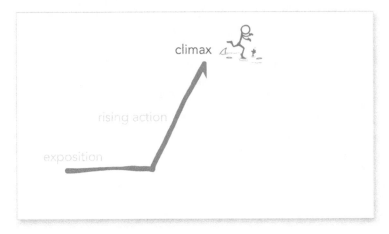

FIGURE 5.4 Narrative arc step: the climax

TIP

> Most importantly, this is also where you want to show them what they stand to lose by not taking decisive action.

This is where you want to show your stakeholders the most impactful or uncomfortable part of the insight. They see just how challenging this problem may be to solve if immediate action isn't taken. That it's not going to get better or it's only going to get worse.

You agitate the feeling of loss, which triggers them into doing something about it. I'll explain how to agitate loss in Chapter 8.

Step 4: Falling Action (The Plan)

Now, a good story won't leave an audience dangling at the precipice or else they'll have a heart attack. **The tides inevitably begin to turn in favor of the hero, and victory is on the horizon!** The tension begins to dissipate like air from a balloon. Trinity's love resuscitates Neo out of his brush with death, and he comes alive with the power to control the Matrix and defeat Agent Smith. (See Figure 5.5.)

FIGURE 5.5 Narrative arc step: falling action

This phase is where your action plan, or list of recommendations, really shines. You bring the audience's agitation down with your calm and collected strategy. Never fear, help is near! You show everything they need to make this recommendation a reality and demonstrate what they will gain by enacting it. And now that you've deftly walked them over the arc, they are super receptive to hearing your plan because they want a solution and they want it *now*.

Step 5: Denouement (Resolution)

Denouement is fancy Français for "resolution to the conflict." This signals the hero's transformation and story conclusion. Neo has defeated the agents, and the system behind the machines now knows they have a formidable new opponent on their hands. He is on his way to helping the Resistance fight for their freedom.

This is where your recommendations are discussed, approved, and assigned. The plan is now in place. They should leave the meeting with a pronounced feeling of collective relief, knowing that solutions are on the horizon, and they're in the driver's seat of making them happen.

Figure 5.6 shows this arc in full.

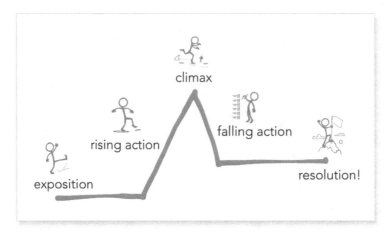

FIGURE 5.6 Full narrative arc

Now, notice how in the final Resolution step, our hero lands on a level above the place they started. This signifies their transformation. Whether the ending to the story is happy or not, the hero has evolved in some way; they will never be the same again with their newfound knowledge, wisdom, abilities, and perspectives.

So, always ask yourself this: what is the transformation you want to inspire? Begin with the end in mind, and you begin the journey on the right foot.

Like Neo's white rabbit, your story will find you once you know what to look for. I encourage you to come into greater awareness of this tool as you come across stories in this book and how stories are woven into the tapestry of our lives. Look for the arc in movies, television, and even your kids' bedtime reads.

Your audience won't see the difference the arc makes in your data stories, but they will *feel* it. And their feelings are crucial to achieving your objective. To be clear, I'm not saying decisions should be driven from a purely emotional place, especially not our dubious "gut instincts." I'm saying that trying to influence decisions from a purely rational place is not as effective as leveraging emotion as well—especially through the power of story.

Avoid the Three "Kiss of Attention Death" Opening Phrases

There are three presentation elements that open most live business presentations.

- Agenda
- Overview
- Executive summary

These artifacts are deeply embedded into corporate meeting culture and are expected by executives. Yet in my extensive observations, their phrasing can induce instant chompie-zombieitis.

During my journey, I wondered what would happen if I revised the script that we're so accustomed to as a corporate collective and tried a few new lines. I'll warn you: these ideas are unconventional and may require finessing with your stakeholders.

I began replacing my "Agenda" titles with variations of the following:

- What we're going to learn today
- How we're going to improve XYZ
- How we're working together on XYZ

Then I replaced my slides titled "Executive Summary" and "Overview" with phrases like these:

- Here's the big story
- What we've learned since last time

Do you see how differently these phrases land with you, as a human being wired for story and entertainment? Then why are we talking to other humans as if we're robots?

Notice that in almost all these phrases, I've used the pronoun "we." This creates a feeling of collaboration and teamwork between you and your audience, which will go a long way to developing rapport and effecting change together.

Carefully give these phrases a try with more open-minded audiences, and observe the effects.

The Role You Play in This Story

To close this chapter, I'd like to use several storytelling techniques to empower you with a helpful mindset for the roles you and your stakeholders play in the story of data presentation. I'm going to reference what is arguably the most excellent story of all time.

Of course, it's *Star Wars*. Picture your favorite *Star Wars* characters, if you're a fan. We start with the central protagonist and antagonist, Luke Skywalker and Darth Vader. The classic incarnations of good (the hero) and evil (the villain).

Let's begin with Darth Vader, the quintessential villain. Based on how south business meetings can go, everyone has an opinion on who the villain is. But in this story, Darth Vader isn't a person sitting at the conference table.

Vader represents the challenges and obstacles your stakeholders face that are interfering with success. Vader is the nosediving conversion rate, the broken product images, the increased competition driving up your advertising costs. The true villain in every presentation is whatever is standing in the way of your audience's success.

Now, I'm getting the sense that you, the practitioner presenter, want to be Luke. Everyone wants to be the hero. But, alas, we are not. Rather, your *stakeholders* are Luke! Remember, your audience is the centerpiece of the presentation process.

If you're going to do this right and show up to the presentation process from a lens of service, then you'll treat your stakeholders like the hero of your data story. Well, if the audience is Luke and their obstacles are their challenges, who does that make us, the practitioner/presenter?

If you said Master Yoda, you're correct! You are the audience's guide. You are their Sensei, their Master Splinter, their Mister Miyagi. You and your insights (your lightsaber) will lead them to their own victory!

I hope that is a useful mindset for understanding how to approach your role in the presentation process. When I began incorporating story and narrative arc into my data presentations, everything changed. This is precisely why I decided to inform data-driven decisions with story-driven data.

> **NOTE**
>
> Your numbers make up your data, but it is your story that will create insight and inspire action.

Chapter Recap

- Story structure and narrative arc are the most crucial and most often missing components of business data presentations.
- Make your audience the hero of the data story by guiding them to overcome their villainous obstacles and claim victory with your insights.
- Freytag's five-point narrative arc offers an effective structure for business data storytelling:
  - Exposition (situation context/refresh what happened)
  - Rising action (what happened and what's surprising)
  - Climax (the cost of not taking action)
  - Falling action (your recommended solutions)
  - Resolution (assigning next steps and roles)

Sandbox Assignment

- Access the Narrative Arc worksheet in the Resource Center (see `https://LeaPica.com/pbm-resource-center`).
- Complete the exercise with your overall message, breaking down the supporting data points into each narrative step.

Create Conceptual Clarity with Analogies

6

"An analogy is like a thought with another thought's hat on."

—Gillian Jacobs

Ever notice how most data presentations are like a box of chocolates because you never know what you're going to get? That can be a good thing and a bad thing, where you need to walk the fine line between clarity and information overwhelm.

The purpose of this book is to help you create as much surprise and delight with your presentations as a classic Whitman's Sampler, without the unpleasant sugar hangover!

The way I just opened this chapter was quite intentional. Do you see how I related the book's topic to something relatable (and munchable) in the real world? And that it referenced the wildly popular catchphrase from the movie *Forrest Gump?* **That was an analogy, and analogies are your best friends for getting less technically savvy stakeholders to understand complex concepts.**

An analogy is a powerful tool for comprehension, especially during a technical presentation. It is a micro-story, defined as "a comparison between two things, typically for the purpose of explanation or clarification."[1]

The easiest ideas to relate between two things are tangible and familiar objects, activities, places, and systems. Those two things could be data lakes and real lakes, or website tracking cookies and triple-chocolate chunk cookies. Not all analogies are as straightforward as these, but you get the idea.

Russell Brunson is the author of the bestseller *Expert Secrets*, which has helped thousands of entrepreneurs successfully sell to audiences using neuroscientific and neurolinguistic programming (NLP)–based principles. He is a big fan of using analogies and simple stories to explain things, often beginning them with something he calls the *kinda like bridge*.

---

[1] "Analogy," Oxford dictionary.

Brunson uses this bridge to explain confusing or obscure ideas such as ketosis, which is a metabolic state of our bodies where we burn our own fat instead of carbohydrates. He "bridges" the gap of understanding by starting with "It's kinda like. . ." and then relates ketosis to the game of Pac-Man, where chomping on a power pellet gives you a strong boost of lasting energy.[2]

During an interview on my podcast, analytics expert Christina Stathopolous shared that she sets up her analogies with "imagine that. . ." and then paints as visual a picture as possible for the audience. Phrases such as "it's kinda like" and "imagine that" set a stage in the audience's brain for processing verbal information in visual terms that they can easily understand.

My favorite way to set up an analogy is with "you know how. . . ." In fact, I do this throughout this book to help you more quickly comprehend the more abstract concepts. One of my favorite analogies is explaining the difference between dashboards and data stories, which are often thought to be the same thing in the analytics field. In it, I relate data dashboards to real-life car dashboards for making simple decisions quickly or addressing bigger issues with an expert, and why a data story has a completely different purpose, structure, and environment.

If you're lacking analogy inspiration, look to your audience's personal interests and hobbies, especially ones you have in common. Does your VP love baseball? Try to relate the rules of the game to how your new advertising platform works. Got a client who loves to cook? Translate a complex testing scenario into a "recipe" they'll grasp right away.

Find some common ground with them or subject matter they're familiar with and get creative with how your numbers relate!

Podcast Sound Byte: Jim Sterne (Ep. 005) Godfather of digital analytics and author of *Artificial Intelligence for Marketing*

"If your stakeholders just don't 'get it,' then you're trying to teach them the wrong thing. As in the classic saying, "Don't try to teach a pig to sing; it will never work, and you'll only annoy the pig."

---

[2]Brunson, Russel. *Expert Secrets: The Underground Playbook for Converting Your Online Visitors into Lifelong Customers*. Hay House Inc., 2022. ISBN # 978-1401970604

> If you're talking to somebody whose job is not connected to analytics, don't try to convince them that the analytics is fabulous. Try to convince them that you have a unique perspective on their job, and you've got some information that will help them make a better decision, which will make them *look good*.
>
> Your job is to understand your goals and help them achieve their goals. But if you're trying to explain cookie deletion and cache files and proxy servers, you're having the wrong conversation."

Communicating Relatable Scale with Large Numbers

You can also relate figures that are difficult to grasp (such as uncommonly large numbers of people or dollars) to concepts that enable the brain to comprehend their scale. Nancy Duarte expands on how you can help an audience visualize large numbers in her book, *DataStory*.[3]

She suggests that these are the four most effective ways to demonstrate scale:

- Size (bigger than a breadbox, a beach house, or the Burj Khalifa)
- Distance (inches, feet, yards, miles, outer space)
- Time (seconds, minutes, days, eons)
- Speed (miles per hour, knots, light years)

One of the most powerful analogies I've ever heard was when a professional speaker illustrated the difference between a million dollars and a billion dollars. The topic was how the coronavirus amplified income inequality, which was both fascinating and sobering. To demonstrate just how abstract that distinction is and the sheer enormity of $1 billion, he related money to time by asking us to imagine earning $1 million dollars per week.

Then he asked the audience to guess how long it would take us to earn $1 billion. Guesses were thrown ranging from several months to several years, with an obviously low degree of confidence.

---

[3]Duarte, Nancy. *DataStory: Explain Data and Inspire Action Through Story*. Ideapress Publishing, 2019. ISBN # 978-1940858982

His answer stunned the audience: if we earned $1 million per week (an inconceivable idea for most), it would take us almost *20 years* to stockpile $1 billion!

This was mind-boggling, and that was the point. His comparison had the exact intended effect to demonstrate the staggering magnitude of income inequality. He continued to astonish us by proceeding with the analogy toward $1 trillion, which would take us more than *19,000 years to earn* at the same rate! Just slightly longer than my average tenure during my digital agency days, am I right? This is an incomprehensible scale for most of us—except perhaps the accounting teams at Apple, Amazon, and government banks.

Powerful stuff, right? Try equating large numbers with these ideas: distance (like miles around the Earth), speed (like walking or flying), volume (like the number of people a movie theater holds), or time (like running the dishwasher). Make the comparisons mentally accessible.

My closing thought on analogies and metaphors is that while they are wildly effective storytelling devices, that doesn't make every analogy right for your idea or your audience.

Take care that the metaphor you're using is easy to understand and that its relevance to your concept is crystal clear. Else, you run the risk of confusing your audience with a technique that was designed to prevent their confusion.

> **NOTE**
>
> You'll know you've nailed helping them grasp the magnitude of your number when they respond with a thoughtful "whoa."

Chapter Recap

- Analogies are a powerful tool for helping your audience relate to complex and technical concepts through real-world ideas and objects.
- Four ways to effectively help them related to large-scale numbers are size, distance, time, and speed.

Sandbox Assignment

- Review your data for any complex or confusing concepts or figures that are exceptionally large or small in magnitude.
- Contemplate different analogies for explaining complexity in simpler terms and helping to envision numerical scale.

Suit Up Your Recommendations for Action

7

"A little less conversation, a little more action, please."

—Elvis Presley

Action should be the primary reason that data presentation exists. The actions we bring to our stakeholders come in the form of recommendations, and they are the key to moving the business forward based on the area you're charged with measuring.

This, if you remember, is what your stakeholder is silently asking for.

In the aforementioned *DataStory*, Nancy Duarte explains the imperative of mastering the art of recommendation: "When you use your data to provide timely and critical guidance to decision-makers, you change organizational outcomes. You become the mentor, and your data is the magical tool that gets them unstuck on their journey. Giving others data in the nick of time brings greater success in reaching a desired goal."

I find that presentation recommendations are often vague, uninspiring, unrelated, and, at times, crammed into the back of the deck as an afterthought. In making and reviewing countless recommendations over my years as an analyst and consultant, I've identified five criteria that ensure a recommendation's survival past the end of the workday and completion with even the toughest stakeholders.

These criteria were inspired by a popular framework for professional and career goal setting. Hint: they can make you and your recommendations sound a whole lot SMART-er.

That's right, they are an adaptation of the SMART criteria, first discussed by George Doran and commonly associated with Peter Drucker. The SMART system is often used for employee performance evaluation.[1] The next sections look at how they can be used for recommendations.

---

[1]en.wikipedia.org/wiki/SMART_criteria

S for Specific: The Recommendation Outlines a Clear Course of Action

Make it abundantly clear what you think the team should do. I've found that the clearer the path to completing the recommendation, the more likely it will get completed. I've encountered recommendations like "complete migration of accounts," "lower ad spend," and "improve conversion." These are okay starting points, but much too vague: *how* are you going to do these things? What's the first next step that needs to happen? Make it Windex clear.

The classic recommendation standby of "we'll continue to monitor performance" also falls squarely into the valley of vague. Continuing to monitor performance is not a strategic recommendation; it is a job description. So, choose more strategic directives that stretch beyond what's beyond your daily tasks.

I'll show you a few examples and build upon them using the criteria in turn:

- "Decrease ad spend on ABC website"
- "Conduct five new subject line tests"
- "Create five new FAQ articles on account management issues"

Notice the specificity of the tasks suggested, as well as how each recommendation begins. Each of these starts with an action verb, which creates clarity around what exactly is to be done. Figure 7.1 shows a table of action to use with your recommendation (a compilation inspired by Nancy Duarte's *DataStory* and Cole Nussbaumer Knaflic's *Storytelling with Data*).

Accept	Commence	Empower	Facilitate	Invest	Persuade	Receive
Agree	Create	Encourage	Familiarize	Invigorate	Plan	Recall
Begin	Decide	Engage	Form	Discern	Promote	Report
Change	Differentiate	Establish	Implement	Learn	Pursue	Respond
Collaborate	Do	Examine	Influence	Lean Into	Recommend	Review
Secure	Support	Simplify	Restore	Start	Complete	Try
Attempt	Investigate	Understand	Validate	Verify	Wait	Zero In

FIGURE 7.1 Recommendation action verbs
Adapted from Nancy Duarte's *DataStory* and Cole Nussbaumer Knaflic's *Storytelling with Data*

Now, while I hope you go big at work and in life, I also advise grounding your suggestions in the reality of your organizational or client constraints.

If you suggest that the VP of marketing approve a new email software vendor migration within three weeks when your vendor approval process spans three months, then there's a good chance it won't happen. Be realistic about what you're asking everyone to do.

M for Measurable: The Recommendation's Impact Is Feasibly Measured and Motivating Toward Action as a Result

I theorize that many recommendations are too "soft" or fail to galvanize an audience because they aren't clearly measurable. It's essential to communicate the "why" behind the recommendation and gather consensus on what you are measuring and how it will translate to success. I'm not talking about "vanity metrics" like website visits and time spent on site. The usefulness of those measures has long been called into question.

Measurable recommendations make clear the impact they will have on the project or business. Here's how to build upon the previous examples:

- "Decrease ad spend on ABC website + to lower cost per conversion"
- "Conduct five new subject line tests + to increase email open rate"
- "Create five new FAQ articles on account management issues + to reduce customer service inquiries" (secondary success measure = page views of articles)

When you assign measurement as a concrete way to revisit a recommendation, your audience will understand its impact and feel more confident executing it. Honestly, who wants to act on a suggestion with low impact or low measurability? In this age of extreme busyness, who has time for that?

Measurability is a good indicator that a recommendation meets the *Specific* criteria, killing the first two birds with the second stone.

A for Assigned: A Person or Team Is Accountable for Task Completion

When a recommendation is given the green light during a meeting but assigned to no one, guess who completes it? Exactly—no one. Until someone invents a magical AI "Recommendation-ator" machine, a specific person or group of people must be tasked with execution.

That may look like any of these:

- "Decrease ad spend on ABC website + to lower cost per conversion + **Assigned to digital ad team**"
- "Conduct five new subject line tests + to increase email open rate **+ Assigned to Ellen on email team**"
- "Create five new FAQ articles on account management issues + to reduce customer service inquiries" (secondary success measure = page views of articles) **+ Assigned to customer content team**

With this, no one will exchange awkward glances when the VP asks whether the recommendation was completed at the next meeting. I'm not suggesting that you assign all your recommendations to people before going into the meeting.

That's because some of your suggestions may not get the green light, and delegating the task may not be your call to make. I'm also not suggesting you order your CMO to complete a task in public.

Stewarding that process puts you in a position of power and influence, which is a good thing. It can also be super intimidating for practitioners.

This is where a senior advocate can be helpful as a resource for pushing assignments through bureaucratic red tape. Your stakeholders include peers whose jobs may be made more complicated or task list longer because of your recommendation, and they may resist. An advocate can help grease the wheels of change.

TIP

If a recommendation is approved, it should have an owner by the end of the meeting.

R for Relevant: The Recommendation Is Tied Directly to an Insight in the Presentation

More often than I'd like, I'll watch a presenter suggest something that completely catches me off guard. That's because I can't figure out why they're recommending it. Then I realize it's because the recommendation had nothing to do with any of the insights presented.

This habit of quietly sliding a recommendation "across the conference table" is a tricky play because it can confuse the audience. While I appreciate the effort to use the meeting to cross off any niggling to-do list items, it isn't the time or place if they're not directly related to the presentation objective and throughline.

Make sure any recommendation you make directly references an insight you've already shared.

T for Time-Bound: The Recommendation Is Given a Reasonable Deadline

Remember how if no one is assigned to a recommendation, no one handles it? The same goes if the deadline for the recommendation is never.

Deadlines help prevent what I call "hangnail" recommendations. They persist on every readout, but no one does anything about them, so they never go away. "We will continue to monitor performance" and "Optimize results" are prime examples of a hangnail. The key is to make the deadline achievable with enough room so there's no cutting it close to major marketing events. Deadlines are critical for meeting seasonal or holiday objectives, such as launching Fall Fashion creative on time for Fashion Week.

Here's how to round out the recommendations with time:

- "Decrease ad spend on ABC website **+ by August 31** + to lower cost per conversion. + Assigned to: digital ad team"
- "Conduct five new subject line tests + **within next 10 weeks** + to increase email open rate. + Assigned to Ellen on email team"
- "Create five new FAQ articles on account management issues + **by end of Q4** + to reduce customer service inquiries" (secondary success measure = page views of articles) + Assigned to customer content team

A truly SMART recommendation will read like this: "Decrease ad spend on ABC website by August 31 to lower our cost per conversion. Assigned to: digital ad team." Now that's a mighty fine recommendation right there!

When you compare the previous recommendations to our earlier example of "complete account migration," do you see how much more motivated a stakeholder may be to act on it?

How great would it feel to see action taken on your recommendations? I firmly believe that the SMART-er they are, the bigger the impact you'll make.

> **Podcast Sound Byte: Nancy Duarte (Ep. 050) CEO of Duarte and bestselling author of *DataStory*, *Resonate*, and *slide:ology***
>
> There are two different energies around why we need to communicate. One of them is getting decisions made quickly. It's in service of making a decision, which means making the data stick. Once the decision is made, that spins out a lot of action, a lot of activities, and a lot of things that need to happen based on that decision.
>
> That's when you need to inspire with data. Decision-makers want a strategic adviser. They don't want somebody kicking up dust with a bunch of charts and without a finely tuned data story.
>
> If you're communicating up and they don't see your insights or recommendations as something that they are personally measured by and if they don't see it as something that is going to help their performance, they're not going to be interested.
>
> If what you're presenting doesn't tie to what matters most to them, you probably shouldn't even be in front of them. But if you can tie your idea to one of those things and your data solves it, then you should have a seat at the executive suite table.

Chapter Recap

- Recommendations are the fuel for business progress and demonstrate your value beyond being just a "number cruncher."
- Crafting your recommendations using the SMART criteria will give them the best chance to earn the green light.

Sandbox Assignment

- Locate two or three of your data presentation recommendations.
- Run them through the SMART criteria, found in the Resource Center (see https://LeaPica.com/pbm-resource-center).

Translate Your Content into a Persuasive Outline 8

"Without a solid foundation, you'll have trouble creating anything of value."
—Erika Oppenheimer

This is a critical juncture in the conceptualization process. You've assessed your audience's needs, identified your core message, gathered supporting insights and put them in story format, and suited up your recommendations for action. It might be tempting to fire up PowerPoint, but I ask you to resist the urge to crank out a slide deck this early, and I'll tell you why.

There is another invisible force present in every memorable and successful presentation: a narrative structure. No, I'm not referring to the narrative *arc* from Chapter 5. They are different.

Whereas the arc shows the rising and falling of action and resolution within each story point and the overarching story as a whole, **narrative structure organizes and arranges all the presentation's content into one cohesive and persuasive framework.**

If you think of your presentation storyline, data points, and recommendations as a car's internal components (the engine, carburetor, fuel tank, and so on), the narrative structure is the chassis. A chassis is the vehicle frame that holds each component in its rightful place so the car doesn't embarrassingly fall to pieces when you pull out of the driveway.

Ideally, a narrative structure guides an audience through a message and story to arrive at a recommendation or request, which requires organization and influence. In my experience, there's no better structure for creating order and influence than the Presenting by Boxes framework, invented by presentation guru Olivia Mitchell.

One Method to Rule Them All

Mitchell created Presenting by Boxes to help startups organize their pitch deck content into a persuasive structure to secure venture capitalist funding. While that may seem like not the right fit for informing and explaining data to stakeholders, let me make something abundantly clear.

When you present to your decision-makers, you are *selling* your insights and recommendations to them. You're selling why they should pay attention to and act on your data, which may require them to shift their priorities, mobilize and realign their human resources, and part with their budget. So, a sales-oriented paradigm is a "pitch-perfect" match for your goals!

Over time, I gradually tailored the Boxes framework to fit the unique objectives and expected components of the typical corporate data presentation to inform or persuade (such as a campaign readout, a conversion rate test, or a quarterly business review).

It became a game-changer in creating focus, clarity, and motivation for my audience. I now use this framework in every presentation I create. It *works*.

The Boxes' persuasive power may also be used to pitch a business case for project approval or even training staff on a new platform. By the end of this process, you'll have a complete outline of your presentation content where your objective will be crystal clear, and every idea and insight will have a suitable home.

The Presenting by Boxes framework looks precisely as it sounds: it is a series of boxes arranged in a way where the presentation components are logically placed. Figure 8.1 shows what that structure looks like.

Note that this structure is not how your presentation slides should look. It is meant to be invisible to your audience and acts only as an organizational guide for your content. And never fear, young Jedi; if you're scratching your head at how to translate this to a linear deck format, I show you exactly how to do that in Chapter 10.

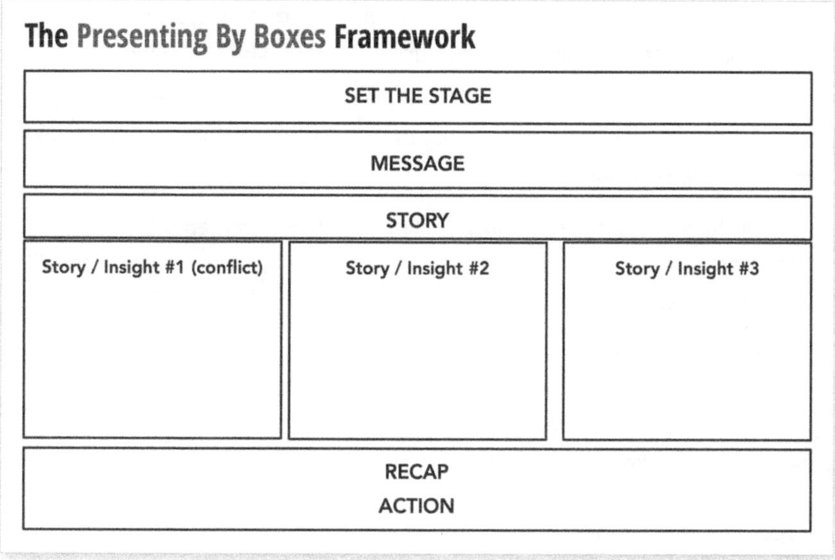

The Presenting By Boxes Framework

SET THE STAGE

MESSAGE

STORY

Story / Insight #1 (conflict)	Story / Insight #2	Story / Insight #3

RECAP ACTION

FIGURE 8.1 Blank Presenting By Boxes outline

The Data-Friendly Presenting by Boxes Framework, Step-by-Step

For clarity, I walk you through each step of this process using an example from a real digital marketing readout.

THE HOOK/SETTING THE STAGE

Every memorable story begins with a compelling "hook"—something that grabs and holds the audience's attention. I do this by declaring the objective of the meeting and hinting that there are exciting insights ahead.

Example: My opening script would go something like this: "Hello, everyone! We're gathered here today to decide upon the Q3 optimization plan for our paid search campaign. We have some interesting findings to share with you, so let's get started!"

Next, I create anticipation by giving my audience a cursory understanding of the presentation content and piquing their curiosity about what's coming.

Example: "First, we're going to cover what we optimized in Q2, what happened as a result, and what surprised us along the way. Then we'll discuss what we recommend going forward."

Can you already feel the focus and confidence in that statement? I haven't given the whole plotline away, but I've set the stage for the audience in a way they'll likely have not experienced before.

This is also where you paint the backdrop needed to understand the rest of the presentation. You can show expected key performance indicators, the current campaign ad creative, relevant landing pages, test parameters, market research, financial figures, or anything required to contextualize your findings.

THE MESSAGE/THROUGHLINE

Here, you'll announce the unifying element of your presentation: your throughline. This, if you recall, summarizes the entire presentation in a single sentence. **At this point, your audience should grasp what the meeting is about and be able to share it with others.** Declaring the message this way serves to complete the hook and bait your audience into wanting more.

I'm often asked where the agenda slide goes in this framework. I don't have a hard and fast rule for that; however, I have found that revealing the meeting's full agenda after the throughline maintains momentum, kind of like a TV show's opening credits after the "last episode" refresher.

Example: "So the big story is, our Q2 digital advertising optimizations increased our landing page conversion rate by 14 percent, which did not meet our target goal increase of 20 percent as we'd projected. However, we dug into the data and found three main reasons why performance fell short, and we have three ideas for meeting our target."

This relays what could be considered "bad news" (a term I don't subscribe to) and reframes it as a potential learning opportunity (the term I do subscribe to). This solution-oriented framing exudes confidence while alleviating any anxiety the audience may feel over the results.

THE STORY

Remember that the story is the substance of your presentation. You'll now deliver the supporting evidence of your throughline with your analytical insights, ideas, projections, and recommendations.

The goal of this section is not to just demonstrate your number-crunching prowess. Rather, by the time you have finished this section, your audience should be thoroughly informed, convinced, and prepared to act.

Think of the distinct insights or stories in your presentation as a set of Russian nesting dolls; you have a large mama story that cradles a nest of baby stories. Your mama story is the throughline, while your baby stories support the mama so that people believe the mama.

You might be asking, how many baby stories should you include?

THE MAGIC NUMBER

If you refer to the previous Boxes diagram, you'll see that the Story section is broken into three distinct modules. Now, I want you to count how many Story modules are there. Only three, right? Yes, and that's the point.

I recommend presenting no more than three to five main insights or areas of evidence to your audience. Why? First, three is a number of significance in storytelling, dating back to ancient myths of old. The three-act play, the three muses, the three little pigs, three questions to get past the Bridgekeeper in *Monty Python and the Holy Grail*. But why is the number 3 so prevalent?

More modern research indicates that three is an ideal number for enabling recall of information from memory. Specifically, the working memory, which is a psychological system that can temporarily hold a limited amount of information for processing.[1]

We'll explore the working memory further in Act II; what matters most here is understanding that the working memory can hold only three to five "chunks" of new information at one time.[2] Any more than that, and their attention becomes an endangered species. Why does this matter?

When you present much more than three to five main chunks, you run the risk of overwhelming their working memory. I'm not saying that you're limited to three to five single data points in total. I mean three to five main areas of insight, where you drill down into each area. This prevents you from hauling a "kitchen sink" deck into your meeting.

Presenting 50 random and disjointed data points on a conveyor belt of slides can short out your stakeholders' attention spans and result in an army of darkness. That is precisely what this framework is designed to help you avoid.

---

[1]Miyake, A.; Shah, P., eds. (1999). *Models of working memory. Mechanisms of active maintenance and executive control.* Cambridge University Press. ISBN 0-521-58325-X.

[2]www.ncbi.nlm.nih.gov/pmc/articles/PMC2864034

As such, you need to be discerning. You must search your data haystack for the most impactful data needles that will *move* the needle for your stakeholders. That will answer your burning question of what data to include!

If you're struggling with which three areas to focus upon, think back to the list of interview questions. Remember how you prompted your stakeholder to "ask the data three questions" in human-speak? That isn't a coincidence. Often those three questions have formed the basis for my analysis because I knew they were sourced from specific stakeholder needs.

TELLING THE STORY THROUGH THE FIVE-STEP INSIGHT JOURNEY

Just like there is a narrative arc throughout the mama story, there's a narrative arc in each of the baby stories. The following translates the narrative arc into questions you can apply to these individual insight journeys. You'll see how to apply it as I continue the example.

#1 Exposition: What's the Topic, and What Happened?

You'll begin each of these modules with the insight, idea, or section of your presentation. I like to first present the insights my stakeholders have already asked for, especially ones where the findings are commensurate with past performance. If they haven't asked, I present the findings that are either expected or least surprising.

This sets the stage, eases them into the story, and identifies the characters in the data. But it also sets the audience up for twists and turns in the next arc step, which will raise their tension.

Example: "We've evaluated three content sites in our digital ad campaign for optimization. First, let's look at Site A. This site has been in our campaign portfolio for quite some time, but we've never really focused on it until now."

#2 Rising Action: What's the Conflict or Opportunity, and Why Did It Surprise Us?

Now you turn up the heat by revealing the conflict (a problem or opportunity) the data is showing. You throw in an unexpected twist to further raise tension and thus, attention.

Example: "When we took a closer look, we noticed that Site A has been gradually increasing in cost per acquisition. Its CPA has increased fourfold in the last three months and is currently the most expensive site in our portfolio. Last month, we spent 30 percent of our total ad budget on Site A, but it generated only 5 percent of conversions. Luckily, we caught it this time."

#3 Climax: How Bad Could It Get, and What's at Stake If We Do Nothing?

This is where your audience's tension is maximized by agitating just how dire the situation is. Even more important than how bad things are is to show how bad things could get if no one takes action.

In other words, what's at stake for them to lose? Exposing the stakes to your audience leverages an important psychological dynamic: loss aversion.

Loss aversion was coined by Daniel Kahneman and Amos Tversky to describe the human tendency to prioritize avoiding pain and loss. In Kahneman's book *Thinking, Fast and Slow*, he characterizes loss aversion where "the response to losses is stronger than the response to corresponding gains."[3]

Meaning, we would rather sacrifice a potential upside to prevent a potential downside. Nailing the climax is about getting in your audience's heads and articulating what they won't want to lose in the terms they understand.

Let's say your lead generation landing page analysis reveals that your conversion rate has dropped by 15 percent over the last two months due to a major layout change. The change was pushed through for cosmetic reasons by executive management; unfortunately, what they gained in good looks has cost them in new leads. But you know they're not going to take this news well.

So, before the meeting, you carefully calculate the estimated number of lost leads, factoring in weekly and seasonal trends. Then you assess your average lead value. Then you run it past a colleague or two to ensure your calculations seem on point. After you unveil the not-so-great news, you raise the stakes by showing them what will happen if nothing changes.

Here's how we would raise the stakes for our ad optimization scenario:

Example: "If we do nothing, things stand to get worse. At our current run rates, we estimate that we'll spend three times more on our ad budget for conversions than we need to. When we translate our potential lost conversions to dollars (with the assumption of an average $1,500 value per lead), we could be leaving

---

[3]Tversky, A., Kahneman, D. *Advances in prospect theory: Cumulative representation of uncertainty.* J Risk Uncertainty 5, 297–323 (1992). doi.org/10.1007/BF00122574

up to $250,000 on the table." (Obviously, these numbers are here for educational purposes only.)

As you'll see, loss aversion is a potent tool of influence. If you can reasonably estimate what inaction will cost, you stand a better chance of lighting a fire under your audience. And it's the perfect way to hold tension at the climax point before you proceed with the story.

Now, how should you handle positive opportunities where there's something to be gained? Here's where reading your audience's personality is helpful: does your audience respond more to positive or negative spins? Each opportunity can be framed as a cost if no action is taken, so test different angles to see which frame your stakeholders are more responsive to.

Take care not to abuse loss aversion; don't go overboard by overdramatizing the results with a doomsday prediction that isn't grounded in fact. Keep the story in service to the truth. This strategy won't work if they don't trust what you say. Just avoid being neutral or tepid because if they don't care about the story, they don't give you the green light.

#4 Falling Action: What Should We Do About It?

Once the audience is clear on what they stand to lose if they do nothing, you've primed them to receive your recommendations with open ears and arms.

I'm often asked how many recommendations one should give for each insight. The best answer I've heard was during my podcast interview with analytics rockstar and psychology nerd Evan LaPointe of CORE Consulting. **LaPointe suggests that for every major insight, offer at least two recommendations.**

He posits that if you give only one, you could pigeonhole the audience into a corner. If they disagree with the single choice, it may create tension among you. Giving stakeholders options provides space for them to evaluate.

Offer more than three, and you run the risk of analysis paralysis. Should stakeholders have their own suggestions, give them the floor to share openly with the team.

Example: "To get our conversion rate performance back on track, we recommend proceeding with one of these two options: we either completely pause Site B for a three-month probationary period or reduce our spend by at least 75 percent to stem the bleeding."

There are several paths the conversation can take at this point; your audience could enthusiastically nod in agreement, be on the fence, or flat-out object to your position. Should the last happen, I've got you covered in a moment.

#5 Resolution: How Can We Enact the Plan Together?

Now, I usually suggest moving on to the next story module without a full resolution at this point. Sometimes your modules will link together and be part of a cohesive strategy, so making decisions at this point wouldn't make sense. Deciding on the specific steps the team will take is best served with a closing discussion at the end of the meeting.

Podcast Sound Byte: Rand Fishkin (Ep. 018) *CEO SparkToro, Founder of Moz, and Whiteboard Friday Legend*

"I've worked with a number of speakers for our Mozcon series. I tried to make every set of slides that is conveying a piece of information (or concept or tactic or a tool) fit into this model: 'Before I heard your advice, I was doing things this way. But after I heard your advice, I'm going to now start doing this thing differently, which will improve my results.'

I think if you can honestly assess all the elements of your slide deck in that fashion, whether it's an individual slide that's describing one tactic or an overarching theme that your presentation is giving, if you can assess from that perspective, then I think you can build something truly actionable."

Bonus Step: Anticipate Audience Objections

You know that super irritating thing that audiences sometimes do where they challenge your findings, poke holes in your methodologies, and object to your suggestions?

Ugh, who do they think they are, right? Are they *trying* to undermine you in front of your team and managers? I empathize, as I know this frustration well. This might seem hard to believe, but your stakeholders may not have such nefarious intentions.

Chances are, you've been confronted by two invisible yet potent adversaries in their brain: **confirmation bias** and **resistance to change**.

Confirmation bias **is the psychological tendency to interpret new evidence as confirmation of one's existing beliefs or theories.**[4] This translates to a habit of seeking out information that "confirms" current beliefs and rejecting information that collides with those beliefs.

Confirmation bias is one of many "cognitive biases," which are at the root of every misunderstanding, disagreement, and conflict on this planet. In a perfect world, our audience is listening only with their logical, rational left brain. But we now understand that they're not, yes? Like it or not, your audience's emotions are inextricably linked to their biases.

In our example, perhaps Site A, the site you want to push pause on, is the darling of a certain executive. Site A has been a mainstay of the marketing portfolio for several reasons, such as the following:

- They're a key strategic partner.
- They used to be a top performer.
- The executive's son "loves that site and thinks we should advertise on it" (not a made-up scenario).

Emotion-driven decisions happen in business all the time, and it's important to remember this human truth: the most indisputable, iron-clad data will never overcome the fact that no one wants to hear their baby is ugly.

The other villain you'll encounter is *resistance to change*. Despite how much the business world wants to effect change, the reality is that not everyone will be on board if it means changing their priorities, how they do their work, or adding work to their already overloaded plate.

Your recommendations will most likely lead to more work, so it's important to prepare a convincing case for change. It involves a bit of psychological counter-intelligence on your part.

Your mission, should you choose to accept it, is to identify and address your audience's potential objections *before* they raise them. This means using communication techniques to "walk them across the bridge" from their

---

[4] Oxford Dictionary.

perspective to yours. Here's my top-secret formula and scripts for anticipating and preempting objections:

1. Acknowledge and validate the potential objection.

   - "It's commonly believed that. . ."
   - "We know this may raise concerns. . ."
   - "We realize that we expected this to look like. . ."

2. Validate why they feel that way or that you used to feel that way.

   - "It's completely understandable to think that. . ."
   - "We can see why this is. . ."
   - "I also used to think that, until. . ."

3. Transition to your counterargument.

   - This is the pivotal moment, when you're about to counter their counter. We often rebut with "but," which has an inherently disagreeable connotation. I find a more productive phrase to be "and yet," which allows for both sides to peacefully coexist.
   - "And yet, the most recent data is showing. . ."
   - "And yet, our analysis showed otherwise. . ."
   - "Despite that, emerging research is revealing. . ."

4. Reveal that you've already considered a solution to their concern.

   - "We've already taken that into account in our solution. . ."
   - "We know this might sound uncomfortable, so. . ."
   - "Luckily, we believe we've found a solution. . ."

5. Encourage their participation in the process (the key to overcoming resistance).

   - "Could that work for you?"
   - "What else can we provide?"
   - "How can we collaborate with you?"

This demonstrates that you've thought of every angle, including how to allay their concerns by mitigating the risks of accepting your recommendation.

Here's a step-by-step example:

Acknowledge: "Now, we realize that our recommendation to pause Site A may raise a few concerns. We know there are special considerations around continuing to work with them."

Validate: "Site A has been a strategic partner in our portfolio since we first launched, and there's a special relationship there."

Transition: "And yet, our most recent analysis clearly shows the steady decline in performance, despite our team's best efforts to optimize our ads and placements."

Alleviate: "We want you to know that we've already considered a backup plan by preparing to reactivate Site A if our performance doesn't improve. We'll be watching very closely to ensure this move is made carefully."

Encourage: "Could that work for you? What else can we do to collaborate on this?"

Now *that.* . .feels like a bulletproof counterargument to me.

If someone has an objection you didn't predict, don't sweat it. We're data practitioners, not mind readers. Always give them the floor to express their concerns. It's vital that your stakeholders feel seen and heard, especially if their beliefs and biases are challenged.

The ability to navigate cognitive bias and resistance to change is a valuable tool for paving your path as a change agent. If this sounds too ambitious, don't worry. This step isn't critical to your success, but if you can swing it, you'll have a major edge in pushing your ideas through.

And that closes out your first story module, phew! Understanding how story unfolds and intersects with your audience's psychology is crucial to developing story-driven data presentations. You may have noticed that I didn't include the Resolution phase of the narrative arc within this story module. That's because we'll resolve the entire story at once in the next Boxes module.

Once you've completed your first story module, then simply wash, rinse, and repeat for two to four more stories or sections. Consistency is essential for keeping the audience in lock step with you; it also takes out the guesswork to figure out how to organize it all.

Once you've gone through your three to five story modules, the Story section of the Boxes framework is complete. You are ready to bring it all home!

THE RECAP

Remember in the beginning of this book, I mentioned that repetition is a mechanism that helps the brain commit information to our memory? If you didn't remember before, you now have a much better chance thanks to the power of repetition!

Repetition leverages a mental processing method called *maintenance rehearsal*, which helps extend information held in the working memory.[5] I think of how repetition works this way: imagine you're installing a new floor, and each floorboard is one of your insights or ideas.

Afterward, you'll apply a layer of shellac to seal and protect the floor from scrapes and scuffs. The mind works the same way: recapping serves as a coating of shellac for the brain to "seal in" your information.

The more repetitions, the better. This is the reason why I sound like a broken record in this book (like reiterating the importance of action in your presentations). It's why I include a recap of each chapter, each act, and the entire book. If you read this book again, say, in six to eight months, you'll retain even more.

When you've finished your story and supporting evidence, begin to wind down the session. Do this with a recap or summary slide that you preface with, "So, let's take a moment to look back at the major points we covered today."

Example: Let's take a moment to review what we've learned and discussed here today! We covered insights 1, 2, and 3, and recommended XYZ courses of action. Are there any other questions before we move on to discussing our next steps?

ACTION PLAN

This is where the rubber of your story meets the road of recommendations. You've made your case, pitched your plan, and now you'll bring resolution to the full story.

If you're high enough on the team food chain, I encourage you to establish a power position for yourself by leading the action discussion (with your manager's advance approval, of course). **As you talk through each recommendation, you'll gather a consensus of yay or nay; remember to identify who is accountable for completing it and by when.** If you don't feel confident leading that discussion, prepare to hand it off to a more senior team member.

> **NOTE**
>
> Repetition is a key vehicle for learning.

> **TIP**
>
> Repeating your key points will help your audience retain your valuable insights, which will help you achieve goal #2: being memorable! (Remember?)

---

[5]www.verywellhealth.com/elaborative-rehearsal-a-better-way-to-memorize-98694

Finally, finish strong by thanking the audience for their time and announcing when you'll deliver the handout. One of the biggest mistakes I see is a mushy closing characterized by a mumbled, "Um, so, that's it. Thanks." No, no, no. Imagine an edge-of-your-seat *Stranger Things* episode concluding with one of the characters turning to the screen and saying, "Uh, I guess that's it," and then a fade to black. Would that *ever* happen? No! Not if they want to get renewed for another season, that is.

Don't leave the room without signaling definitive closure.

By the end of this section—and the meeting—everyone in the room should have clarity on the information presented and the plan for going forward. Signs you've gotten this right are generous compliments, enthusiastic requests for follow-up, high-fives, and hearty goodbyes.

Figure 8.2 is a visual representation of the complete Boxes framework.

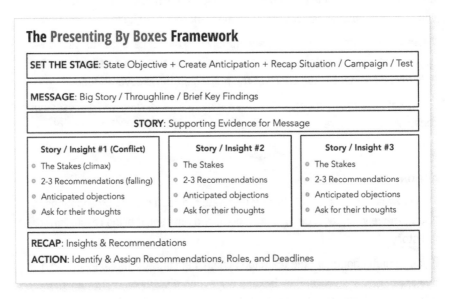

The Presenting By Boxes Framework

SET THE STAGE: State Objective + Create Anticipation + Recap Situation / Campaign / Test

MESSAGE: Big Story / Throughline / Brief Key Findings

STORY: Supporting Evidence for Message

Story / Insight #1 (Conflict)	Story / Insight #2	Story / Insight #3
○ The Stakes (climax)	○ The Stakes	○ The Stakes
○ 2-3 Recommendations (falling)	○ 2-3 Recommendations	○ 2-3 Recommendations
○ Anticipated objections	○ Anticipated objections	○ Anticipated objections
○ Ask for their thoughts	○ Ask for their thoughts	○ Ask for their thoughts

RECAP: Insights & Recommendations
ACTION: Identify & Assign Recommendations, Roles, and Deadlines

FIGURE 8.2 Completed Boxes Framework

To see this framework in action with a real business data scenario, Figure 8.3 shows a completed Boxes outline from one of my workshop participants.

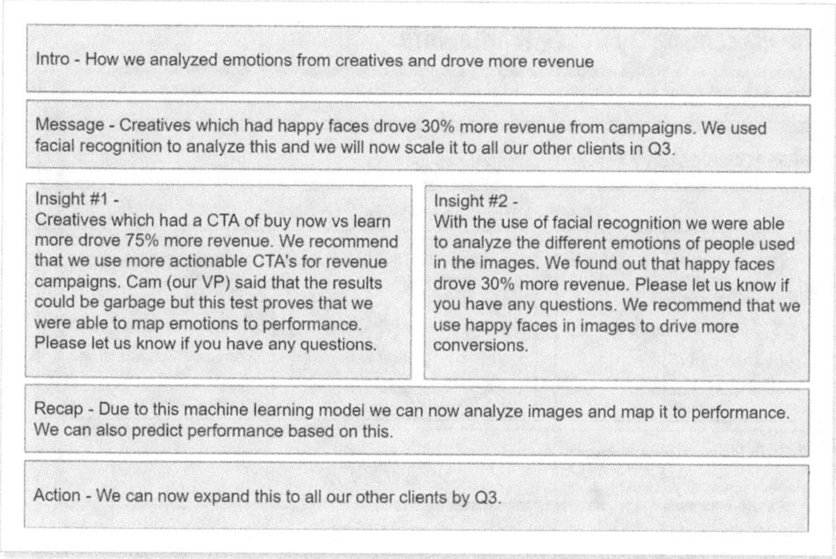

Intro - How we analyzed emotions from creatives and drove more revenue

Message - Creatives which had happy faces drove 30% more revenue from campaigns. We used facial recognition to analyze this and we will now scale it to all our other clients in Q3.

Insight #1 -
Creatives which had a CTA of buy now vs learn more drove 75% more revenue. We recommend that we use more actionable CTA's for revenue campaigns. Cam (our VP) said that the results could be garbage but this test proves that we were able to map emotions to performance. Please let us know if you have any questions.

Insight #2 -
With the use of facial recognition we were able to analyze the different emotions of people used in the images. We found out that happy faces drove 30% more revenue. Please let us know if you have any questions. We recommend that we use happy faces in images to drive more conversions.

Recap - Due to this machine learning model we can now analyze images and map it to performance. We can also predict performance based on this.

Action - We can now expand this to all our other clients by Q3.

FIGURE 8.3 Example of Boxes outline from a workshop participant

Notice that this is a way to truly corral the wild herds of data typically found in business data presentations, finding clarity, succinctness, and a less over-whelming way to create the presentation.

Now that you can see the big picture, I'll show you the multiple narrative arcs woven throughout your presentation. There is the overarching mama arc that begins with your intro and throughline, which rises during the Story section and reaches a final resolution through the Recap/Action sections. Then there are the baby arcs, or nested narratives, which allow your audience to process each on its own. Figure 8.4 shows what that looks like.

The Role of the Appendix

Ah yes, you may have noticed I didn't mention the appendix in the Boxes framework. That's because it's not a core component of your story but, rather, a useful *supplement*.

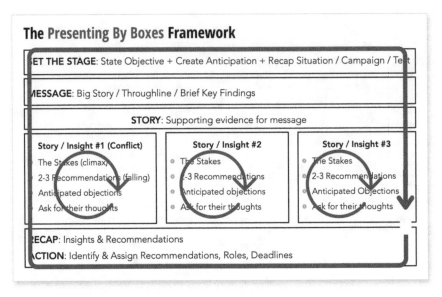

FIGURE 8.4 Nested narrative arcs in the Boxes Framework

The appendix should be the most voluminous and nonessential section of your deck. It's called that because, like a real appendix, it is not a critical organ of the live presentation. For me, the purpose of the appendix is to hold data, diagrams, screenshots, or content I want in my back pocket that won't derail the main presentation topic. Kevin Hillstrom offered a simple guideline for the appendix during our podcast interview: "If I know the majority of my audience will benefit, I'm going to put it in my presentation. If I know the minority of my audience will benefit, I'm going to put it in the appendix."

There you have it: this is the most effective and focused framework I've found to date for creating persuasive business presentations. I guarantee that once you implement this technique, you will never again be wringing your hands about where to begin and what to include.

Chapter Recap

- The most successful data presentations have a narrative structure that organizes content in a meaningful and action-oriented way.
- The Presenting by Boxes framework consists of these sections:

■ **Intro/Hook:** Set the stage and create anticipation.

■ **Message:** Declare your throughline for total meeting clarity.

■ **Story:** Three to five chunks of supportive insights and recommendations.

■ **Recap:** Repeat your information to "seal" it in your audience's brains.

■ **Action:** Open the discussion for your recommendations.

Sandbox Assignment

■ Set aside at least 30 minutes to an hour on your calendar.

■ Access the Boxes Outline worksheet in the Resource Center (see `https://LeaPica.com/pbm-resource-center`).

■ Complete the outline using your existing content. Where should everything live? What should stay, and what should go?

Brainstorm Your Content into Slide Format

9

"Creativity is intelligence having fun."

—Albert Einstein

Now that you have an organized outline for your ideas, you're ready to start expanding and translating them into a linear, slide-by-slide sequence.

This is important: your presentation slides should not *look* like the modular Boxes outline; the audience should never see the boxes. So, how do you take a modular model and transpose it linearly? Don't worry about that yet; I'll show you in the next chapter.

For now, your mission is to generate as many ideas as possible to create your slides.

Again, you might feel tempted to open PowerPoint for a slide fiesta. I'm going to stay your hand once more, because believe it or not, a digital screen isn't the most constructive medium for generating ideas.

Screens? Where we're going, we won't need screens. We're going analog, as in *offline*!

Why You Should Brainstorm Offline

A large volume of research by Indiana University shows that the act of writing by hand stimulates creativity in a way that no other brainstorming method can.[1] Garr Reynolds, revered master of the presentation stage, popularized the Post-it Note brainstorming method in his seminal work, *Presentation Zen*. This book became the dojo of my creativity and presentation process, and I suggest making it one of your next reading destinations.

Handwriting has also been found to activate the same neural centers triggered during meditation, explaining why manual brainstorming and journaling enables slower, more deliberate ideation.[2]

Another benefit to offline brainstorming is that you're working on your presentation in a distraction-free environment. It minimizes the risk of getting roped into aimless watercooler chats on Slack or interrupted by a so-called "hot" request from the boss. You'll be amazed at how productive you become at brainstorming when you give it your undivided attention!

How to Brainstorm Offline

Before you begin, gather the following items:

- An offline version of your Boxes outline, printed or drawn on a whiteboard
- A stack of *rectangular* sticky notes
- A trusty, well-inked pen
- Your brain
- Not your cuddly yet distracting pet

Here's your brainstorming process:

1. Block an hour on your calendar and turn away from your computer. This prevents last-minute meetings from burgling your precious time. I know this sounds hard, but I know you can do it!

---

[1]canlab.sitehost.iu.edu/handwriting.html
[2]www.wsj.com/articles/SB10001424052748704631504575531932754922518#articleTabs%3Darticle

2. Look at your Boxes outline and bring a clear picture of your ideas to the forefront of your mind.

3. Start to think about each idea you'd want on your slides. For every single thought that pops up, write it down on one sticky note. The idea could be your presentation title, an insight with a chart, a recommendation, a process, a bold statement, or even a question for the audience. Then, put the sticky note aside.

   It may take a few moments to get your creative juices flowing, as you may not be accustomed to free-thinking methods like this. I promise that once you get going, it will become easier.

4. For ideas with visuals such as charts or images, draw a rudimentary sketch as a placeholder or write a word representing the image, like "conversion rate bar" or "img of laptop." Don't worry about visual execution at this stage.

5. Write down all your ideas on notes—every single one that comes to mind. No filtering or editing yet. Write them down even if you think they suck. This is a vital aspect of brainstorming to facilitate the flow of ideas, so let 'er rip! You don't need to figure out which section each idea belongs to or the order of ideas; there's plenty of time for organization later.

6. The only time you should be tempted to check your computer is to verify a data point or fill in an idea gap. That's it. No sneaking over to check email!

7. I find it useful to set a timer for 25-minute increments with 5-minute breaks in between. This is known as the *Pomodoro technique*, a handy productivity hack that maximizes creative output and minimizes interruptions.[3] I use a Mac app called Be Focused (https://apps.apple.com/us/app /be-focused-focus-timer/id973130201) with this timing built in, but there are many timer apps for phone and computer to choose from.

8. Try to have fun with it! This is where you get to flex your creative muscles, so take advantage of your freedom of thought.

9. Keep going until you've exhausted your ideas. If need be, take breaks and spread the process out over a few days. I find that when I get blocked, a longer break can "unkink" the creative firehose.

That is brainstorming in a box, my friend!

You know when you're in the middle of a project and that million-dollar idea pops up when you're driving, commuting, or watching TV? And you tell yourself

TIP

For now, I recommend giving yourself at least two to three days to brainstorm. Sometimes great ideas bubble up a while after you've flipped the creative switch. You also want to find a way to capture random thoughts that surface when you're not actively working on the presentation.

---

[3] francescocirillo.com/pages/pomodoro-technique

that you'll remember it when you get back to your desk? Then you completely forget because you've thought about a million other things since then? Yep, I have no idea what that's like.

That's why I create a "Parking Lot" note in a virtual notebook app for every in-progress presentation to capture rogue ideas before they evaporate (I prefer Evernote). Better yet, you can ask Siri (or your voice assistant) to add your idea for you if you're hands-free. Now you'll never forget another great idea again!

The Single Idea per Slide Philosophy

As you're going through this process, you may notice that there's not much room to put stuff on each sticky note. There's only enough space for just one idea, a title, maybe a relevant chart, and not much else. That's entirely the point.

You don't realize it, but you've just been indoctrinated into one of the most prestigious presentation philosophies in all the land: *single idea per slide*.

Why You Should Put Only One Idea on Each Slide

Nancy Duarte's "single idea per slide" credo has revolutionized countless presentations around the world (including mine), which states the following in so many words:

Learn to create ideas, not slides. And communicate no more than one idea on each slide.[4]

Now, when I drop this in my workshops and keynotes, I can hear the faint sound of tires screeching to a halt in the minds of my audience. Just one idea. . .per slide? How does that work? That's going to be so many slides! But, but, what about all that stuff I need to put on there? I understand the concern, and I ask, how's that been going? Hint: Refer to the $541 billion in lost productivity per year (see Chapter 1). Allow me to explain why this is a hefty piece of that puzzle.

Think of your presentation deck like a shopping cart. As you build your deck, you roam around the store haphazardly pulling items off the shelves and dropping them in the cart. The decks I used to present looked a lot like what you see in the carts at Costco: economy-size piles of excessive, jumbled junk.

---

[4]Duarte, Nancy, 2008. *slide:ology: The Art and Science of Creating Great Presentations.* O'Reilly.

Now think of your presentation audience as the cashier. The way your cashier rings you up is exactly how your audience takes in information: **by scanning each item individually and placing it in a shopping bag.** But when we pack our slides to the brim with copious ideas and visuals, it's like flying down the aisles at Mach 10 speed and shoving all our items through checkout at once!

That would lead to a disgruntled cashier and an equally annoyed audience. Why? Because this is not how their brains learn and understand. This often conflicts with what my students have come to believe about creating kitchen sink decks.

A workshop participant once protested: "But Lea, my client believes that the more stuff I put on my slides, the harder I worked!" And yet, his client's biggest complaint was not understanding his insights. This points us to the deeper issue of stakeholders suffering from more-is-better-itis. I believe this affliction results from stakeholders' not trusting that they'll get what they need from our presentations.

So, they ask you to throw every piece of data you have into a busy, overstuffed slide burger. Ironically, I find it takes more thought, skill, and effort to create one slide with a clear focus on a single idea.

This means when you go digital, you'll be blowing up your beefy "McSlides" into more digestible, bite-size "sliders."

Yes, you'll create more slides than you're used to. Yes, it's OK to have a lot of slides in your presentations; last time I checked, we aren't charged per slide. Yes, you'll end up with a mountain of cluttered slides *if* you're putting too much information on each one. No, limiting the number of slides you're allowed to use does not cure information overload.

When you're brainstorming, don't count your slides; just make as many sticky notes as you need to represent each idea that comes up. We're going to revisit this in the next phase, but I want to plant this seed with you early in the process.

I discovered Duarte's "single idea per slide" approach in her book *slide:ology* (or as I call it, the "Slide-ea" tenet) early into my presentation transformation. And wow, it was *not* easy to hear or apply. I found it so confronting as I had to unwind years of conditioned habits of squeezing text, charts, and cheesy clipart into every available pixel.

But when I got the hang of reducing and simplifying, the response to my presentations was so groundbreaking that I've shared this approach in every single keynote and workshop I've ever delivered. So, use the constraint of space available on your little sticky notes as a guardrail to keep your slides simple.

Edit and Organize Your Brainstorm into Your Boxes

Once you've expanded your ideas into tiny slides, you're almost ready to organize, edit, and arrange them into your Boxes structure. I say almost because it's important not to do it *right* after completing brainstorming. Give your brain a break to work out any final ideas and let things settle.

When you're ready to go back and edit, return to your Boxes outline and pile of notes. Pick up each note and place it in what feels like the appropriate box (intro, message, story, etc.). My preference is to draw my Box outline on a whiteboard so that I have room to arrange the notes. If you don't have a whiteboard, simply arrange them on a wall in the structure you have on paper.

The critical question you want to ask for each note is: does this idea directly support or relate to the overarching presentation message and throughline? When organizing, I close my eyes and imagine the throughline as a rope and asking if the idea "hooks" onto it. If it doesn't or is nice-to-have data that may make me look smart but doesn't support or may even distract from the message, I send it to a very special place: the appendix!

I ruthlessly send any nonessential notes to the appendix for cold storage. This keeps my core slides ultra-focused, and I take comfort knowing that should someone ask for that information, I have it at the ready.

Once your notes have fallen in line, you're ready for the process you've been putting off since the beginning: creating digital slides!

Chapter Recap

- Analog (handwritten) brainstorming stimulates creativity better than digital methods.
- While brainstorming, write only one single idea on each sticky note.

Sandbox Assignment

- Schedule at least 30 minutes to an hour on your calendar.
- Grab your Boxes outline, a stack of sticky notes, a pen, and, optionally, a whiteboard.
- With your Boxes framework in mind, brainstorm individual ideas and insights on each sticky note.
- Resist the urge to filter or edit until all ideas are out of your brain.
- Leave it be for a day before organizing.
- Schedule another 30 minutes on your calendar.
- Organize the notes into your outline on a whiteboard or a wall. Keep what supports the message and story and send the rest to the appendix.

Digitize Your Analog Slide Content

10

Oh my reader, I have incredible news: **you are finally ready to create your digital slides!** Have you ever done this much preparation work before opening PowerPoint? If not, this may have felt quite daunting, but I guarantee you're going to see your presentation outcomes transform from this effort.

Once your sticky "Slide-eas" are organized within your Boxes outline, you're finally ready to begin digitizing them into slide form. What I'm going to show you next is how to create an artifact I call the *presentation skeleton*: a nondescript, bare-bones version of your presentation that serves as a scaffolding for you to build upon.

Now, this is extremely important: **Do not design your slides at this stage.** This might seem counterintuitive at first; why the heck wouldn't you just design your slides as you work? Concentrating only on content first is an integral step of my data presentation process, and whenever I choose to skip ahead to design, I end up regretting it. Let's look at why.

Avoid the "Flushed Money Trap"

Before I created this method, my very unscientific process was to create a slide from scratch, design it, and move on to the next one. Create, design, create, design. Then, a manager or stakeholder would ask to review the deck before the meeting, and they'd slice and dice it up in cold blood.

Time and again, I watched in silent horror as a significant portion of my beautifully designed slides would now lay lifeless on the cutting room floor. I call this the "flushed money trap," because this led to pouring a whole lot of work time right down the drain. And as you know, time is money.

That's why it's vital that you do not design your slides during the conceptualization phase. I repeat, you want to focus on content and flow *only*, at least until you're about 70–80 percent of the way there. Let's begin.

Transpose Your Boxes into a Linear Format

Remember how I said that your final slide deck should not look like the Boxes outline? That means you'll need to "transpose" the Boxes to a linear format.

Before I begin to create my digital skeleton, I rewrite my Box checkpoints into what I call the *Box Blueprint*, which is a list of sections that resembles the following:

- **Intro:** State the meeting purpose/recap campaign details/create anticipation.
- **Message:** State the overall key message/throughline/preview key insights.
- **Story:**
  - First section or insight/stakes/recommendations
  - Second section or insight/stakes/recommendations
  - Third section or insight/stakes/recommendations
  - Continue if you have more sections
- **Recap:** Review three to five insights and recommendations.
- **Action:** Confirm next steps and assigned roles.
- **Closing**
- **Appendix**

Review this several times to ensure that you've made the connection between the structure of the boxes and the Blueprint format. Once you have a sense of the overall flow, you're ready to go digital. Return to your computer and have your Box outline and sticky slides at the ready.

Now, I don't build my slides in PowerPoint right away; I create my skeleton in Google Slides first for several reasons.

- Google Slides constantly saves your work in the cloud, so you can access the skeleton from different computers and even your phone.
- Being cloud-based enables slick collaboration features for team presentations.
- I find it less straightforward to design slides in Google, so I'm not tempted to design them at this stage.

If you can't access Google Slides or prefer PowerPoint or something else, then build your skeleton in your tool of choice. Just use the default, no-frills Office Theme design or the most minimalist template available. First, you're going to import your Boxes structure and then your individual slides.

Install Your Boxes Framework into Your Deck

By now, you see that it is possible to have an organizational structure inside of a linear presentation. Here's where you'll see how that translates to your slides.

Import Your Content Structure

- Create a new Google Slides or PowerPoint deck. You'll see in both programs that the title slide is there waiting for you. Fill it out with your objective-based title.
- Insert a new slide and then apply the Section Header layout (select the layout from the toolbar, right-click and choose Apply Layout in Google Slides or select from Layout in the PowerPoint Home ribbon).
- In the Title box, enter the name of the section from your blueprint.
- Duplicate this slide and enter the name of the next section.
- Continue until you have all your sections entered.

Import Your Slide Content

- Create a new slide using a basic layout such as Title + Content. Enter the title or message from your first sticky note in the title, and additional thoughts in the content box. Then move on to the next slide, and so on.

- Hey, hey, no designing! I'm on to you. . .seriously, no designing yet.

- When you're digitizing your stickies with data and insights, I have a killer trick. **Try to write the title in the form of an observation of the data, rather than a statement of what the data is.** For example, instead of "sales by marketing channel" or "landing page test results," write "paid search highest channel" or "landing page B won." In other words, write an observation in shorthand that you'll understand later. I'll explain this approach in more detail in Act III.

- If I want to include an image, I'll type the phrase "IMG (image idea)." The image idea might be a website screenshot, a photo of money, or a technology icon. Later when I'm in the design stage, this allows me to hunt for image slides by searching for "IMG."

- If I want a chart, I'll either create a rudimentary placeholder chart using the default settings of Insert Chart, or I'll paste a rough graph with actual data.

- For now, try to get as many slides as possible into the deck before messing with the order. It's important that you take these steps in phases or else you may end up redoing your work.

- You're done with this step when you've digitized all your sticky notes.

Refine Your Narrative Flow

This step is about providing a logical and seamless progression through your content for the audience. The best way to refine your flow is by getting a bird's-eye view of your slide content through the view that acts as a sort of "storyboard." Each presentation tool has a storyboard view, but they go by different names.

It's Slide Sorter in PowerPoint (see Figure 10.1), Grid View in Google Slides, and Light Table in Keynote. In these, you now have a storyboard view of your story rather than single, discrete slides. Take note of how each slide flows into the next, and ask yourself these questions:

- Does this slide support the overall message/throughline?

- Will this slide help meet the meeting objective?

- Is this slide in the right location, or would it work better somewhere else?

- Does there need to be a smoother transition between this slide and the next?

FIGURE 10.1 Slide Sorter storyboard view in PowerPoint

The storyboard view makes it easy to grab and drag slides around to the most appropriate place in the narrative. When I feel like it's almost there, I exit the storyboard view. I then do something that gives me a huge edge in mastering my content before I even get to the design phase: **I do a verbal practice run with my slides.**

Yes, I rehearse my presentation before I even design my slides. I speak through each of my slides and put any ideas or statements that I really don't want to forget in the speaker notes of each slide. This helps me make sure of these two things:

- That everything I'm saying has my audience needs and savviness levels in mind
- That my slide transitions are velvety smooth

Preparation this early may sound unappealing when it comes to your valuable time, and I get it. However, investing this effort now pays off huge dividends by the time you're ready to present. Practicing now prevents one of the most irritating tendencies I see in presentations today: that painfully awkward moment when the presenter advances to the next slide, gets caught off guard by it, uncomfortably stares at it for too long, and tries to remember why they put it there. . .out loud.

So, don't do that, and run through your content once at this stage if possible. When you have your content and flow about 70–80 percent finalized, you're ready to move on to the next step.

Transpose Your Box Outline in Your Slide Deck Using Sections

If I'm using PowerPoint to present, I download my skeleton from Google Slides as a PowerPoint file (skip this if you're presenting with Google Slides). I then group my slides into sections that match each box in the Box outline. Hold up; did you just hear me say that you can group slides in PowerPoint? Indeed! It's not commonly known that there's a way to put structure around digital slides in linear tools.

Creating slide sections helps you see if your slides are in the right order and in the right areas. You can create sections in PowerPoint using the same steps in either the Slide Sorter view or the Slides pane (which is the area to the left of the main slide that shows your slides in succession). Here's how:

1. In either Slide Sorter view or the Slides pane, right-click in the blank area between two slides (you'll see a line flash where you clicked) and select Add Section.
2. Enter the name of one of your sections into Section Name.
3. Click Rename.
4. You'll now see the name of the section in between slides. Every slide after that section name is a member of that section, until the next section. You can expand and collapse the sections as you work, which I find extremely helpful during storyboarding and design (see Figure 10.2).

In Keynote, you can similarly group slides in the Slide Navigator. Note that at time of writing, Google Slides does not offer a sections feature, which is one of several reasons I still prefer to present in PowerPoint.

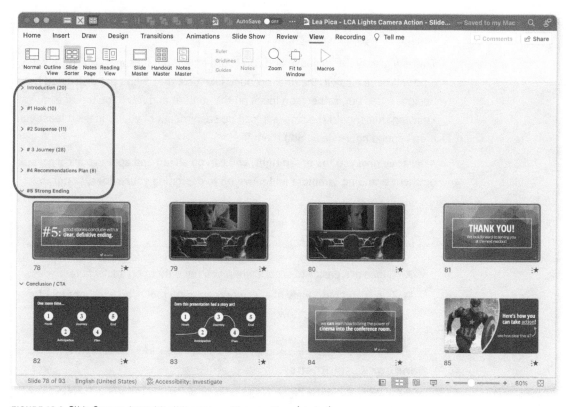

FIGURE 10.2 Slide Sorter view with slides grouped into sections (circled)

To reiterate, your list of sections may resemble this:

- Introduction
- Message/Throughline
- Section/Insight 1
- Section/Insight 2
- Section/Insight 3
- Insights & Recommendations Recap
- Action Plan
- Closing
- Appendix

What you now have in front of you is an incredibly well-conceived, well-constructed collection of cohesive ideas and insights. You are so far ahead in the data presentation game that the game is running after *you*. And you are ready to begin thinking about design. At long last!

This is a great time to pause and run your content past a supervisor or anyone who will have a say in the final product. Like you, they won't get distracted by design issues but, rather, can focus on the content and flow. You'll rest easy knowing that should they make sliced up sashimi out of your slides, at least you didn't spend hours designing them first.

After they give you the green light, you can go ahead and apply your corporate or client branding template and move on to designing your slides. Congrats!

Chapter Recap

- Slides are easier to create when you have them on sticky notes.
- The storyboard view of every presentation tool is an excellent tool for refining narrative flow.

Sandbox Assignment

- Make a copy of the Google Slides or PowerPoint Presentation Skeleton template in the Resource Center (see https://LeaPica.com/pbm-resource-center).
- Translate your sticky note framework into digital slides.
- Practice your flow and adjust as necessary.
- Get preliminary manager approval on your content.
- Apply your branding template and begin design when 70–80 percent complete.

Act I Intermission

Right about now, your brain is likely exploding with new information. It's possible you've never put in this much effort to prepare your data presentation content before even cracking open PowerPoint.

Trust me, this is a good thing. You're now ready to move on to the phase that most presenters start with.

Now, you know I love a good recap, so here's how to remember the flow of steps in the Conceptualize phase:

- Determine the focal point of the presentation.
- Identify the needs and desires of your audience.
- Establish the overarching message with a clear throughline.
- Support the message with evidence and narrative arc in your story.
- Identify the action your audience should take and how to execute.
- Flesh out your Boxes outline with your content and insights.
- Brainstorm your content onto sticky notes (your "slide-eas").
- Organize and edit the notes into the Boxes outline.
- Digitize your "slide-eas" into a minimalist Google Slides or PowerPoint deck.

And now for our next act: SLIDE DESIGN!

Act II: Design Your Slides

Slide Graphics, Layout, and Emphasis

Why Bad Slide Design Is Not a PowerPoint Problem

11

"Everything is designed. Few things are designed well."

—*Brian Reed*

In 2008, the New York Giants defeated the New England Patriots in a dramatic Super Bowl upset. This caused a deep inner conflict for me, where my homeland of the Shore of Jersey scrimmaged against my newfound love for the Town of Bean. (I've now exhausted my football vocabulary.)

But more notable than my East Coast love triangle was a hilarious Super Bowl commercial aired by Tide called "The Talking Stain." It portrayed a hopeful job candidate who inadvertently brings an embarrassing and sizable coffee stain on his shirt to his job interview.[1]

Every time the candidate answers one of the interviewer's questions, the stain suddenly starts unintelligibly shouting over him. Unbeknownst to our job seeker, the vocal stain completely steals the interviewer's—and the TV viewers'—attention.

Once my belly-laughing died down, it struck me that the stain was the perfect analogy for what happens when you create presentation slides that are so visually "noisy" that they drown out your message. That's why the way you use your presentation tools is a critical juncture.

It's the difference between inviting a trusty, supportive wingperson versus bringing in a digital Kanye West who climbs up on stage and steals your thunder.

To contrast the difference between what the stain did and what a true visual wingperson does, consider the following.

---

[1] www.youtube.com/watch?v=X2cs8gnb42A

I recently purchased my first iPad. (Yes, over a decade after its debut. I am *not* a first mover.) Perhaps more wondrous than the technology behind a computer the width of a lasagna noodle was the experience of unboxing it.

As I carefully unpackaged the compu-noodle, I marveled in amazement at the thought and attention Apple devoted to an act that is usually a nonevent. Not a single detail was left to chance: from the plastic flap that unwraps the box in one smooth motion to the sliver of the iPad side shot on the box to the pull tabs revealing the cleverly nested charger and manual. The elegance of the process took my breath away.

I didn't feel like I had just bought any old device. I felt like I was now part of a design movement.

And as you'll see noted here and throughout this book, Apple design represents the essence of simplicity and intentionality, and presenters would do well to take notes.

Design Matters

Something important unconsciously happens when an audience watches a presentation. Most corporate and conference presenters use a slide deck or similar tool to visually guide both the audience—and the speaker—through the talk.

That means there are not one but two focal points for the audience during your presentation: you *and* your deck. And while multitasking is a sought-after skill on job requisitions, human brains are actually terrible at it.

One of my favorite books of all time is *Brain Rules* by neuroscience researcher John Medina. (This book will make you a better human.) His 12 "brain principles for life" hold invaluable wisdom for presentations.

Medina's 10th rule is especially relevant, which is that human beings' vision trumps all other senses. He posits that our visual dominance harkens back to our days on the Serengeti, where our survival depended on our seeing eyes.[2]

---

[2]Medina, John, 2014. *Brain Rules: 12 Principles for Surviving and Thriving at Work, Home, and School*. Pear Press.

Vision helped our ancestors make life and death decisions like spotting a lion in the bush, remembering where they buried those berries last summer, and remembering not to eat *those* berries. And when survival is at stake, our attention becomes laser-focused on the task at hand.

As a result, we've evolved where our attention is deeply intertwined with our vision and is captured by what we see. Let me explain how that plays out in presentation.

When you advance to your next slide, there is a fractional moment of split focus. The visual change on-screen prompts your audience's eyes to shift their attention because that's what their brains are wired to do for survival.

You may still be talking, but their attention is now on the slide just for the moment, or, rather, *should be* just for the moment. Ideally, their attention comes right back to you to hear you speak. But to do that, **your slide must instantly support the idea you're communicating and then release their attention back to you.**

The question is, is that what your slides are doing? Or, like most presentations today, are your slides a visual vortex that sucks the audience in and holds them hostage, silently activating zombification?

To answer this question, I'm going to kick off this phase with two important words that are even more important when they're next to each other:

Design. Matters.

Good design is invisible; it doesn't make itself obvious, but rather, it naturally evokes pleasure and arouses our senses. Bad design is *not* invisible. Many of us can immediately detect bad design when we see it, and it creates unease, discomfort, and even disgust.

What's important to understand is that as time passes, our tolerance threshold for bad design exponentially lowers. Social media has dramatically raised the bars for our working generation's eyeballs. We live in an Instagram world where elegant design aesthetics are a new standard in everything from exotic home decor to exotic cat apparel.

Unfortunately, corporate presentations are one of the last bastions of visual communication that is still, for the most part, trapped in last century. How do you know if your presentations are stuck in a time warp?

The answer depends on whether you've used intentional presentation design techniques. In technical fields like data analytics, digital marketing, and data science, design can be an afterthought behind good, solid, trusty ol' data. If the numbers are good, who cares what it looks like, right?

Truthfully, your audience's brain cares a great deal about the design of your information, because good design fulfills a golden rule: **to make them do less work**. How I came to learn this was the catalyst for my entire journey to presentation enlightenment (cue story time!).

In 2010, I was working as a digital analytics manager for a Fortune 500 finance firm. I had spent my 7-year career crunching data and spawning zombies with my presentations with no clue as to why.

Then one fateful day that April, everything changed. I received an email from the dean of my graduate school where I was on track to earn my MBA the following month. He was inviting students to deliver a capstone presentation to the class as part of graduation week.

Because I am a certified overachiever, I volunteered to do a presentation on social media, which was still pretty nascent. Then I decided to make my life even harder by choosing a radical new presentation tool you may know as Prezi.

Prezi was a cloud-based tool that had social media elements, so I thought, *hey, what a great way to talk about social media! Great idea, Lea! Yet when I first logged in, expecting to see an interface somewhat resembling PowerPoint, all I saw was the "canvas" in Figure 11.1.*

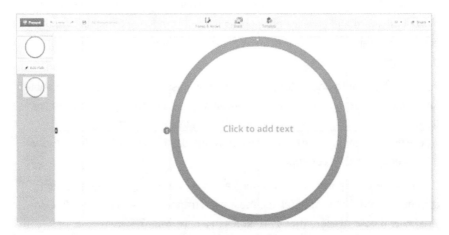

FIGURE 11.1 Blank Prezi presentation design canvas

It was a grid-like void with a giant circle that stared me in the face. For a while, all I could think was, "What the heck is this? What is this infinite scrolling thingy and zooming whatsit? Where are the single, discrete slides I'm used to where I can drop all my discombobulated junk in an illogically linear fashion?"

It dawned on me that I had no idea how to execute a presentation here the way I'd done with PowerPoint. I was going to have to completely rethink my approach. *That* was my watershed moment. Utterly baffled at how to start my talk, I began Googling "presentation design" and came across a book that would not only change my approach to presenting, but it would also change the trajectory of my entire life.

That book was *Presentation Zen* by my friend and master of the slide, Garr Reynolds. Reynolds has consulted on some of the most memorable talks in the world, so he knows his stuff. At first, I was challenged by his seemingly over-simplified and high-drama approach to the art of presentation. Giant single numbers instead of pie charts? No decorative elements like logos and water-marks? And no bullet points, huh?

I eventually understood the many ways that Reynold's distillation of Japanese Zen principles like *kanso* (simplicity), *shizen* (naturalness), and *shibumi* (elegance) could elevate my presentations. By the time I was finished with the book, I was absolutely hooked.

I used his Zen principles to create my capstone presentation in Prezi, abandoning the linear format and instituting a completely new paradigm that incorporated structure and narrative flow. I delivered my talk and was blown away by the reaction. Students and faculty in the audience approached me throughout the rest of the week thanking me for such an engaging presentation.

I realized I had created a moment for the audience, one that would change the way they thought about social media forever. I felt exhilarated and validated for deciding to take a crazy risk on a new platform with a new approach. This system worked.

Once I returned from my victory bubble and got back to work, I knew there was no going back to my old ways. Except, I realized I wasn't allowed to use Prezi for my work presentations. So, I was determined to figure out how to apply what I'd learned from the forced design constraints of Prezi to my work in PowerPoint.

In *Presentation Zen*, Reynolds states what effective design means:

"Design is necessary and a way to organize information in a way that
makes things clearer; it is also a medium for persuasion. Design is not a
decoration. If anything, design is more about subtraction than addition.
Visually, we do not want to include too much, nor do we want to exclude
too much."

In essence, effective slide design is about discernment: finding a balance
between what to include and what to leave out visually so that the audience
understands your message. Discernment isn't an instinct we're born with, nor a
feature built into any tool or template.

Prezi Is Not the Solution to PowerPoint

One of the most common questions I'm asked by audiences is whether Prezi is a
"better alternative" or "the solution" to PowerPoint. This question indicates a
sweeping perception that PowerPoint is at the root of presentation
zombification.

My answer often raises a few eyebrows, which is that it's not the solution
because PowerPoint isn't the problem. To understand my perspective, we must
step into the way back machine and examine how we got here with PowerPoint
(and similar tools) to begin with.

PowerPoint was birthed into the world in 1987 for the Apple Macintosh, believe
it or not! And it was designed to innovate on ye olde overhead projector and
plastic transparency system.[3] (This was *not* a system designed with cognitive
comprehension in mind.) It caught fire as the de facto tool for presenting visual
information during meetings and is still arguably the undisputed champion of
global presentation domination.

Now, whether that's a good thing is highly debatable, because with PowerPoint
becoming the Kleenex of presentation software, meeting audiences are inun-
dated with hordes of slides that are super boring. Check out Figures 11.2
through 11.4.

---

[3]Britannica, The Editors of Encyclopaedia. "Microsoft PowerPoint". Encyclopedia Britannica, 29 Mar.
2019, www.britannica.com/technology/Microsoft-PowerPoint. Accessed 25 February 2021.

Section 6.1 Momentum and Impulse - 1

1. **Calculate the magnitude of the linear momentum for the following cases:**

    a. A proton with mass 1.67×10^{-27} kg, moving with a speed of 5.00×10^6 m/s. **Answer** ☞ {8.35×10^{-21} kg·m/s}

    ☒ The image cannot be displayed. Your computer may not have enough memory to open the image, or the image may have been corrupted. Restart your computer, and then open the file again. If the red x still appears, you may have to delete the image and then insert it again.

FIGURE 11.2 Super boring technical slide

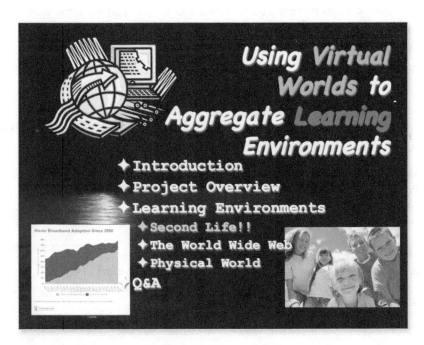

FIGURE 11.3 Super ugly business slide
Source: Marzanna Syncerz / Adobe Stock

FIGURE 11.4 Bizarre data slide correlating a rabbit and hot dog
Source: lifeonwhite / Deposit photos

I'd like to point out that there is a bunny rabbit and a hot dog on the same slide here, and they are apparently correlated in some way with weird asset business models.

PowerPoint has steadily traveled two paths of both presentation domination and vilification; it's blamed for everything from conference room naptime to passive-aggressive behavior to the tragic 2003 NASA Columbia explosion.[4] In fact, a journalist named Angela R. Garber unaffectionately coined a term that you may be familiar with: "Death by PowerPoint."[5]

To be transparent, I think this is an unfortunate witch hunt. I no longer see this as a PowerPoint problem. Or a Keynote problem, or a Google Slides problem. But rather. . .

---

[4]www.edwardtufte.com/bboard/q-and-a-fetch-msg?msg_id=0001yB

[5]www.smallbusinesscomputing.com/biztools/article.php/684871/Death-By-PowerPoint.htm

Presentation Zombification Is a
People Problem

As a global population of business professionals, we are categorically not using our presentation tools to their full potential for one simple reason: *we were never taught how to use them properly.* For me, blaming PowerPoint for our world's woes is like blaming a scalpel for a botched surgery. A scalpel is a neutral object, but the outcome of its usage depends on two factors: the skill and intention of the user.

Then along comes a Prezi, which many believe is the "solution" to PowerPoint because of how incredibly different it is. This belief is a slippery slope, because it permits us to shirk the responsibility of learning how to use these tools correctly.

Even though Prezi inspired my entire data storytelling journey and has facilitated some truly breathtaking visual journeys, I don't find it the most practical choice for delivering in a typical business meeting context. Its interface and paradigm require a fundamentally different approach to structural and design execution, which requires skills that far surpass what you need to be successful within PowerPoint.

I've borne witness to nausea-inducing visual death spirals and mortifying technical snafus with Prezi, so proceed with caution and master the design tools in this book with the basics first.

Time to Put on the Right Mindset

Believing that presentation zombification is PowerPoint's fault is completely missing the point. The unfortunate irony of the corporate world is that with design being an integral tool for visual communication, most employees aren't equipped with it when entering the workforce.

Jeff Weiner, CEO of LinkedIn, announced in 2018 what the biggest gaps were between what skills companies are seeking and what candidates are equipped with. Most believed the skill gap is software coding, but the truth is far from it.

It turns out that the largest skills gaps are soft skills like communication and "digital fluency" skills such as designing business presentations.[6] Well, who would have imagined! This points to a huge opportunity to gain a healthy competitive advantage. . . should you choose to equip yourself.

Let's do just that.

Chapter Recap

- Presentation zombification is a visual design skills gap problem, not a PowerPoint problem.

---

[6]www.linkedin.com/pulse/jeff-weiner-explains-how-linkedin-diversify-global -nicholas-thompson

Sharpen Their Vision with Preattentive Attributes

12

"You can't see the picture when you're in the frame."

—Les Brown

One of the most fascinating—and frustrating—aspects of presenting information is that there is so much unconscious mental processing going on behind the scenes of the audience's brain. Remember that by "unconscious," I mean not aware of. And that lack of awareness is something most presenters are unaware of, which is an unfortunate irony.

How Memory Works

Our brains send information through a series of memory stages to keep what we need or discard what we don't, mainly for survival purposes. We have three stages of memory that enable us to visually intake, process, and store information. The three stages are as follows (see Figure 12.1):

1. Iconic memory
2. Working memory
3. Long-term memory

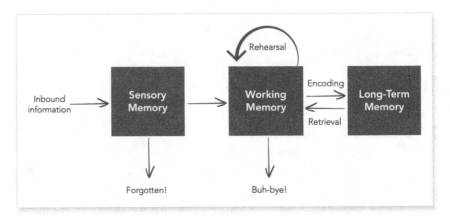

FIGURE 12.1 The three stages of human memory

Iconic memory refers to the short-term visual memories we store when seeing something very briefly, like pictures in the mind.[1] Unlike long-term memories, which can be stored for a lifetime, these iconic mental images last only milliseconds and then quickly fade.

Working memory is where the information that the iconic memory passes in is actively evaluated for either long-term storage or the mental trash bin.[2] This stage is temporary and has a limited capacity for storage, which will become important in Chapter 13.

---

[1]examples.yourdictionary.com/examples-of-iconic-memory.html

[2]Alan Baddeley and Graham J. Hitch (2010) Working memory. *Scholarpedia*, 5(2):3015.

Long-term memory is the last stop for a filtered subset of information for archival. Remember our presentation goal #2: be memorable? Long-term memory is the destination for that goal. It's where we aspire to send our valuable insights and recommendations so that our audiences are inspired to act after the presentation.

What we want to focus on now is a form of automatic, unconscious processing that happens in the iconic memory, called **preattentive processing**.

Preattentive Processing: In the Blink of an Eye

Preattentive processing refers to the "body's processing of sensory information (such as light, temperature, noise, etc.) that occurs before the conscious mind starts to pay attention to any specific objects in its vicinity."[3]

In human-speak, this translates to the brain's intake and parsing of information without conscious awareness. We detect various sensory stimuli subconsciously (unaware) before we detect them consciously (aware). Subconscious detection is lightning fast and happens *outside* of our awareness.

For example, if we walk into a dark room, we *subconsciously* detect that it is dark and so we reach for a light switch. We don't first consciously exclaim, "It is dark in here! Whatever shall I do? Oh, I should turn on the light!" and *then* decide to turn on a light. Our reach for the switch is on autopilot. This is happening the whole time that you are presenting slides, where you visually stimulate your audience and direct their attention in ways that they aren't conscious of.

If we as presenters are unaware of this unawareness, we run the risk of misdirecting their attention and interpretation with unconscious design decisions.

How you direct your audience's attention visually is *everything* when presenting data. It's why certain words in this book are in bold and why diagrams have color highlights. This reading experience was carefully designed to guide your

---

[3]Preattentive Processing. (n.d.). In Alleydog.com's online glossary. Retrieved from: www.alleydog .com/glossary/definition-cit.php?term=Preattentive+Processing

attention and emphasize what matters most, not out of manipulation but out of a mission to help you learn the material and place the most weight on certain concepts.

If you're going to learn this right, then you must make acquaintance with two of the most important figures in the information communication space: Stephen Few and Colin Ware.

Few and Ware: Perceptual Powerhouses

Stephen Few is universally considered one of the top authorities in the data visualization field, having penned two outstanding and essential volumes, *Show Me the Numbers* and *Now You See It*. In the former, Few explains how our visual perception came to be:

"Because of its evolutionary roots, visual perception is fundamentally oriented toward action, always looking for what we can do with the things that we see. As designers of tables and graphs, we should understand how to use attributes of visual perception to encode information in ways that others can easily, accurately, and efficiently decode."[4]

What this means is that within our visual perception, there are visual properties that trigger preattentive processing. These properties are known in the information design sphere as *preattentive attributes*.

In his book, Few calls upon the work of our other data viz guru, Colin Ware, author of *Information Visualization: Perception for Design*. He offers this rationale of the importance of understanding preattentive processing in data viz:

"If we can understand how perception works, our knowledge can be translated into rules for displaying information. Following perception-based rules, we can present our data in such a way that the important and informative patterns stand out."[5]

Preattentive Processing in Practice

Let's put your preattentive detector to the test. Look at the graphic in Figure 12.2; it shows a series of numbers.

---

[4]Few, Stephen. *Show Me the Numbers*. Analytics Press, 2012. ISBN #978-0970601971
[5]Colin Ware, *Information Visualization*. Morgan Kaufman, 2019. ISBN #978-0128128756

FIGURE 12.2 Series of numbers with no preattentive emphasis

None of these numbers should particularly stand out to you, so it almost appears like a solid wall. Now look at a slightly modified view of the same number series, shown in Figure 12.3.

FIGURE 12.3 Series of numbers with one number 3 in preattentive emphasis of bold weight and the color orange

Notice anything different? What number were your eyes immediately drawn to first? If you said the number 3 on row 3 and column 7, your preattentive processor is online and operational!

What exactly are these mysterious attributes we don't know we're processing? Ware describes four key areas of preattentive attributes as:

- Form
- Spatial positioning
- Color
- Movement

The following sections take a cursory look of the four areas of attributes and preview how they'll come to your visual storytelling aid, with examples to help you distinguish each attribute.

Form

The attribute of form leverages **length, width, orientation, shape, size, and enclosure** to distinguish between visual markings. See Figure 12.4.

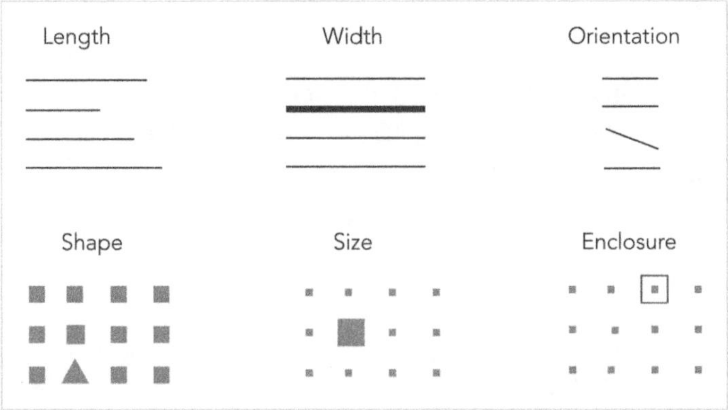

FIGURE 12.4 Diagram illustrating form attributes, inspired by Stephen Few's *Show Me The Numbers*

Note how certain components of each attribute jump off the page. Which one has the most pronounced effect on you? Form attributes are likely the ones you're most familiar with, such as the length of bars, the width of treemaps, the shape and size of bubbles, and so on. Orientation is less common, while enclosure comes into play when annotating data.

Spatial Positioning

The spatial positioning attribute uses an object's location in space to communicate meaning. An example of this is placing text at the top of a slide, rather than at the bottom, to indicate importance or hierarchy, or, using a scatter plot for positioning data points to communicate meaning.

Color

Color possesses a singular power to draw a viewer's attention and even trigger an unconscious interpretation of your information. That's one major reason why the 3 in Figure 12.3 jumped out at you.

The color attribute may be further segmented into hue and intensity. **A hue is what we think of as the color itself** (blue, magenta, or burnt sienna, if you're a Crayola crayon aficionado like me). See Figure 12.5.

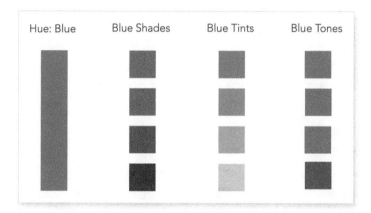

FIGURE 12.5 Examples of shades, tints, and tones of the pure hue of blue

Intensity is the saturation or brightness of that hue. Saturation refers to what percentage of the color is present, and brightness is how bright or dark the color is. Here's how colors shift when you add black, white, or gray to a hue:

- ■ Hue + black = shade
- ■ Hue + white = white
- ■ Hue + grey = tone

The way I think of these subattributes is that saturation decreases when you mix in the color white, and brightness decreases when you mix in black.

Movement

Remember that our brains are visually attuned for survival, which is especially true in terms of motion and movement. Our evolutionary attunement to movement helped our ancestors detect predators in their midst and still does for us today. Live presentation offers the perfect opportunity to leverage this attribute, but only when you put intentional thought toward its execution.

In Chapter 17, I discuss my favorite (and pretty much only) animation techniques I use to utilize movement for maintaining attention and pacing for the audience.

Gestalt Principles: The Relationship of Objects

Gestalt is a fancy-sounding word for "pattern." Gestalt principles are related to, yet different from, preattentive attributes in that they describe the relationship between objects, rather than the design qualities of each individual object. These principles also subconsciously influence our perception of visual information (sometimes positively, sometimes negatively)—see Figure 12.6.

- **Proximity:** Objects are close to or far from each other.
- **Similarity:** Objects are alike or different from each other.
- **Enclosure:** Objects are in a box or in a defined space together.
- **Closure:** Objects (like shapes) are incomplete, prompting the brain to mentally "finish" them).
- **Continuity:** Objects (like lines) are fragmented, prompting the brain to mentally "continue" them.
- **Connection:** Objects are linked and belonging in the same group.

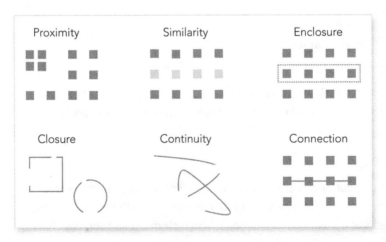

FIGURE 12.6 Diagram illustrating Gestalt principles
Source: Wirestock, Inc. / Alamy Stock Photo

How these principles interact with your audience's brain is crucial to designing slides for accurate and clear comprehension; therefore, you must use them intentionally. Haphazardly grouping certain elements will signal meaning in their minds when it may have no inherent meaning. Or leaving a gap around a photo may cause the brain to invoke closure and continuity, which could be distracting.

As you will see throughout this phase, there are many choices you can make in visually presenting information that affect your audience's perception. These choices may not have been apparent to you before embarking on this journey, but by the time you're complete, preattentive attributes and Gestalt principles will play a starring role in your practice.

TIP

Visit the Bookshelf in the Resource Center (www.LeaPica.com/pbm-resource-center) for more resources on the visual cognition of information.

Chapter Recap

- Preattentive processing occurs beneath your awareness, and its attributes can help you direct the audience's attention and interpretation.
- The main forms of preattentive attributes you'll learn to create visual meaning are form, spatial positioning, color, and motion.
- Gestalt principles enable you to create additional visual meaning with the spatial relationship of objects to each other.

13 De-fluff Your Slides and Embrace White Space

"Simplicity is the ultimate form of sophistication."

—Leonardo da Vinci

Facilitating visual understanding is less about what is there and more about what is not there. What do I mean by this cryptic fortune cookie aphorism? Take a look at an ad for the Apple iPhone X in Figure 13.1.

FIGURE 13.1 Apple iPhone X advertisement
Source: Haymarket Media Group Ltd.

What do you notice about it? Not much there, right? Do you feel like your brain is sighing a big "ahhhhh" of relief right now? So calming, so serene, yes?

Now compare that with this hilarious tongue-in-cheek parody of a "Microsoft I-pod Pro 2005 XP Human Ear Professional Edition" product box[1] in Figure 13.2.

---

[1] www.darren-price.com/2006/03/01/ms-ipod

FIGURE 13.2 Parody iPod advertisement mimicking Microsoft design[2]
Source: [13], Microsoft Corporation / www.nuvonium.com/blog/view/parody-of-microsoft-redesigning-ipod-packaging-still-makes-me-chuckle last accessed 5 May,2023

Do you see the, erm, "slight" difference between these design approaches? What's in the Microsoft parody ad that's missing from the real Apple ad? If you said loads of unnecessary visual junk, you're right.

That's because Apple knows what's up when it comes to feeding a viewer's brain something it craves: **white space** (and Microsoft is catching up nicely). Unfortunately, white space is not on the agenda of most business presentations today simply because presenters don't know how important it is.

You've learned that the audience's brains silently run all kinds of software programs during your presentations that potentially help or harm your ability to deliver information into it. A key psychological theory to know is called *cognitive load*, which affects how well the working memory (stage 2 of the information processing sequence discussed in Chapter 12) does its job. Here's where understanding the working memory matters.

> **NOTE**
>
> Visual white space (also known as *negative space* or *blank space*) gives your audience's brains room to breathe.

Overworking the Working Memory

The working memory is a sort of holding tank for the information the brain has taken in, and it gets to decide whether the information stays (and remains embedded in long-term memory) or goes (discarded for all time). Recall the

[2]www.nuvonium.com/blog/view/parody-of-microsoft-redesigning-ipod -packaging-still-makes-me-chuckle

earlier diagram of how information processing works, shown again in Figure 13.3.

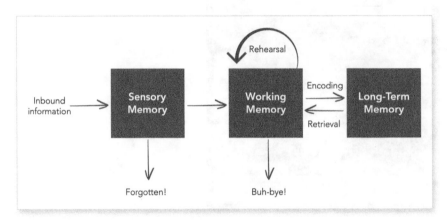

FIGURE 13.3 Information processing and memory stage diagram

Cognitive load is defined as the amount of effort used by the working memory.[3] The working memory has a limited capacity; it's able to actively process only between three and five pieces, or "chunks," of information per type of information (such as verbal versus visual).[4]

Verbal information chunks can include a statistic, a question, or a recommendation, while visual chunks include graphs, photos, or logos. When you present many visual chunks, you increase the load on the viewer's brain, forcing it to work harder until it potentially "overloads."

I picture an overloading working memory like this: Imagine someone juggling a ball or two (not a professional juggler). Now imagine throwing more balls at the juggler, one after the other. They're working hard to keep the balls in the air, but eventually, there are simply too many balls. The juggler slips up and drops all the balls at once, resulting in ball pandemonium.

Translation: The more visual balls you throw at someone to juggle, the higher the load on their brain, and the harder they must work to pay attention to you (ahem, goal #1!) And guess what is throwing a whole lot of balls at your presentation audience? Busy, crowded, noisy slides. That's why you must learn, young Padawan, to do something you've never been taught to do, covered next.

[3]en.wikipedia.org/wiki/Cognitive_load

[4]Colin Ware, *Information Visualization*. Morgan Kaufman, 2019. ISBN #978-0128128756

Resist the Fluff and Embrace White Space

When I say talk about fluff, I don't mean fluff in the form of fuzzy kittens and puppies. Never resist *that* fluff. I mean slide fluff, which I call the repetitive and ancillary visual elements found in most business presentations today. Slide fluff is in your branding templates and your presentations and is perhaps the most sinister silent villain sneaking into your slides.

This is because fluff creates visual work for the audience while not communicating anything of value. Slide fluff that doesn't add value during live presentations includes but is not limited to:

- Company logos
- Watermarks
- Textured or patterned backgrounds
- Prominent page numbers
- Background header and footer bars
- All other fluffy doodads that do not belong on *every single slide* of your live presentation deck.

The slide in Figure 13.4 houses a whole gaggle of fluffies.

FIGURE 13.4 Busy slide loaded with slide fluff like logos, watermarks, and ancillary objects

While this truth bomb typically cues protests from branding departments, understand that most branding templates are not designed with cognitive load in mind. Fluff does one thing quite well: it visually distracts your audience and interferes with your insights. The fluffier your slides, the more they become Tide's shouting stain.

The solution: embrace the white space and let your slide (and your audience's brains) breathe. The saying "less is more" applies here in spades. White space naturally restricts the number of chunks you're tempted to stuff your slides with.

I learned this concept from *Presentation Zen*. Garr has a tough stance on company logos used on every single slide of a live presentation:

> "We don't begin every new sentence in a conversation by restating our name, so why should you bombard people with your company logo on every slide?" Hear, hear, Zen Master.

My best advice: for a live presentation, keep logos on the first and last slides, and keep your interior slides fluff-free. You're free to bring the logos back in the printable handout you'll send after the meeting, which I cover in Chapter 34.

Animated Slide Fluff/Looping GIFs

There is a growing trend in using animated GIF images during presentations (especially in the conference arena). And while they can be hilariously effective when perfectly timed with the presenter's speech, they create an adverse effect if they begin infinitely repeating.

I call this effect the *loop vortex*, and it is a sinister form of fluff. I recall getting trapped in the vortex during a conference session where one particular GIF looped at least 14 times while the presenter didn't notice the audience beginning to chew on their seats.

The repetition created a hypnotic visual "droning" effect that left me blanked out on everything the presenter said in those minutes. In other cases, GIFs have a frenetic "shouting" effect that irritate the eyes. I suggest that if you're going to use animated GIFs, that you use them sparingly, choose ones with slow animations, and that you don't allow it to excessively repeat. One way to solve this is to upload your GIF to a tool called EZgif to limit the number of loops.

Animation can be an amazingly effective tool when you're conscious about it. Don't let a GIF lure your audience to the vortex.

Distracting Object Misalignment

The alignment of slide elements, or *relative positioning*, doesn't add extra stuff to your slides; however, improper alignment can add mental work. Take note of how the objects in Figure 13.5 are arranged in the visual space.

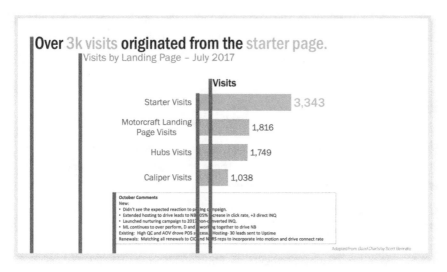

FIGURE 13.5 Data slide with objects centered and multiple alignment points

The arrangement of objects on this slide creates five distinct alignment points, which force the eyes to jump from point to point. That can lead to slower processing and broken attention. I've observed a tendency to center everything on slides without a clear structure, and this can scramble the eyes.

The slide shown in Figure 13.6 is faster and more pleasant to process.

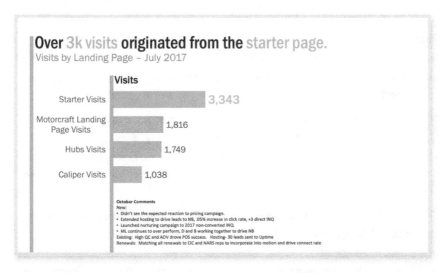

FIGURE 13.6 Data slide with objects aligned to minimize alignment points

This layout aligns the slide title, subtitle, chart labels, and source text box into one point. The chart title and bars align to a second point. This creates a more orderly layout with less eye jumping and more attention on you!

Effectively Effecting Change

Presenters must be mindful of the visual decorations on their slides that don't add value and subtract from attention. There are two places where you need to *effect* change in order to *affect* change:

- Your own work
- Your organizational/client culture

In your own work, routinely review your templates and remove any unnecessary and repetitive visual elements you can (including logos) from the interior slides. And when adding visual elements like background bars, shapes, clipart, and so on, ask yourself this question: does this have a purpose? If so, what is it? If it doesn't have a purpose, then prepare to beam it out of there, Scotty.

Effecting change in organizational culture is easier said than done. One of the most common objections I get when training data presenters is that they anticipate resistance to these changes from their stakeholder audience. Here are several strategies to overcome that.

First, make small changes gradually, which eases your audience through the transition and adds up to big results at the end. James Clear, productivity expert and author of bestseller *Atomic Habits*, explains the exponential power of consistently making "1 percent improvements" to a process or habit.

"If you can get 1 percent better each day for one year, you'll end up 37 times better by the time you're done. Conversely, if you get 1 percent worse each day for one year, you'll decline nearly down to zero. What starts as a small win or a minor setback accumulates into something much more."

Translation: slow and gradual change works in big ways. Unless everyone on the team is 100 percent bought in to this evolution, it is best treated like a marathon, not a sprint. It means getting creative with your branding department and sussing out the degree of flexibility with your company guidelines for live presentation decks.

Take this opportunity to become a change agent for the good of your internal and external presentations as a champion of your audience's brains. Remember to take a collaborative approach with visual decision-makers to have your best shot at effecting change.

Keep It Clean—and Legal

The asterisk on removing branding template fluff is to not remove something that's legally required. We live in a digital age where there are laws around labeling electronic corporate documents with terms like "Proprietary and Confidential" and "Copyright." Be sure to check with your legal department about what is required on all electronic documents and include that language in the smallest font and faintest gray text allowable in the bottom of the slide master.

> **Pro Tip**
> For industry and conference presentations, it's common for audience members to snap photos of your slides and share them on social media. Rather than being a hypocrite and putting my logo on every slide, I request that the audience copy my Twitter handle on any tweets, which I also include on my most quotable, "tweetable" slides.

With every slide design decision you make going forward, ask yourself: **Is this making the audience do more work than they need to?** If the answer is yes, simplify or forgo it without hesitation. Be ruthless. I know you can do this, and your audience's brains will thank you!

Chapter Recap

- Ancillary and repetitive visual elements on every slide such as logos, watermarks, page numbers, and title bars increase cognitive load and distract your live audience.
- Branding templates are typically not designed with the brain in mind.

- Animated GIFs can unintentionally cause a "loop vortex."
- Small, gradual changes gently ease your stakeholders into your newly simplified approach.

Sandbox Assignment

- Review your current slides and branding template for potentially repetitive and ancillary fluff.
- Develop a strategy for removing the fluff in a way that accommodates your guidelines.
- Consider facilitating a conversation with your management and branding department around streamlining the deck template.

The Lethal Downside of Bullet Points

14

"Bullet points are not the point."

—*Seth Godin*

We've arrived at possibly the most pervasive and challenging slide design habit to kick. It's a form of slide fluff so deeply ingrained in our practices that I routinely observe visceral resistance when I call it out during workshops. So I'm going to be direct and state it outright:

Bullet points are murdering your presentations. That's probably why they're called *bullets*, because I can't think of any other logical reason for their name.

Allow me to illustrate: take a look at the real PowerPoint slide in Figure 14.1.

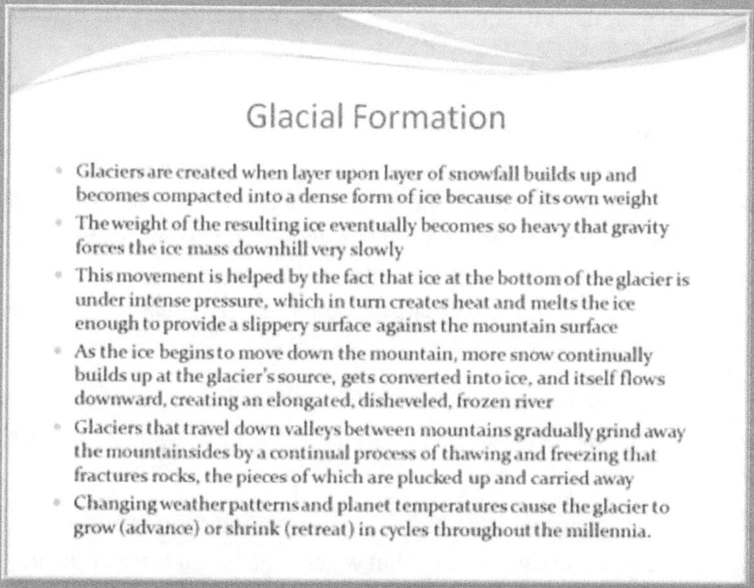

Glacial Formation

- Glaciers are created when layer upon layer of snowfall builds up and becomes compacted into a dense form of ice because of its own weight
- The weight of the resulting ice eventually becomes so heavy that gravity forces the ice mass downhill very slowly
- This movement is helped by the fact that ice at the bottom of the glacier is under intense pressure, which in turn creates heat and melts the ice enough to provide a slippery surface against the mountain surface
- As the ice begins to move down the mountain, more snow continually builds up at the glacier's source, gets converted into ice, and itself flows downward, creating an elongated, disheveled, frozen river
- Glaciers that travel down valleys between mountains gradually grind away the mountainsides by a continual process of thawing and freezing that fractures rocks, the pieces of which are plucked up and carried away
- Changing weather patterns and planet temperatures cause the glacier to grow (advance) or shrink (retreat) in cycles throughout the millennia.

FIGURE 14.1 Slides with a wall of bullet points describing glacial formations

Pop quiz: who is the only person in the room who wants to see all these bullets at once like this? If you're thinking it's the audience, think again.

The answer is. . . you, the presenter!

This all-too-familiar slide is artfully arranged into a structure I call "the Wall": an oppressive block of long-winded, run-on sentences written in PhD thesis language. And I guarantee if you display your insights in wall form, the only glacial formation in the room will be your stakeholders' icy stares.

This is because blocks of bulleted text expose all your information at once. This locks up their attention as they are subconsciously triggered to read the entire slide word for word to themselves and completely tune you out (or fall asleep). Imagine that when watching a TV show, instead of seeing one visual scene at a time, it projected a wall of bullet points describing the entire plot of the episode.

So write this across your heart: **Friends don't let friends kill their audience's brains with bullet points.**

Once you become aware of the Wall, you will likely observe it in almost every presentation you see going forward. The effect is truly dastardly. But awareness doesn't make it an easy habit to change.

Why We Love Bullet Points

As with all the other habits discussed, the first step is unpacking how the bullet point habit got here. I believe there are two culprits at work: the more obvious of which is that everyone else is doing it, so it's what we learn to do ourselves. You put everything you plan to say verbally on your slides and then read it aloud to the audience! Easy peasy.

But the less conspicuous and more sinister villain is that bullet points help us avoid doing something we generally don't want to do: **we do not plan to prepare and practice our content.**

Instead, we put all of our speaking points, observations, and conclusions in expository format directly on the slide so that we can read from them verbatim during the meeting since we don't know our material well. This is unfortunate because when I ask my workshop students what makes them nervous about presenting data, the top reason is usually that they feel unprepared.

There are a million and one justifications and rationalizations of why we don't prepare for our presentations, the most prevalent being that there's not enough time in the day. I believe that this is an excuse sitting on top of a skill gap. While the surface reason is that we don't know how to build in the time for it, at the root, we don't know *how* to effectively prepare or how to create time to prepare. Therefore, we cut corners and the Wall is born.

I discuss the importance of preparation more deeply in Act IV. For now, I invite you to rethink this behavior by repeating this mantra over and over:

Your slides are for your audience. *Not* for you.

Your slides are not a line-by-line script. They are a tool to help you visually deliver your message into your audience's brain. Your stakeholders don't want you to read them a bedtime story during your meeting; they can go home and do that with their kids. They want you to *share* with them. Collaborate with them. Ideate with them.

If you're feeling resistant to this idea, try to remember the last presentation you sat through. Do you remember that moment when an overstuffed bulleted slide flashed on-screen, and suddenly your post-lunch food coma set in? Or while watching the words swirl and melt together, suddenly you blank on where you've been for the last 15 minutes?

My theory is that the food coma we blame for audience slumps is a scapegoat for slides riddled with bullets. What's the solution? We've already discussed it!

One Idea Per Slide

Remember Nancy Duarte's "single idea per slide" philosophy from Act I? Using one slide to communicate one main idea is the most effective antidote to bullet walls. This means taking one heavily bulleted slide and exploding it into more digestible "slide-eas," leading to a higher count of slides. This means less text on each slide that doesn't compete for your audience's eyeballs.

Now, practitioners often complain that they are commanded to "fit everything into 10 slides or less" to keep presentations "simple." This mandate is possibly inspired by PechaKucha, the popular Japanese presentation storytelling format of showing only 20 slides for only 20 seconds of commentary each.[1] While I appreciate the spirit of creating fewer slides to simplify a presentation, I feel this totally misses the mark for business presentations.

---

[1]PechaKucha

NOTE

My philosophy is to use as many slides as you need to fully express your narrative in an engaging manner. If you're doing it right, no one will be counting how many slides you have because each slide will support the idea you're communicating *at that exact moment*.

In PechaKucha, slides are highly visual and designed to be moved through at a rapid clip to maintain audience engagement. In corporate presentations, however, I see slide limit mandates resulting in slides that are exponentially more jam-packed with graphics, text, and fluff because the presenter is now attempting to fit a McMansion into a studio apartment. I believe the reason stakeholder audiences are demanding fewer slides is because they're trying to reduce the overall overwhelm they expect to see on each slide, per the examples you saw earlier.

If your slide is starting to look like a synopsis of the *Odyssey*, cut that text and place it in the Speaker Notes section. Then take the most salient phrase or sentence from the text and make it a single statement on the slide. Figure 14.2 shows an after example of Figure 14.1.

FIGURE 14.2 Simplified slide about glacial formations with striking photo of iceberg
Photo: Cassie Matias
Source: Cassie matias / EyeEm / Adobe Stock

This practice is *transformative* because your audience's zombifying brains won't be lurching around the slide to take it all in while you watch in helpless horror. Less is truly more here.

A Compromise: The Story Point Solution

Now, it's easy for me to sit here and tell you to ditch the bullet points and just place every single idea on its own slide. This was one of the hardest habits to break during my transformation, and I don't want to leave you stranded.

There are also situations that call for wordier list formats, such as recapping insights and recommendations, illustrating steps in a process, or reviewing lists of related items.

That's why I created the Story Point Solution as an antidote to bullet points. I replaced "bullet" with "story" since that word has no meaning here. This method is an effective bridge between the single-idea-per-slide philosophy and the Wall habit, leveraging mechanics of your audience's mental limits on multitasking while preserving your slide sanity.

Guidelines for the Story Point Solution

The following are the guidelines for the Story Point Solution:

- All story points on the slide should be related to one main idea. The purpose of this method is to dive deeper into related ideas, not a bunch of disconnected points.
- Keep each story point to one line. Don't write in full sentences that run on to the next line, because that encourages the brain to read and disengage.
- Use concise phrases with no more than five to seven words.
- Try not to exceed more than five story points per slide (or you run the risk of overwhelming your stakeholders' brains).
- Use a small image or icon on the slide that is *unquestionably relevant* to your list of ideas to trigger visual reinforcement (more on this in Chapter 16).
- Try not to exceed one story point slide for every five visual slides. This method is not intended as a one-to-one ingredient swap in the bullet point recipe; rather, it's designed to mitigate the stress of trying to break every idea out individually and accommodate list-oriented content. Remember that the more visual your presentation is overall, the more engaging and memorable it will be.

- Don't use bullet point symbols. A numbered list is fine, or even a checkbox symbol for a checklist. But bullet symbols don't add any visual information to the slide, which qualifies them as slide fluff. And yes, I'm using bullet points right now because this is a book, not a live presentation!

Figure 14.3 shows how I represent these guidelines to my audience when I'm teaching in a live environment.

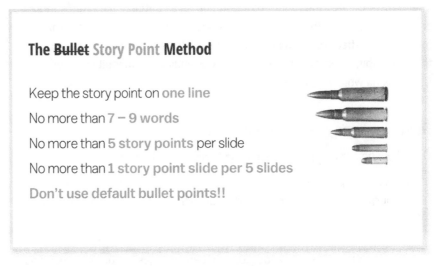

The ~~Bullet~~ Story Point Method

Keep the story point on one line

No more than 7 – 9 words

No more than 5 story points per slide

No more than 1 story point slide per 5 slides

Don't use default bullet points!!

FIGURE 14.3 Example of properly formatted Story Point Solution slide

Executing the Story Point Solution

What's lost in book format is the movement mechanism I use to reveal these story points live. This mechanism leverages basic animation and meets the audience's brains' preference to process one idea at a time. Here's how it would display during your meeting:

1. You advance to a blank slide with a title that discloses your next topic.

2. You click to animate each story point in one at a time using a quick fade in.

3. When you click to animate in the next point, you'll dim the text of the prior point. This is the key to the method. When you dim the prior point, you're shifting your audience attention down to the text that you want them to shift to. **The dimmed line serves as a reminder of what you've already covered,**

but you've signaled that you're moving on. This is a powerful way to keep you in the driver's seat of your audience's attention while still using a text-based slide.

Download my Story Point Solution checklist from the Resource Center to try this at home.

Now that you understand why presentation bullets are lethal and what to do instead, I guarantee you are going to witness a dramatic improvement to your audience's attention spans, their engagement, and the health of your presentation career.

It is my dream that bullet point walls will become an endangered species in presentations. And while on the journey toward that goal, the Story Point Method provides a solution that still works to keep all eyes on you and your insights.

Chapter Recap

- Your slides are for your audience, not you.
- Bullet points expose all your information to your audience at once, prompting them to read to themselves and tune you out.
- Adopting the "single-idea-per-slide" philosophy will help you keep the pace for your audience and maintain their attention.

Sandbox Assignment

- Review your current slides for walls of bullet points.
- Rethink how you can simplify and break these out into a series of slides.
- Consider using the Story Point Method for text-heavy lists and processes.

NOTE

At the time of writing, Google Slides and Keynote do not offer a dimming animation feature for text boxes, which is a major reason why PowerPoint remains my tool of choice.

Create Hype with Your Type

15

"Helvetica, Times New Roman, and Comic Sans walk into a bar. The barman turns to Comic Sans and says, 'Sorry, we don't serve your type in here.'"

—*Original Source Unknown*

In my early days as a data storytelling educator, I got embroiled in an online forum debate with a well-known analytics practitioner when I brought up how presenters think about type and fonts. Their argument was that fonts don't matter in presentation; only the content does.

My research and experience with design couldn't differ more. I would make an educated guess that if Apple decided to randomly switch its sleek, minimalist iPhone font of Helvetica Neue to juvenile Comic Sans without warning, the world might melt down into chaos.

iPhone owners may not even realize what changed exactly, but you better believe they'd know *something* was off. Remember, good design is invisible; bad design is glaringly obvious. Typography and font choice are no exceptions to this rule.

The truth is that fonts matter because they influence the emotions you elicit and the credibility of your content. In fact, fonts matter so much that a typography consultant named Sarah Hyndman wrote an entire book on it called *Why Fonts Matter*! Hyndman offers proof that type can influence our mood, our personality, and even our buying habits. She explains:

"Typefaces and magic tricks both take place right in front of our eyes, but somehow they can seem invisible. Type sets the tone and gives you clues to what you're about to read. It works much like the music in a film, which sets the scene for what you are about to watch."[1]

In this chapter, I explore why type is so powerful and how you can leverage it to communicate your insights.

---

[1]Hyndman, Sarah. *Why Fonts Matter*. Gingko Press, 2023. ISBN: 978-158-423-6313.

The Power of Type

Kevin Larson is an MIT psychologist who specializes in studying typefaces. He conducted a landmark study that demonstrated how font choice and layout affect human emotion. Amazingly, both font choice and text layout appeared to influence how *good* the reader felt. And as it turns out, feeling good is a critical piece of inspiring action.

"People exposed to the well-designed layout were found to have higher cognitive focus, more efficient mental processes, and a stronger sense of clarity."[2]

Wouldn't you want your slides to have that effect on your audience? **The first step is choosing the right fonts for your brand, subject matter, tone, and readability.** That means making your fonts an intentional choice and not leaving that decision up to your presentation tool!

One thing to know about me is that I have a beef with Calibri. It's still the most prevalent font I see in business presentations today. Why? Because it's the default font in every new PowerPoint presentation. And because we were never taught the power of type, we often don't think to change what's already there.

Because Calibri is everywhere, it is perhaps the most *unremarkable* font in the stable. Worse yet, many corporate brand templates still use Calibri, perhaps not realizing that there are many more updated and on-brand choices out there.

In our Instagram world, there is an explosion of creative font faces infusing ads and memes with bold, stylized, and vivid energy. And thanks to open use foundries like Google Fonts, the sky's the limit in infusing your deck with a potent and unique personality.

This is gradually improving in the increasingly popular Google Slides; however, even its default presentation font is set to Arial, which is also considered by some experts to be overstaying its welcome. As such, seeing Calibri or Arial in a presentation is a signal that the creator likely didn't consciously consider their font choice.

---

[2]affect.media.mit.edu/pdfs/05.larson-picard.pdf

The key to leveraging type to your advantage is to gain a cursory understanding of its elements and features. Now, there's some confusion over the difference between fonts, and font families or typefaces. Here are the technically correct definitions:

- A *typeface* is the name of a collection or group of fonts of varying weight, width, and style. It's also known as a *font family*.
- A *font* is a particular weight or style within the typeface or font family.

What we normally think of as a font, such as Open Sans or Helvetica, is really a typeface, while Open Sans Condensed is a specific font. But don't worry; if you use them interchangeably, I won't tell!

Typeface Classifications

Typefaces have a classification system that's sort of like a taxonomy of species. There are a number of typeface "genera" to get fancy, but for practical reasons, I'm going to have you focus on the three most common classes (see Figure 15.1).

- Serif
- Sans Serif
- Slab

1. Serif

2. Sans Serif

3. **Slab**

FIGURE 15.1 Three main classes of typeface

Serif typefaces include fonts whose lettering is characterized by a tiny stroke or line on the end of every letter, called a *serif*. Serifs reportedly originated in ancient Roman times and are still used today in print and newspaper publishing because they are considered to facilitate readability.[3] The serif assists the human eye in readability by visually connecting each letter without being in script.

Some people debate whether serif fonts are appropriate for presentations because it is a digital medium. However, Garamond, Quattrocento, and Merriweather are all highly rated by experts like Jeremiah Shoaf of Typewolf for online readability.

Sans serif typefaces are the fraternal twin of serif; the body of the lettering is the same, but it does not have the serif (*sans* is French for "without"). They are generally thought of as better for readable body text in presentations. Arial and Franklin Gothic are examples of sans serif typefaces. Lucida and Museo are examples of larger, more versatile typefaces that have both serif and sans serif families.

Slab serif typefaces have stylized and block-like serifs and are generally of thick weight. They are an excellent choice for large type and headings in presentations, but not as many would work well for body text. Roboto Slab and Adelle are two examples that are popular for presentation and web design.

There are even more typeface descriptors called Grotesque, Modern, Rounded, Humanist, and Monospaced, all of which you can explore at your leisure. For now, I would suggest keeping to the previous three for the sake of simplicity and readability.

TIP

Shoaf is one to follow if you're interested in keeping up on cutting-edge type trends.

Fonts in Families

What distinguishes each member in a font family are certain attributes of emphasis, including width, weight, and italicization. Font families are easy to spot in PowerPoint if you haven't already noticed them. If you highlight text on your slide and go to the Font drop-down in the Home Ribbon, look for a font with a small arrow pointing to the right such as Franklin Gothic or Georgia.

---

[3]Merriam-Webster's Manual for Writers and Editors (Springfield, 1998), p. 329.

You'll notice familiar treatments or weights of the same font, such as regular, italic, and bold. You may also notice unfamiliar variants like condensed, narrow, and heavy. It's in these variations where you'll find the most flexibility in expressing the tone and importance of your content.

In addition to limiting the number of distinct font families in each presentation to two, you'll want to limit the number of font weights to two or three. This will create a cohesive look and allow you to minimize the visual "switching" your audience's brain must do when reading.

And, if you use clean and versatile font families with a wide variety of weights, such as Open Sans, Montserrat, and Playfair Display, you can create complementary and dramatically contrasting looks for your headings and body text using the same family!

Font Pairing

One of the arts of presentation is pairing fonts, much like the art of pairing gourmet food with the perfect fine wine. The wrong pairing can visually sour a viewer's experience.

For even more consistency, choose one font family with a variety of weights including thin, semi bold, and condensed. You'd be amazed how much variety you can bring to your text content by using varied weights within the same family.

Recommended Font Families

I have several guidelines for practitioners to select presentation fonts, in this particular order:

1. Defer to whatever corporate branding guideline your company/client uses.
2. Use standard Microsoft fonts if you're using PowerPoint.
3. Try custom fonts in Google Slides or installed into PowerPoint if you don't share your deck with anyone else (do this at your own risk).

The reason I suggest standard fonts first is because it safeguards you from font malfunctions when you share decks between computers. If the host computer for your meeting doesn't have your custom font, it will use the program's default font, and the translation process can get ugly.

This happened to me during a last-minute computer switch at an agency summit, and my mangled slide text looked like my toddler had designed it. Ironic considering I was literally teaching about. . .slide design (smacks forehead).

Best Standard Fonts

Figure 15.2 shows my favorite font choices for business presentations with flexible families.

- Franklin Gothic
- Gill Sans
- Segoe
- Century Gothic
- Corbel
- Tahoma
- Garamond or Georgia

FIGURE 15.2 Recommended standard presentation fonts

I know it might seem yawn-inducing to stick with such old standbys, but know that these typefaces have a nice variety of font weights that you can experiment with to create an updated and unique look (such as pairing Franklin Gothic Condensed Demi for headings with Franklin Gothic Book for body content).

Do your best to avoid Calibri, Comic Sans, Times New Roman, and even Arial to keep text looking fresh.

Custom/Nonstandard Fonts

Once you get bitten by the font bug, you may feel constrained by the choices available in PowerPoint. As I mentioned, there is a mind-boggling array of typefaces waiting to be discovered to inject a wider range of personality and expression into slides.

My favorite source for nonstandard type is Google Fonts, which are incredibly easy to install onto your computer. For business presentations (including my own), I use the following combinations most often:

- Open Sans (my top choice for a fresh and flexible font family; I love to use Semi-Bold Condensed for headings and Light for body text)
- Montserrat or Raleway (crisp, modern, and ultra-readable)
- Roboto Slab and Roboto Sans (a readable and modern pairing of related serif/slab and sans serif)
- Oswald (a bold, impactful choice for headings, too strong for body content)
- Quattrocento and Merriweather for readable serifs

If you use Google Slides, you're in luck! Google conveniently offers its own fonts by default, so there's no need to install them on your computer.

> This is super important: if you use custom fonts in your PowerPoint deck and you must send it to be presented on another host computer, **remember to send your fonts as well!** Do this only if you are 100 percent sure the host can install your fonts. You've been warned. And a tip: if a font gets missed on the host computer, change your deck's default fonts from Calibri (the secret default) to something else like Franklin Gothic so that at least the backup looks appealing enough.

Now that you know which fonts to choose, your typographical to-dos don't end there. You must also consider how you visually treat the text on your slides as a tool for helping drive your key messages home. So next, you emphasize!

How to Emphasize Text

Fonts are flexible design tools for emphasis. There are several font characteristics you can use to help your message stand out. One of the biggest mistakes I see in data presentations is the haphazard treatment of text. You're going to see these pitfalls in the next few examples and learn how to avoid them.

Text Size

Let's play a quick game. I'm going to ask you to look at the slide graphic in Figure 15.3 and think of how fast you're able to read the text. Ready. . . go!

Go big or go home.

FIGURE 15.3 Slide with tiny text that says "go big or go home"

Maybe you can read it, but it might have taken you a second. And that second is the one where I lost your attention. You don't want to speak to an audience who is squinting at your slides. Now, stop and think for a moment about why we would use such teeny tiny type. . .if you said because we can cram more and more text onto the slide, you're right! Oftentimes, small text is a result of too much information in one view.

That's why the expert consensus is to set text size to no less than 20pt for body text in live presentations. This ensures adequate readability for most audiences in any size room, including conference venues. Obviously, this is less of a concern for virtual presentations, yet that is not a license to pack the screen with tiny type.

Let's fix the earlier slide's micro-text; see Figure 15.4.

FIGURE 15.4 Previous slide with "go big or go home" in much bigger font

This time, the text is an easily readable size. And, it may leave you with a feeling of. . . meh. Nothing particularly stands out. Remember, if everything looks the same, the audience will mentally treat it the same.

Emphasizing the text you deem to be most important is a presentation A-Team skill. And speaking of attributes, leveraging those preattentive attributes discussed in Chapter 12 is exactly how you'll do it.

Remember that the main preattentive attributes are form, spatial positioning, color, and movement. In the context of text, you leverage the form attributes of size, weight, and capitalization, as well as the attribute of color.

Text Form

Remember the slide that quite tepidly told us to go big or go home? Now look at the same text emphasized with form attributes of size, width, and capitalization in Figure 15.5.

Can you immediately feel the difference? A bit more ka-POW? This is where your message gets "meta"—I'm making my text "go big" by literally going BIG!

FIGURE 15.5 Previous slide with "go big or go home" dramatically emphasized with size, width, and capitalization

Text Color

The impact that the preattentive attribute of color has on our audience's perception of information cannot be overstated. The key to using it effectively is using it intentionally, meaning you're using it to communicate something specific. When I say use color intentionally, I don't mean like Figure 15.6.

FIGURE 15.6 Slide with random and unappealing text and background colors

Like random or default font choosing, arbitrarily applying color is one of the least productive presentation habits we pick up. An effective technique I learned from *Presentation Zen* is to pick up a color from an image I'm using and match it to the most important text on the slide, as shown in Figure 15.7.

FIGURE 15.7 Slide with image of red pencil standing out from black pencils and matching text saying "STAND OUT"
Source: cosma / Adobe Stock

Notice how the bold red pops out from the slide. Not only does this technique attract the eye, it creates a connective tissue between the image and the message. Just like going big, I'm getting "meta" and using the color that stands out to color "stand out!" Catching my drift?

You can easily do this by using the eyedropper tool in PowerPoint to snag a color value. You'll find the eyedropper in the Color settings of your element by choosing More Colors ➢ Colors. Click the eyedropper and use the "magnifying glass" to pinpoint the exact hue you're seeking. See Figure 15.8.

At the time of writing, Google Slides does not have an eyedropper tool, so you'll need to install a Chrome extension like ColorZilla to grab the color from your browser. Then you input the hex value into the Slides text or shape by clicking Fill color and then the + sign under Custom.

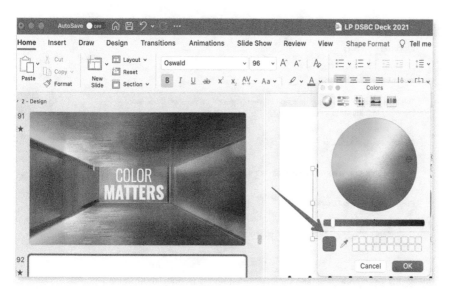

FIGURE 15.8 Location of the color eyedropper tool in the PowerPoint Colors menu

Establish a Visual Content Hierarchy

One way to help your audience understand your text content is through a visual hierarchy, which is a system of organization where content is emphasized based on its importance or rank.

Visual hierarchy is necessary for the brain to quickly parse the important ideas on each slide. Look at the slide in Figure 15.9 and ask yourself how quickly you can pick out the most important or overarching ideas.

I would guess that other than reading from top to bottom, you're not exactly sure what matters most because nothing stands out. And if you start by reading the middle of the slide, you may not be sure which text belongs to what headings, or even which lines are headings versus text.

As discussed in the emphasis section, using size and weight is one way to set apart the title and heading text, as shown in Figure 15.10.

Now you can tell which lines are higher-level headings and which are lower-level body content. But the new issue is that you don't instantly know which content belongs to which heading. The even spacing between each line fails to assist the viewer in determining the hierarchy.

> **CAUTION**
> I advise against using more than one color to highlight text in the same slide, unless there's a specific reason to do so, such as showing two different brand names. Try your best to keep to just one emphasis color per slide.

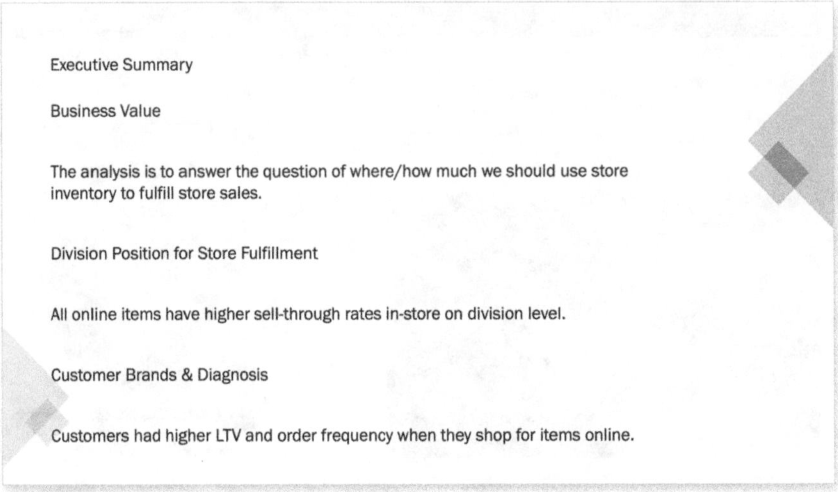

FIGURE 15.9 Executive summary slide where all text is formatted the same

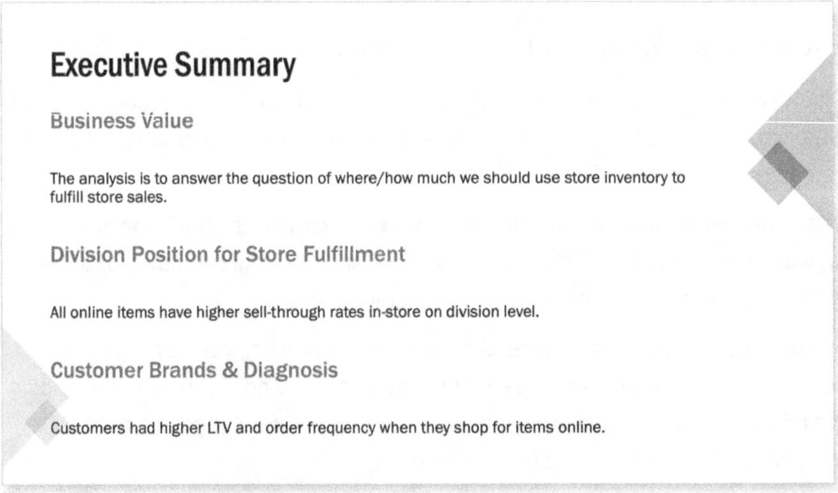

FIGURE 15.10 Same executive summary slide with improved text formatting for hierarchy

Here's where the spatial positioning attribute of proximity, or closeness, can assist. Figure 15.11 shows what happens when you group the lines using proximity (relative distance).

Do you see how you can immediately tell which body line belongs to which heading? That's the power of proximity!

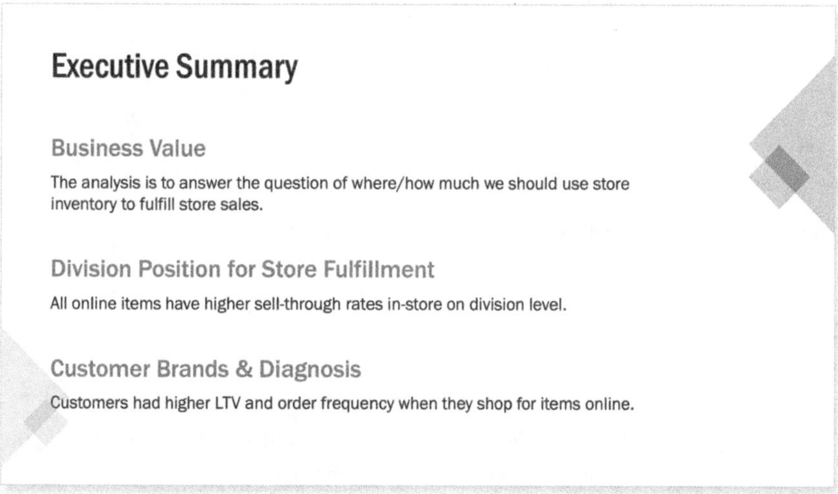

Executive Summary

Business Value

The analysis is to answer the question of where/how much we should use store inventory to fulfill store sales.

Division Position for Store Fulfillment

All online items have higher sell-through rates in-store on division level.

Customer Brands & Diagnosis

Customers had higher LTV and order frequency when they shop for items online.

FIGURE 15.11 Same executive summary slide with properly grouped lines using proximity principle

Putting It All Together

Figure 15.12 shows how you can use all these attributes either alone or in layers for the biggest punch.

In this example, I layered multiple attributes to emphasize the words "your key message" because that is what I wanted to stand out to you the most. I often use this styling mix for what I call *statement slides*, or slides containing one or two sentences designed to interrupt the story and land something important with the audience.

use color, font size, **weight**, **width**, and CAPITALIZATION to emphasize **YOUR KEY MESSAGE**

FIGURE 15.12 Slide showing different techniques to emphasize text

A Few Final Type Tips

■ To ensure adequate readability, change your view mode to Slide Sorter in PowerPoint (Grid View in Google Slides, Light Table in Keynote). If you can read everything in the small slides, the audience at the back of the room can too, and no one expends unnecessary effort to read.

■ Have you ever decided to change your font choice at the last second, or did the client change their mind? Going crazy tracking down every instance of that font? Well, stop right there! Did you know you can search and replace fonts in PowerPoint just like specific text? **Just go to the Edit menu and choose Find ➢ Replace Fonts.** Select the font you want to replace, then select your new font, and *voilà*! PowerPoint hunts down every instance of the old one and swaps it out for you. You're welcome.

■ Keep an eye on color contrast, which means choosing a shade or hue of your text color that is different enough from your background color. For example, don't use a blue font on a green header bar, as in Figure 15.13.

■ I do not recommend handwriting fonts unless there is an excellent reason to do so, such as extremely simple titles for lifestyle brands where that makes sense. They are generally hard to read, which creates work for your audience.

TIP

Use the Color Contrast Checker in the Resource Center to verify that your choices pass with flying colors.

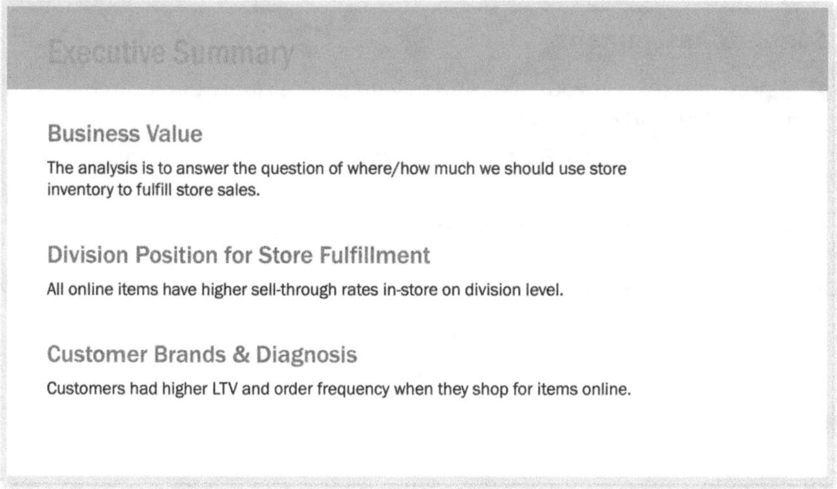

FIGURE 15.13 Slide with difficult-to-read title because of poor background color contrast

As you can see, there is a multitude of techniques to make your text drive your message home. I hope you are continuing to see that none of this is rocket science; rather, it's quite simple and intentional, just as promised.

Chapter Recap

- The typeface you choose for your presentation can greatly influence how your information is perceived in terms of credibility.
- Always follow your brand guidelines for font selection; within those guidelines, experiment with different font weights and styles to emphasize your message.
- The three best typeface classes to choose from are serif, sans serif, and slab.
- Use a mix of preattentive attributes such as size, weight, color, and intensity to emphasize important text.

Sandbox Assignment

■ Review the text on your slides and evaluate the clarity of hierarchy, readability, and emphasis.

■ Ensure consistency of font usage between headings, body, and other text.

■ Use different mixes of font attributes to emphasize and enhance your key message.

Harness the Power of Real Imagery

16

"Photography is the only language that can be understood anywhere in the world."
—Bruno Barby

Let's play a little game: close your eyes and recall the last text-heavy slide you remember in a presentation. Here, I'll wait. Hmm. . .is it taking a while? Having trouble dialing one up? Gosh, I didn't expect that.

Now close your eyes again and call up the last impactful or memorable image or photograph you remember. Boom! I'll bet one is coming to mind for you almost right away. There's a good reason for that, one we're about to exploit for you and your audience's benefit: to increase memory recall and elicit emotion from your audience.

When we think of imagery in corporate presentations, certain types come to mind first: charts, diagrams, and my personal nonfavorite. . .clipart. I believe focusing on only these kinds of images is a missed opportunity in persuading through presentation because of a psychological effect that many practitioner presenters aren't aware of.

The Picture Superiority Effect

Picture superiority is a phenomenon based in Allan Paivio's dual-coding theory, where he posited that pictures have an advantage over words alone because they encode both a visual and verbal message, which enables longer memory storage.[1]

Pictorial superiority is a powerful ally in your presentations and is highlighted at length in John Medina's aforementioned *Brain Rules*. Medina's research declared that if a piece of information was delivered with text alone, the recall (or ability to remember) sat at around 10 percent three days later. But if presented along with a powerful and relevant visual, such as an image or chart, the recall of that information jumped to more than 65 percent![2]

Medina explains that this is the result of our evolution as a visual-dominant species whose survival depended on our vision.

Now, this factoid has been the subject of some dispute in the data presentation expert community as the originating source has not been definitively located. However, pictorial superiority is an accepted psychology concept, and I've witnessed its effectiveness in action.

One can observe the massive difference in audience attention and recall when using imagery; the slides that are most often cited in my keynotes and workshops are the ones with dramatic images accompanied by simple text.

But here's the key: plopping any old image onto a text-based slide isn't going to trigger this effect and improve recall. **The image must be powerful and relevant to the message you're trying to convey.** And there's nothing more powerful and relevant than imagery of the world around us. By that, I mean full-color, full-bleed, high-res shots of people, places, and technology.

Medina says that real images are also your besties because **they have the uncanny ability to evoke emotion and empathy.** Think about how memorable a single photo can be, like the famous "Afghan Girl" of *National Geographic* legend.[3] According to Medina, evoking emotion *also* increases the recall of information. Win-win!

---

[1] www.sciencedirect.com/science/article/abs/pii/S1053810002000077
[2] Medina, John. *Brain Rules*. Pear Press, 2014. ISBN #978-0983263371
[3] en.wikipedia.org/wiki/Afghan_Girl

Imagery Elicits Empathy

Imagery is the most powerful visual tool for achieving the underlying mission of the presenting data: telling the customer's story so that your stakeholders will take action on their behalf.

Remember, humans make decisions using a blend of logic and emotion. Empathy is a compelling motivator toward action, because when the audience can feel the pain of the customer, they are more inclined to troubleshoot their pain.

Consider this example: perhaps you're sharing "bad news" of how most of your mobile visitors are abandoning a key sales page. You could communicate these findings as I once did in Figure 16.1 and then watch your VP proceed to check their email in front of your face. . . .

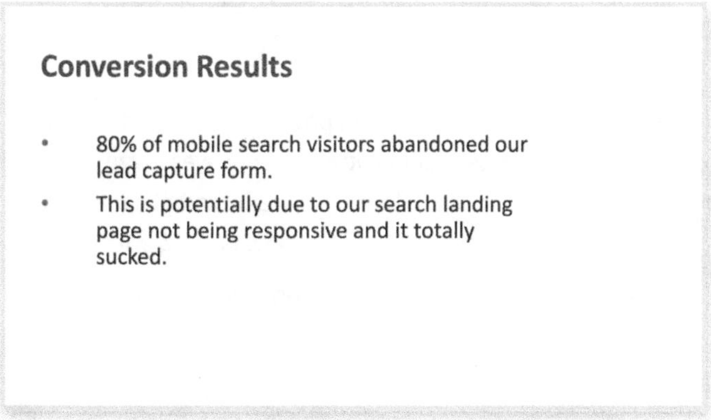

Conversion Results

- 80% of mobile search visitors abandoned our lead capture form.
- This is potentially due to our search landing page not being responsive and it totally sucked.

FIGURE 16.1 Boring landing page results slide with bullet points

If that doesn't sound appealing, why not *show* them someone who looks like a would-be customer and is struggling engaging with the company? Something along the lines of Figure 16.2.

Yowza! Doesn't the visible frustration and tension on the "customer's" face help send home just how dire it is that 80 percent of our visitors are ghosting the page? Many practitioners' first instinct is to represent any single data point or statistic in a chart. The previous technique is called *large number*, and displaying the data point this way is an eye-catching alternative. It's even more impactful when combined with an image aimed to evoke emotion.

FIGURE 16.2 More visually stimulating results slide with image of typical customer and large number statistic
Source: Eugenio Marongiu / Adobe Stock

Imagery Stimulates Their Attention

Perhaps the most valuable function a real image can provide is pure and simple visual stimulation. When acting as a presentation attendee, my eyes glaze over when I'm subjected to an endless parade of bulleted text walls, complicated charts, and convoluted diagrams. Images instantly snap an audience back to attention.

Consider the slide in Figure 16.3, which presents the concept of power.

FIGURE 16.3 Boring slide with bullet points describing power and a floating image of a lion
Source: Imaginechina Limited / Alamy Stock Photo

Now consider how the simplified and visual slide treatment in Figure 16.4 lands for you.

FIGURE 16.4 Simpler slide with full-bleed image of lion and simple text
Source: Imaginechina Limited / Alamy Stock Photo

It's the exact same idea with the exact same photo. But a different *feeling*, yes? Did you need all that bulleted text to understand the idea of power, or perhaps the lion was enough? Was it even more impactful with how the image filled the entire screen?

My guess is that the spirit of the message came through louder and clearer, simply by saying less and showing more. This is the superiority that imagery holds over text, and it's the way you treat your imagery that wins the day.

Basic Design Techniques for Images

This section covers several of the simplest and easiest image treatments that will inject your slides with emotional and memorable verve.

The Rule of Thirds

This guideline is yet another gem I learned from *Presentation Zen* and is considered an essential photographic composition technique. First written about by John Thomas Smith in 1797, the Rule of Thirds is the practice of dividing a visual space into three columns and three rows, creating a grid of nine squares or rectangles.[4]

---

[4]en.wikipedia.org/wiki/Rule_of_thirds#cite_note-7

The idea is that when you overlay this grid onto your slides, it creates four intersections between the lines, which are called *power corners*. The rule directs the designer to place important focal points in the image or text on or along these corners. It posits that our eyes tend to move to one of these power corners before other areas such as the center or outlying spaces. These points supposedly contain more power and energy and create natural balance and interest.

Figure 16.5 is an example of a slide where everything is centered. The image is striking enough, but it doesn't provide the maximum balance that it could.

FIGURE 16.5 Slide with image of mountain and text centered
Source: Tyler Lastovich/Pexels

And now, Figure 16.6 shows a slide leveraging power corners, which are marked with yellow dots.

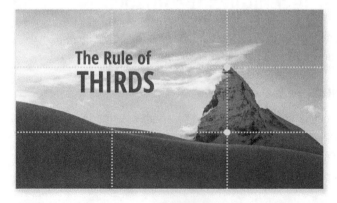

FIGURE 16.6 Slide with image of mountain and text balanced with power corners
Source: Arnab_Datta_7 / Shutterstock

Do you see how the peak of the mountain and the slide text overlap with three of the power corners? If I had placed all focal objects in the center, the effect would be different. I see this rule as a visual "scale" balanced by each object.

To try the rule of thirds, go to the View ribbon in PowerPoint and click Guides to activate. You'll start with a crosshair; hold the Shift key on one of the lines to duplicate it and drag the new line to mark a third of the slide. Repeat one more time and adjust the lines to create the grid. (In Google Slides, choose View ➤ Guides ➤ Show Guides ➤ Add Horizontal / Vertical Guide.)

Copy Space

A common practice in advertising design is to use an image with a visual focal point in the foreground, like a person or object, and then place "copy" (marketing text) in an offset position in an empty "space." Hence, you can think of "copy space" as the white or negative space in a photo.

Copy space often uses the rule of thirds, and it's a simple and elegant way to help your text stand out and be reinforced by the image. Figure 16.7 shows an example.

FIGURE 16.7 Slide with image of desk and items surrounding text in copy space
Source: Andyone / UnSplash

You see how I've placed my slide text in the empty space above the focal point, the desk objects? That's it, it's that simple. When you use copy space correctly, it will look like the photo was snapped specifically for your message and you'll pave your path toward magazine ad greatness.

Now, you'll note in the image in Figure 16.7 that I centered my text and aligned it with the eyeglasses and laptop. But didn't I just talk about not centering everything with the rule of thirds? Yes, yet I believe the rule of thirds is meant to be more of a guideline toward more energetic and impactful slides, but you do not have to use it for every image-based slide.

WHERE TO FIND THE BEST IMAGERY

Once my workshop students get bitten by the photo bug, the first question they ask is where to find photos. There is a growing stable of image sources out there, but the key to using them is knowing whether you're *allowed* to use them.

If you want to use an image you found on Google in a public-facing conference or sales presentation or on the Web in a blog post, you must check its copyright restrictions. Many images aren't permitted for public and commercial applications, and there is technology to track down unapproved usage.

If you use Google or an image aggregator like Flickr, make sure to activate the Creative Commons license filter, which in most cases means the photo is free, but you are required to attribute credit for the image to the creator. The safest setting is "commercial use and modifications allowed," especially if it is on a public website.

My go-to photo website is Unsplash, an ever-growing collection of stunning images that are completely free to use *and* don't require attribution if you forget (although it is a kindly gesture). Your imagination is the limit for filtering by keyword, orientation (portrait versus landscape), and even specific color tones! Pexels and Pixabay are fine free sources as well.

When you're looking for more corporate-oriented stock photos, illustrations, or video and are striking out on free sites, there are plenty of commercial stock photo sites available. My top choice is Deposit Photos, which offers periodic package deals, lots of graphical formats, and the ability to search for a specific professional model in a photo series (great for consistency).

Use the Right Image

Remember that the magic formula for selecting an image is that it's powerful and relevant to your message; else, it won't click and can even confuse the audience. When facilitating my slide design workshop for a group of digital analysts, one of them took my imagery advice a bit out of context during our meeting simulation exercise.

On one slide, the analyst displayed a bar graph of a client's paid search click-through rate broken down by search engine (e.g., Google, Yahoo!, etc.). But rather than labeling each bar with the search engine's name, he used a small headshot of each search engine's company CEO. This led to more than a few of us scratching our heads.

While he won points for creativity, a typical stakeholder audience may have no idea how to distinguish Sergey Brin from Jerry Yang in a lineup. He explained that I had encouraged him to use images, so he used as many as possible. This prompted an important note on discernment: it's not about always using images; rather, it's about using images that align with your concept—*or not at all*.

While I'm on the subject, be discerning with the images you find on stock photo websites. Just because a photo was professionally snapped and listed on a paid site doesn't mean it's going to be a good choice.

That means avoiding oddities like the photographic, erm, "specimens" shown in Figure 16.8.

(a) (b) (c)

FIGURE 16.8 Silly stock photos
Source: (a): auremar / Adobe Stock   (b): Ariel Skelley / Getty Images
    (c): iridi66/Adobe Stock

Yes, these are actual stock photos you can purchase on actual stock photo websites. But as you can see, it's hard to imagine a business or data scenario where these are appropriate.

So, how do you find the right photo? For literal ideas such as smartphone usage or retail shoppers, obviously use photos of smartphones and retail shoppers. This is less straightforward when finding images to convey more abstract or theoretical ideas.

I find that this is easier when you connect the idea to something tangible and relatable in the real world. Remember in Chapter 6 the discussion on using

TIP

Jot down ideas for the first visuals that come to mind when you think about the subject and see where that leads you. You can also jump on the AI prompt technology train with a tool like ChatGPT to get ideas for image concepts!

relatable analogies? That thought process can assist here. Are there objects, animals, places, sports, etc., that evoke the concept or feeling you're aiming for?

For example, if you reference the speed of information, what about a high-speed highway or an Olympic runner? Or in my case, referencing power with a lion?

Use the Image Right

Once you've selected the perfect image to reinforce your idea, haphazardly slapping it on your slide isn't going to cut the mustard. There is a set of guidelines for treating photos that leverages how the brain works.

I'll explain using the slide example from my signature keynote, shown in Figure 16.9.

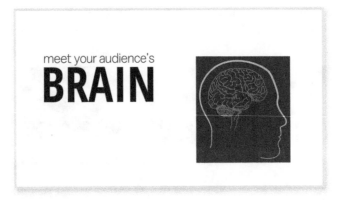

FIGURE 16.9 Slide with basic text and illustration of a head with brain
Source: justinkendra / Deposit Photos

Notice that I chose an illustration of the human brain to reinforce the text mentioning the audience's brain. Now, I see photos in presentations treated like this all the time, with two main issues.

First, this is what I call a "floater," where the image is adrift in space, rather than properly anchored to the edges of the slide. Remember the Gestalt principles from earlier? This image treatment triggers the principles of closure and continuity, where the brain will divert energy to mentally "completing" the object by filling in the gaps on the sides. This effort occupies mental horsepower and attention, which is then diverted away from you speaking. So what's the solution?

DO BLEND YOUR IMAGE INTO THE SLIDE BACKGROUND

In the revision shown in Figure 16.10, I used the PowerPoint eyedropper tool to "sample" the background color of the graphic and match it to the background color of the slide. Then I inverted the text color to white to create proper contrast.

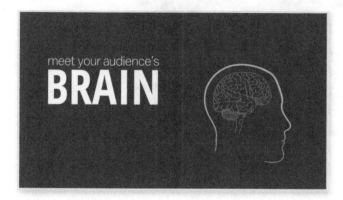

FIGURE 16.10 Brain slide with matching background color
Source: justinkendra / Deposit Photos

The second issue is that you may not realize it, but this image may be making your eyes give the message the cold shoulder. So next. . .

DO ROTATE IMAGES TO FACE YOUR TEXT

Research suggests that our brains tend to track the gaze of others, in person or in imagery.[5] Your first unconscious eye motion may have been to follow the head's gaze off the slide. **That's why presentation principles advise turning any image with a face toward the slide text.**

This creates the effect that the face is "looking" at your message, which can help give it more importance in the eyes of both the image and the audience; see Figure 16.11.

DON'T STRETCH SMALL OR LOW-QUALITY IMAGES TO FILL THE SLIDE

Low-resolution images are a no-no for your slides, and when you stretch out smaller images, the resulting pixelation can "age" your content and degrade

---

[5]www.nationalgeographic.com/science/article/what-are-you-looking-at-people
-follow-each-others-gazes-but-without-a-tipping-point

its credibility by evoking Super Nintendo–era graphics, as shown in Figure 16.12.

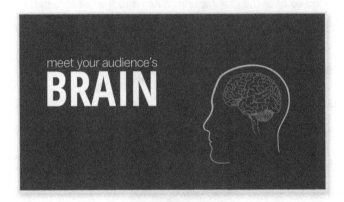

FIGURE 16.11 Brain slide with head facing text
Source: justinkendra / Deposit Photos

FIGURE 16.12 Stretched brain slide and pixelated, low-res image of New York City
Source: justinkendra / Deposit Photos and Adobe Stock images

DO USE HIGH-RESOLUTION IMAGES THAT FILL THE SLIDE

Whenever possible, fill the slide with the image and eliminate gaps. I play it safe by using images at least 2000 pixels wide, which is slightly larger than the now-standard 16:9 widescreen presentation aspect ratio of 1920 × 1080.

DO CREATE A WINDOWPANE EFFECT FOR PORTRAIT (VERTICALLY ORIENTED) IMAGES

Rather than awkwardly stretching and warping a portrait-oriented image, keep the image in its original aspect ratio and put a rectangle shape with the same background color so that the image seamlessly blends in. See Figure 16.13.

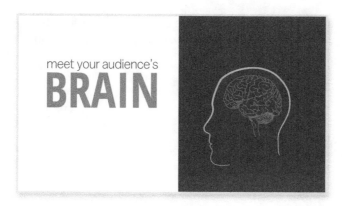

FIGURE 16.13 Brain slide with windowpane effect
Source: justinkendra / Deposit Photos

This creates a striking contrast between the "panes," which could further rein-force the idea of the brain by representing its two hemispheres (right and left).

DON'T DISPLAY DISEMBODIED PEOPLE AND LIMBS

A common and disturbing boo-boo I see in presentations is images of incomplete people or floating limbs. This is an unsettling visual effect, which you can see in Figure 16.14.

FIGURE 16.14 Slide with floating hand and woman
Source: LIGHTFIELD STUDIOS / Adobe Stock

This visual disturbance tweaks our preattentive tendency toward closure and continuity again, where our brain scrambles to "complete" the person to prevent our uneasiness.

The fix here is simple: always align the incomplete edge of a person or limb against an edge of the slide so it looks like the person is "peeking" in from off the slide, as shown in Figure 16.15.

Ahhhh, that's. . . less creepy.

FIGURE 16.15 Slide with hand and woman properly aligned with edges
Source: LIGHTFIELD STUDIOS / Adobe Stock

Put your photos on a diet.

Now, you'll notice something interesting when using these gorgeous hi-res snaps: your PowerPoint or Keynote file size will skyrocket, which may cause frustration in trying to email the hefty deck to colleagues.

That's why I use a nifty tool called TinyPNG to compress my images before I insert them into PPT. TinyPNG strips all unnecessary stuff from an image and compresses it as much as possible without compromising image integrity or resolution. I found that this helps speed up Google Slides as well, despite it being a cloud-based tool.

These dos and don'ts should get you on the right track for jaw-dropping and impactful photo slides. The following are several other ways to incorporate real imagery in your data presentations for visual impact.

Background Shots

Stunning background images are one of my favorite on-trend design techniques. They provide a bit of visual stimulation and "subliminal" context for the slide without hogging the spotlight.

Background images work particularly well for section header slides; they create a consistent look and are a vast improvement in stimulating attention over the more typical solid background colors. Lush landscapes of mountains and oceans and high-wattage nighttime city photos make for especially appealing backdrops.

Sometimes I have a photo I want the audience to see, but it's too busy for my text to be readable. In this case, I place semitransparent rectangle shapes across the slide to help the text "leap" out, like in Figure 16.16.

FIGURE 16.16 Slide with semitransparent text box over a busy, colorful image
Source: Jezael Melgoza / UnSplash

Depending on the photo, you can use dark or light shapes to maximize legibility. This technique is well-suited for "statement slides," where you are stating a simple yet powerful idea without distracting ancillary elements. See Figure 16.17.

Make absolutely sure that the shape is solid enough and provides enough contrast to read the text (not like the beauty in Figure 16.18).

Section Headers

Most section header slides in business presentations are about as exciting as watching a herd of snails crawl through peanut butter. (I wish I could claim that phrase as my own.) Section headers are the perfect opportunity to interrupt the all-too-common parade of chart, diagram, and text-heavy slides.

14.65%
25%
of new hires + promotions will require
DATA STORYTELLING SKILLS

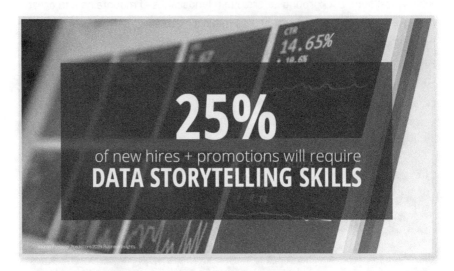

FIGURE 16.17 Example statement slide with semitransparent text panel over an image of dashboard
Source: Stephen Dawson / UnSplash

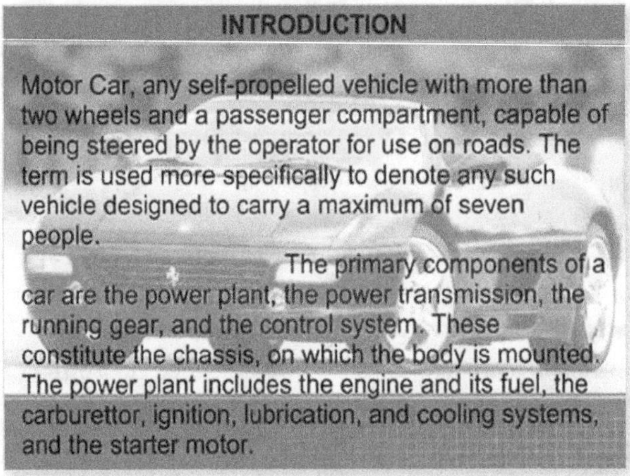

INTRODUCTION
Motor Car, any self-propelled vehicle with more than two wheels and a passenger compartment, capable of being steered by the operator for use on roads. The term is used more specifically to denote any such vehicle designed to carry a maximum of seven people.
The primary components of a car are the power plant, the power transmission, the running gear, and the control system. These constitute the chassis, on which the body is mounted. The power plant includes the engine and its fuel, the carburettor, ignition, lubrication, and cooling systems, and the starter motor.

FIGURE 16.18 Slide with poor legibility from background image of cookies
Source: Nicolás Varela / Unsplash.com

You can use the full background image technique with an overlay or the windowpane effects shown in Figure 16.13. Don't be afraid to get creative here, so long as you follow the photo principles! See Figure 16.19.

FIGURE 16.19 Example section header slide with semitransparent polygon and background image of tropical island
Source: Julian Timmerman / UnSplash

Iconography

An imagery trend taking the web design and presentation world by storm is *iconography*, which is the use of symbols to represent concepts. Icons are an excellent way to visually reinforce your ideas and reduce the volume of less-stimulating text.

Icon design styles range from simple line to filled to gradient to circular to flat (my favorite style). They can be incredibly simple or complex in artistic execution, as you can see in these renderings of a checklist in Figure 16.20.

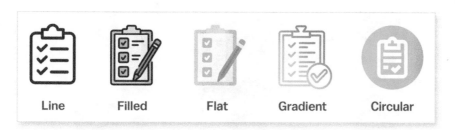

FIGURE 16.20 Various style renderings of a checklist icon
Images source: Freepik

Creative Ways to Use Icons

Two of my favorite ways to use iconography, other than in diagrams, is in lieu of text-based bullet slides and as a visual agenda. First, icons are my favorite alternative to the wall of bullets we're so accustomed to seeing. Figure 16.21 shows the snoozefest of a digital marketing presentation slide I made my audience sit through many years ago.

FIGURE 16.21 Boring bullet point explanatory slide about customer channels

Figure 16.22 shows how I would approach it using icons to represent each bullet.

FIGURE 16.22 Enhanced explanatory slide with channel icons surrounding the "customer"
Source: Angello Pro / UnSplash

See the difference in how the text concepts are visually reinforced? Note: I also layered several techniques, including emphasizing the title text and using a striking background photo of a would-be customer who is gazing up at my title!

Next, icons can reinvent that boring old agenda that we're not calling an agenda anymore (right?). See the example presentation agenda in Figure 16.23.

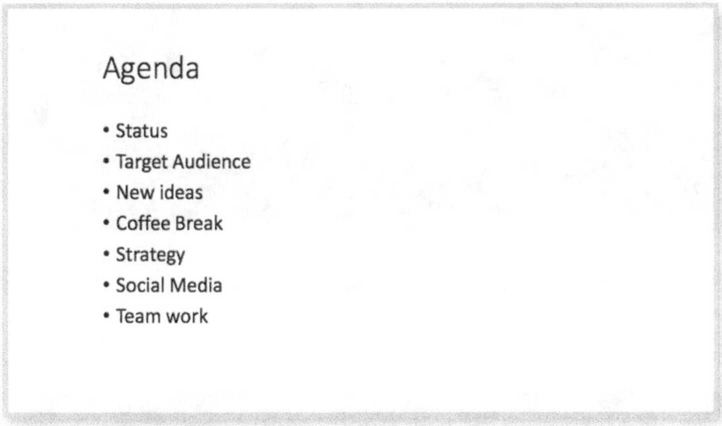

Agenda

- Status
- Target Audience
- New ideas
- Coffee Break
- Strategy
- Social Media
- Team work

FIGURE 16.23 Boring bullet point agenda slide

As common as this format is, it's hard to imagine anyone who could have stayed awake past the 10-minute mark. Figure 16.24 shows a more visual approach that uses icons to communicate each step in the agenda.

Note how the icons are connected in a way that indicates a path or journey, which is what your presentation actually *is*. Also note that I've placed a darkened background image here, which provides dynamic energy and visual context.

You can also repurpose the visual agenda as section header slides. In Figure 16.25, notice how I've darkened most section icons with semitransparent shapes so that the icon of the next section pops out.

This is a simple and inventive way of visually escorting your audience through the journey of your data story.

Icon Caveats

I encourage mostly free creative license with icons, with a couple of guidelines:

FIGURE 16.24 Enhanced agenda slide with icons depicting presentation sections
Source: fabioapferreira / Shutterstock

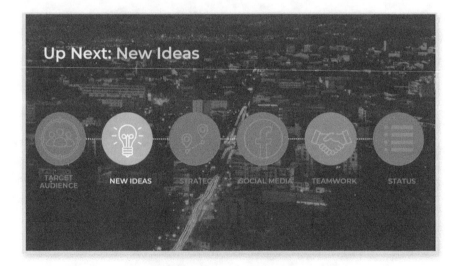

FIGURE 16.25 Enhanced section header slide with highlighted icon showing the next step
Source: fabioapferreira / Shutterstock

■ Once you choose an icon design style, stick to it. To make this easy, look
for icon "packs" that offer collections of icons with the same style and
related concepts.

■ Do *not* use clipart. Clipart does not qualify as acceptable iconography in my book. Nothing says "this presentation was built in 1997" better than those cartoonish smiley faces, disembodied high-five hands, or small, featureless person-shaped blobs lurking in slides. As I mentioned, social media has ratcheted up our threshold for bad design and imagery.

Where to Find Iconography

Almost all commercial stock photo websites also offer icons and icon "packs," which are great for creating visual consistency. However, my favorite source is FlatIcon, where you can search for symbols with different design styles based on a concept, find related icons, and even choose the icon color.

Web-Based Screenshots

Screenshots are a valuable type of imagery to provide visual context, especially for those in the digital marketing and analytics fields. Ad creative tests, search engine keyword results, website mockups, and so on, are all great assets to show your audience exactly what you're talking about.

If you just drop a screenshot of a website or app as is, you can again trigger the Gestalt principles of closure and continuity, forcing your viewers' brains to do extra work. It also doesn't look intentional. The first way I like to treat screenshots is to add a subtle drop shadow at the bottom and right edges of the image to give it a tangible depth. This is one of the few places where I recommend enhancement effects like shadows, so use this sparingly.

The other method I prefer is to situate the image inside the appropriate viewing device, such as a desktop monitor or a smartphone. This contextualizes the customer experience for the stakeholder audience, as shown in Figure 16.26.

This technique most accurately illustrates the interactive customer experience for your audience, facilitating their understanding, familiarity, and comfort with your data.

Now, the practice of dropping screenshots onto slides does not apply to all charts, graphs, and visuals inside of data platforms. This is very, very important: **do not capture tables of numbers from data platforms and use them for slide visuals.** See Figure 16.27.

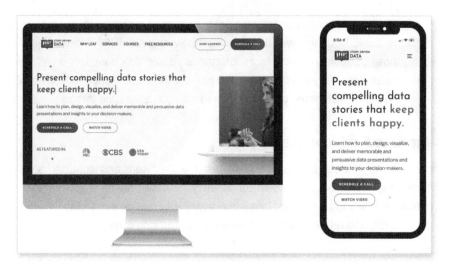

FIGURE 16.26 Website screenshots seated in desktop monitor and mobile device
Images source: Deposit Photos

	Source	Users ↓	New Users	Sessions	Bounce Rate	Pages / Session	Avg. Session Duration
		49 % of Total: 4.56% (1,074)	41 % of Total: 3.95% (1,037)	68 % of Total: 5.87% (1,158)	20.59% Avg for View: 24.01% (-14.24%)	1.90 Avg for View: 1.20 (57.59%)	00:04:07 Avg for View: 00.02.08 (92.80%)
☐ 1.	coolinfographics.com	15 (30.61%)	14 (34.15%)	17 (25.00%)	11.76%	1.24	00:03:34
☐ 2.	juiceanalytics.com	5 (10.20%)	4 (9.76%)	5 (7.35%)	40.00%	2.00	00:02:53
☐ 3.	t.co	5 (10.20%)	5 (12.20%)	5 (7.35%)	20.00%	2.80	00:05:15
☐ 4.	linkedin.com	3 (6.12%)	1 (2.44%)	5 (7.35%)	0.00%	2.20	00:01:24
☐ 5.	coolinfographics-com.cdn.ampproject.org	2 (4.08%)	2 (4.88%)	2 (2.94%)	50.00%	1.00	00:00:04
☐ 6.	facebook.com	2 (4.08%)	2 (4.88%)	2 (2.94%)	100.00%	1.00	00:00:00
☐ 7.	go2.bucketquizzes.com	2 (4.08%)	2 (4.88%)	2 (2.94%)	50.00%	1.00	00:00:12
☐ 8.	go2.bucketsurveys.com	2 (4.08%)	2 (4.88%)	3 (4.41%)	66.67%	1.00	00:00:40
☐ 9.	yandex.ru	2 (4.08%)	2 (4.88%)	3 (4.41%)	0.00%	1.00	00:00:53
☐ 10.	amplitude.com	1 (2.04%)	1 (2.44%)	1 (1.47%)	0.00%	2.00	00:01:38

FIGURE 16.27 Screenshot of report table from an analytics platform

This approach is *not* conducive to immediate visual comprehension. Take a few extra minutes and load the data you're speaking to into a chart, and your audience's brain will thank you. I dive into why tables are not your best bet for communicating data visually in Act III.

I hope you're understanding the power and versatility of imagery as both art form and communication tool. Remember, moderation here is key. Don't go overboard with images, but do make them a regular star in your show, and you will win over your audience with their undivided attention.

Chapter Recap

- Real imagery is a powerful visual tool to capture attention, improve recall, elicit emotion, and inspire empathy in your audience for the customer.
- Images make for more engaging backgrounds, section headers, and statement slides.
- Clipart can detract from the credibility of your content.
- Iconography is an effective technique for replacing text.
- Screenshots are an effective image type to contextualize your data.

Sandbox Assignment

- Look through your slides to see how you can replace text-based content with imagery, backgrounds, screenshots, and icons that visually support your information.

Master Motion with Simple Animation

17

"Motion is the sign of life."

—*Swami Vivekananda*

I'm often asked how I use animation in my presentation slides. My answer: I use it simply, judiciously, and very, *very* carefully.

PowerPoint currently lists more than 65 entrance, exit, and motion effects in its animation arsenal. So many to choose from, right? Well. . .not if you want your audience to stay focused.

The only training in presentation design I ever received was a summer college class on PowerPoint "effectiveness." The class unlocked so much knowledge about all the fantastical features this tool had to offer in the early 2000s, especially animation!

I learned invaluable skills like how to use laser beam in individual letters of every sentence on every slide (complete with laser beam sound effects) and how to use checkerboard slide transitions to "keep it exciting." I mean, PowerPoint even features an "Exciting" category of animations! How exciting is that?

Or at least, so I thought. Several years later, I was working at an internship for a small software company when I was asked to present the capabilities of our sales territory alignment program to a prospect. So, I pulled out all the stops. I used every PowerPoint bell and whistle I could think of.

When I asked for feedback afterward, my boss graciously responded, "Hey, nice job in there. But do you think next time, you can, um, not make me so dizzy?" Yikes! I was crestfallen. I simply didn't understand how they weren't blown away by my incredibly exciting presentation slides!

Today, I do understand. Instead of creating clarity for our client, I trapped them in a dark visual carnival complete with a creepy funhouse; it looked fine going in, but the way out was a nightmare. I learned a hard lesson that day, which is to beware of most PowerPoint animation features.

Animation is a potent tool for attention, but it also has great potential for misuse. I've already discussed how motion is an important preattentive attribute, so leveraging it with intention is paramount. The following are the specific instances of how I use (and don't use) animation.

Slide Transitions

The animation I use most often is the transition between my presentation slides. I have simple guidance here: when I've finished editing, **I select all slides and apply the Fade transition. Then I set the duration to .25 seconds.** After much testing and tweaking, I find that this transition effect and speed provides a smooth and consistent shift between your ideas.

The other transition I've experimented with is Push, which visually "pushes" the current slide in a particular direction to reveal the next slide. You can use this to give the sense that you're navigating subsections of a much larger visual, such as a diagram or customer journey map.

This is also a helpful effect if you want to take an audience through a website or digital experience by creating a clever "scrolling" effect. If you carefully line up your slides, you can achieve what's called a *scrollytelling* mechanism, which is a growing trend in interactive journalism.

The *New York Times* (NYT) regularly publishes outstanding data visualization pieces; one fascinating and sobering example of scrollytelling is the NYT's visual depiction of "How the (COVID) Virus Got Out,"[1] and it is worth a visit.

Object Movement

Path Animation is a class of effects I haven't experimented much with yet; however, they offer interesting potential. You select an object such as an icon or text box and draw a defined "path" along which the object moves. The object can travel along a path of predefined shapes such as lines, arcs, and circles.

I envision paths used in scenarios like with moving a customer avatar across a journey diagram of some kind; however, I would file this in the "Advanced" category that would warrant use by highly skilled presentation designers.

---

[1] www.nytimes.com/interactive/2020/03/22/world/coronavirus-spread.html

Object Reveals for Masterful Storytelling

I also use animation to reveal and remove objects such as charts, text boxes, diagrams, and sections. My essential animation rule is this: **use animation to show the audience exactly what you're talking about in that moment, and nothing ahead of that**. All too often, I see practitioners display a slide showing a complex process like this, with everything displayed at once. See Figure 17.1.

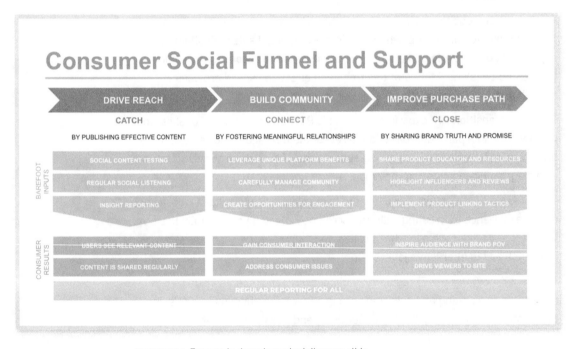

FIGURE 17.1 Extremely densely packed diagram slide

Then the practitioner would speak through each part of the process in a logical order, utterly unaware that the audience has completely tuned them out and is turning into zombie ankle-biters. To prevent this, I developed techniques I call *Object Pacing* and *Shape Pacing*, which animate objects and shapes to pace the audience through a busy slide or complex chart.

Object Pacing

This technique is quite simple and effective at keeping you in the driver's seat of your audience's attention span. Imagine if you only showed this slide instead of the busier version you just saw (see Figure 17.2).

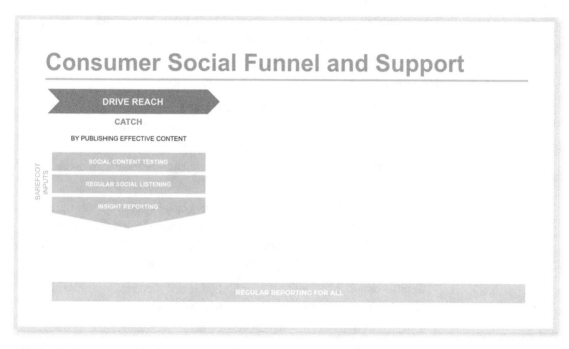

FIGURE 17.2 The same diagram slide with only the first column of objects shown

See how it's less tempting to read the entire slide? Why? *Because you can't read it all yet.* And neither can your audience. This technique is also effective because the blank space on the slide indicates there is more to the story, which builds anticipation. Figure 17.3 shows a sort of "storyboard" of how I would unveil this slide piece-by-piece so that the audience stays hitched to me.

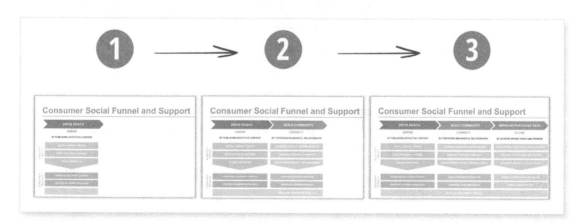

FIGURE 17.3 Storyboard of step-by-step reveals of diagram slide

Even though you see three distinct views here, this is all one slide. I animate in objects with a "click" trigger to reveal them at my pace, just like with my Story Point Method.

Here's how I do it:

1. Click each object and apply the Fade entrance effect with a duration of .25 seconds. (No Swivel, no Spinner, and nothing from the Exciting category, if you please.)

2. Adjust the order of reveals and object groupings in the Animation pane using the Timing menu.

Now you can reveal every object or group of objects at the exact pace you're speaking through. This requires some practice in selecting and applying animation settings. One trick I use is to select all objects at once, apply the Fade animation in bulk, and individually adjust each object's reveal order in the Animation pane.

Your other option is to duplicate your first slide and then repeat it, adjusting what's shown on the subsequent slides. That works well if you want the slide title to change as you reveal new sections.

This pacing technique is so incredibly simple yet *game-changing* when it comes to keeping your audience's attention glued to you.

Shape Pacing

I devised this next approach when asked to present slides that didn't belong to me and the objects were part of one image. I knew I didn't want to overwhelm my audience with everything at once, but I was low on time and needed a quick fix because I couldn't animate discrete objects.

Figure 17.4 shows what the slide looked like.

Ay caramba, what a fiesta for the eyes! But alas, no bueno for their brains. Instead of displaying this all at once, I chose to review each piece of the story by overlaying a combination of opaque (solid) and semi-transparent white square or rectangular shapes. I constructed a path I wanted to take the audience through to arrive at their a-ha moment.

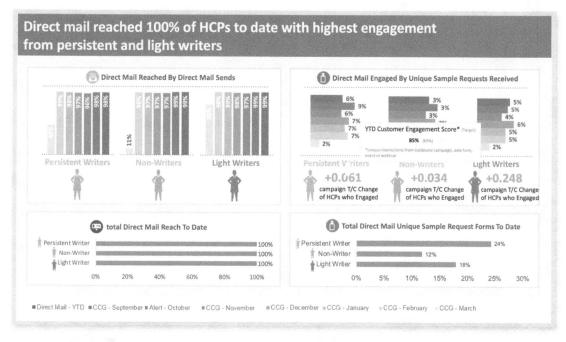

FIGURE 17.4 Densely packed data slide

Here is the mechanism:

1. First, I covered the separate slide areas with solid white rectangles except for the title, which prefaces the theme of the slide.

2. I applied a visible gray dotted border to the rectangles while arranging them and then removed them when I presented my slides (see Figure 17.5).

3. When presenting the slide, I animated out the rectangle shape on the upper left (using a Fade exit) to reveal the first story area of the slide. You'll speak to that section only. See Figure 17.6.

4. When I was ready to move on to the next area, I faded out the next solid white rectangle.

5. At the same time (in one animation stroke), I faded *in* a semitransparent rectangle that covers the first area I revealed. See Figure 17.7.

6. After presenting that section, I repeated the mechanism one last time by fading out the final area's solid rectangle and fading in a semitransparent rectangle over the previous area. See Figure 17.8.

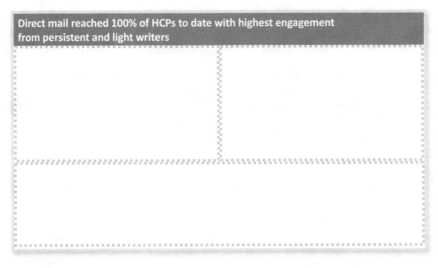

FIGURE 17.5 Densely packed data slide with concealing shapes marked in gray borders

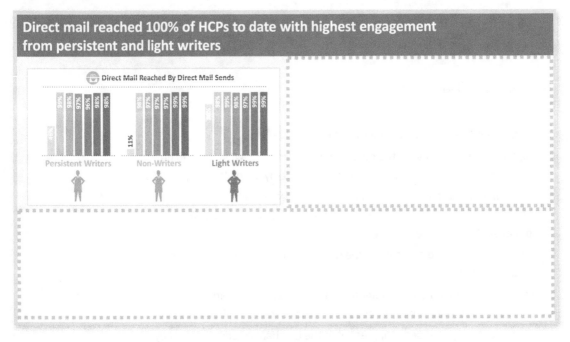

FIGURE 17.6 Revealing the upper-left area of the data slide

This method empowers you to herd your audience through each area of your slide story without watching them jump the attention corral.

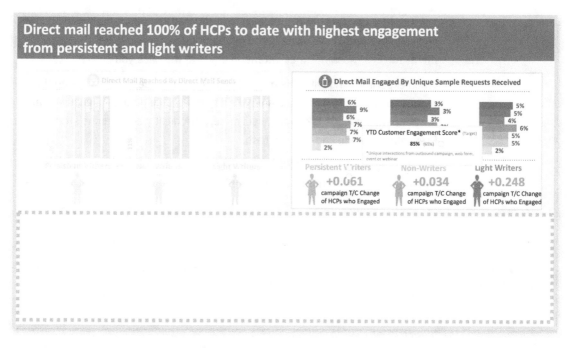

FIGURE 17.7 Revealing the upper-right area of data slide while fading in the shape to partially conceal the upper-left area

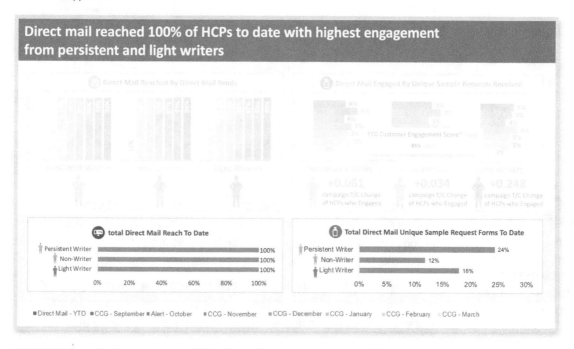

FIGURE 17.8 Revealing the bottom area of data slide while concealing the upper-right area

The semi-transparent shapes fade out the covered sections, which reminds the audience of what you've already presented but doesn't allow them to linger there. You are "pushing" their attention along at the pace you desire.

When experimenting with this method, you'll want to keep a close eye on the order of object animations, the animation type, and the timing. To ensure that the animation doesn't take *you* by surprise, periodically activate the slide in Presentation mode and test the path.

Simply drag each shape into your preferred order and play with linking them with different start timing; see Figure 17.9.

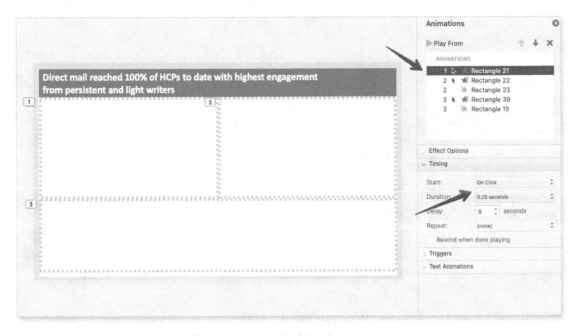

FIGURE 17.9 Shape pacing using the Animation pane

TIP

Visit the Resource Center for a detailed tutorial on how you can use shape pacing.

With this technique, the single idea per slide approach simply becomes the single idea per "click." It helps to get well-acquainted with the Animation pane, so don't be afraid to roll up your sleeves and mess around. Note that you can also do this technique in Google Slides and Keynote.

Whenever possible, use the first object pacing technique of applying individual animation actions to discrete objects on your slides; this makes it easier to work on the slide by seeing its final state. The shape pacing technique obscures everything from your view in the workspace, so one workaround is to duplicate the slide you want to animate, add shapes to the duplicate, and hide the original so it doesn't show during your presentation.

Final Animation Pointers

Here are some final pointers:

- Don't animate any object without a specific intent or purpose in mind ("More interesting slides" does not qualify).
- Absolutely avoid anything under the so-called Moderate and Exciting animation categories.
- In short, animation is one of the sharpest "scalpels" in your surgical presentation toolbelt. You'll get a big payoff when you use it carefully with the right skill and intention. You'll get a big mess when you don't.

Chapter Recap

- Animation should only be used with discerning skill and intention.
- The object pacing and shape pacing techniques can be used to walk your audience through busy and complex slides a step at a time.

Sandbox Assignment

- Look through your slides to see how you can use object pacing and shape pacing to mindfully step your audience through your content without overwhelming them.
- Practice different animation sequences with your slides.

Act II Intermission

You made it through Act II! I hope this phase has shown you exactly why PowerPoint (and other tools) are an unfortunate scapegoat for boring and ugly presentations and how to avoid blaming your slide deck for zombie disasters.

Let's review the steps you just learned in the "Design Slides" phase:

- Understand why well-designed slides are crucial to success.
- Familiarize yourself with preattentive attributes and the Gestalt principles.
- Learn how to organize your visual space.
- Declutter your slides of slide fluff and embrace white space.
- Create single ideas per slide and stop using walls of bullet text.
- Use the Story Point Solution in lieu of busy bullet slides.
- Create hype with your typography.
- Harness the emotional power of real imagery and learn how to use it right.
- Use simple animation techniques for strategic revealing of the story.

Saddle yourself up for the part you've probably been chomping at the bit to get to: data visualization and visual storytelling, woohoo!

Since I'm concluding a phase on new design practices and habits, it's fitting to apply the idea of small moves to everything you've just learned.

As you begin to incorporate each practice into your toolbox, observe how challenging it was to apply and how it seemed to impact your presentation success. Don't overwhelm yourself and go at a pace that suits your learning schedule and your sanity.

It's important to remember that honing and perfecting your craft can be a long game.

Just keep it moving.

Act III: Visualize Data

Data Visualization + Storytelling featuring the PICA Protocol Prescription

18 Data Storytelling: The Intersection of Conceptualization and Design

"The greatest value of a picture is when it forces us to notice what we never expected to see."

—*John W. Tukey*

Ah, at last you've arrived at the part everyone loves most: the data part! Yes, it might have felt like an eternity to spend this much time talking about data storytelling before diving into data, but trust me, it will be worth it.

Remember, this book assumes that you are skilled with analysis, have a starting point for your analysis, or your insights are already prepared. In this phase, you will organize your insights into the specific baby narrative arcs you learned in Act I, while synthesizing them with the design toolbox of Act II. And as with everything you've already learned, to truly master data storytelling, you must first deepen your understanding of it.

I liken the current cult-like obsession with data storytelling and visualization to lusting after a shiny wrapped present under the Christmas tree (or other gifting holiday plant). The twinkling tree lights gleam in the sparkly wrapping, tantalizing us with promises of at least 2 hours of fun before we forget the content's existence.

Oftentimes, it's the mystery of a thing that is most alluring because humans have an insatiable appetite for variety and are determined to crack the code on new toys. And that pursuit can lead us down many precarious rabbit holes of unproductive practices.

To set this stage, here is my definition of essential data storytelling:

Data storytelling is the holistic methodology and practice of communicating events indicated by data in a compelling manner using a persuasive narrative construct supported by visual aids such as images, diagrams, and charts.

In simpler terms, showing and telling a data story with visual stuff so people get it.

When I discovered the field of data storytelling, I became so overwhelmed by the different opinions, approaches, and abstract musings on what *it* is. I craved a practical, methodical, and repeatable approach to creating effective visual aids. So, per my Type A personality, I created one myself!

Introducing the PICA Protocol

This protocol is your prescription for healthy, actionable data stories and is used by practitioners all over the world to engage and inspire their stakeholders. It is designed to cut the fluff from the anecdotal and abstract concepts of data viz and put a concrete methodology in your capable hands.

The PICA Protocol consists of the following steps:

1. P for PURPOSE
2. I for INSIGHT
3. C for CONTEXT
4. A for AESTHETICS

Think of this next phase as the intersection of everything you've just learned and how to apply it to each individual data story in your presentation. I also invite you to think of this part of the process as solving a mystery; we're going to identify a crime, gather evidence, put the evidence in a specific order, and bag the villain using our recommendation plan.

Ready to solve your big data mysteries, gumshoe? The insight game is oh-so-afoot!

Sandbox Assignment

- Choose one particular baby data story, one slide, or one chart from your sandbox. You'll learn and apply each step of the protocol to this example.

19 P is for PURPOSE

As you're learning, when each of us gathers around the conference table, we're all showing up with an assortment of our own needs, desires, and concerns.

"Are we going to miss our quarterly sales quota?" "Why is our email campaign performance declining?" "Where are we overspending?" These are all questions that could be circulating within the minds of the attendees.

The questions we don't want our audience asking are, "What the heck am I doing here?" or, "What's this whole thing about?" Everyone should be abundantly clear on the purpose of the meeting. One of the most common mistakes I see is jumping to create a chart without identifying the purpose of the visualization. And that is what the first step in the PICA Protocol is all about.

Remember how your whole presentation needs a purpose or objective? Guess what? Each of the data stories and individual charts, tables, and diagrams need one as well. Ideally, each purpose directly reinforces and propels your presentation narrative forward while motivating the audience toward the greater purpose.

Purpose Starts with a Q

I believe that every powerful and impactful data story begins with a clear and focused question. I always like to say that curiosity is where ignorance ends and wisdom begins.

Sometimes that question feeds into a dialogue with yourself, your data, or your stakeholder. Remember the list of decision-maker interview questions from Act I? The following questions build on those to explore more deeply what will empower your stakeholders with the right information.

Here are some thought-starter questions to ask each of the visuals you're creating:

- Why do you exist? Do you exist because you're the key to answering a crucial business question? Do you advance the narrative forward? Or do you exist because someone thinks you're important and you don't serve any other purpose (like a vanity metric such as number of Instagram followers)?
- What need are you meeting? Financial security, profitability, brand favorability, market growth, customer retention, ego-boosting?
- What decision(s) are you informing?
- What success are you facilitating?
- What obstacles are you overcoming?
- **How are you going to make my stakeholders' lives better and, thus, my customers' lives?**

My favorite way to approach this process is through a live dialogue either with my stakeholder or with myself. This dialogue will provide the keys to understanding your story's purpose, and the "keywords" in that conversation are just that: keywords. **Like search engine keywords, certain words in the dialogue will help you identify the intent of the inquiry and accomplish a vital step in the storytelling process: selecting the most appropriate visualization for your data.**

Steering the PURPOSE Conversation

You'll want to observe the keywords in the dialogue that will illuminate your stakeholders' intent behind the request and act as a compass to guide you toward the choice that will work best for them. The most important question to arm yourself with for this conversation is a simple, three-letter word: **why**.

A dialogue that properly probes into the heart of what your stakeholder needs might go something like this:

Stakeholder: I want to see the results of our new digital campaign for last quarter.

You: Great! Why do you want to focus on just digital?

Stakeholder: The board has been asking questions around our best-performing digital channels because they're locking in advertising budgets for next quarter.

You: So you're looking for the best-performing digital channels? How do you define "best-performing"?

Stakeholder: I guess. . .I'll want to see where the most sales are coming in! Hmm. . .what **marketing channels** are bringing in **the most conversions**?

A-ha! Now we're getting somewhere. Notice I've highlighted the phrases "marketing channels" and "the most conversions." These are the keywords that will guide your chart selection process. "Marketing channels" is a list of categories that may be compared using a measure, and "most conversions" indicates a measure that may be used to compare and rank a list of categories. We have our first big clue to solving the mystery!

With these keywords in mind, we're able to get to the heart of the inquiry.

Q: How do we visualize a list of categories compared with a measure?

A: Bar none, with a horizontal sorted bar chart! Revealing this answer during workshops is typically met with groans of boredom because it's not exactly the most groundbreaking, innovative, or eye-popping visual. And that's the point when it comes to executive business meetings. The fact is that the bar is still one of the most universally understood and comprehensible charts.

It's a classic because there is no learning curve; stakeholders instantly get it, and this means less mental work for them. As such, it isn't going anywhere soon. Bars are also well-suited for questions about composition (parts of a whole) as well. So we drop our marketing channel data into a bar chart (below) and poof! It-sa da-ta!

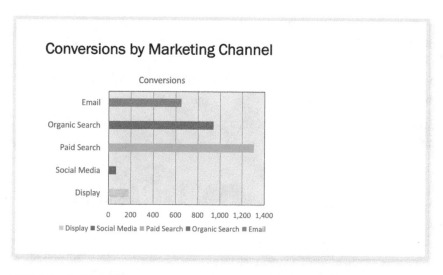

FIGURE 19.1 Horizontal bar chart with list of marketing channels by conversions

We choose a horizontal bar for categorical comparison for two reasons.

- Our brains are wired to interpret a chart that unfolds from left to right as a passage of time (conversely, never use a horizontal bar to display a time series).
- The vertical orientation of column charts can force longer category labels to go on the diagonal, creating a readability issue, as shown in Figure 19.2.

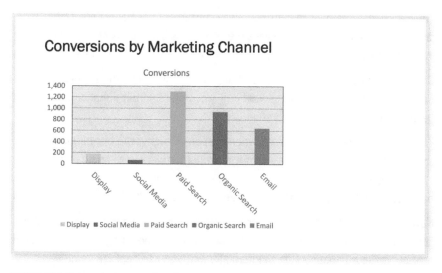

FIGURE 19.2 Categorical comparison improperly rendered as a vertical bar chart

Now, there's an important step to reduce the amount of work on your audience's mental plate. Can you guess what that is? If you said sorting the data by *priority*, Yahtzee! When you don't sort a group of bars, the audience's brain will switch gears to figure out the ranking, likely while you're talking to them. **Remember, make them do less work!**

Sorting also creates a more polished, organized look for your graph. See the difference in Figure 19.3.

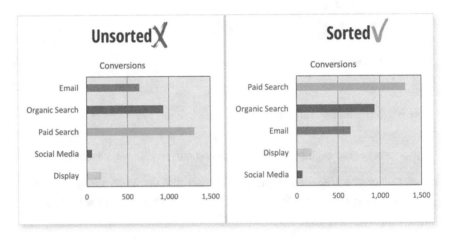

FIGURE 19.3 Unsorted versus sorted bar charts

When sorting, remember that it's not always by largest to smallest but, rather, by priority. For example, you may have a metric such as abandonment rate where the lower the number, the more favorable. In that case, you may want to sort *ascending*.

Quick note: if you're at all chaffed by the "interesting" formatting choices in these initial chart views, don't sweat it. It's completely intentional, and my nefarious plot will be revealed soon.

We know we're on the right track when we see an answer to our initial question emerge this early in the process. Your stakeholder wanted to know which channels generate the most conversions, and immediately we can answer that: paid search with organic search as a close second!

Now, understand that this is an incredibly simple data scenario, and that's the point. I'm not trying to win any big data or predictive modeling awards. The goal is to illustrate an analytical thinking model that you can apply to whatever scenario you're working with, however simple or complex.

At this point in the conversation with your stakeholder, you may decide you have enough information or probe even further. But their direction has already provided a decent starting point for the purpose of your analysis and visual representation of it, all made possible by the magic of curiosity.

Chapter Recap

- Every data visual and story must have a clear PURPOSE tied to the stakeholder needs you've identified.
- Purpose helps you determine the most appropriate visualization for your data and story.
- Keywords in the conversation can help guide you to the best chart choice.

Sandbox Assignment

- Evaluate the purpose of your selected sandbox example using the questions in this chapter.
- Consider the type of chart or data visual you could use to fulfill its purpose.

---

20 I is for INSIGHT

"We are surrounded by data, but starved for insights."

—*Jay Baer*

Ah, this word, insight. Like data storytelling, this is another term used ad nauseum in the data field; stakeholders are always asking for more insights, and no matter how hard we try to give them more insights, we seem to keep missing the mark.

The best definition of "insight" I've found is this: "the capacity to gain a new, accurate, deep, and intuitive understanding of a person or thing." Did you catch certain words there? *Accurate*, *deep*, *intuitive*, and *new*. Let's go back and remember what we've been presenting (up until now) during our meetings; see Figure 20.1.

FIGURE 20.1 A not-so-shining example of a well-visualized data slide

This beauty is one of mine, and I can honestly say it did not cut the mustard. If I asked myself while synthesizing my data story, "Does this facilitate an accurate and deep, intuitive understanding,"? the answer would be a resounding nope.

Brent Dykes, my esteemed analytics contemporary and author of *Effective Data Storytelling*, augments this definition with the element of surprise (new), where an insight inspires an "a-ha!" moment for the audience. The idea is that if you're presenting data to an audience that they already know, you are not presenting an insight. This chapter reviews how you can infuse the *eureka* factor into your data story slides.

Transform Your Data Statements to Storified Insights

Imagine you're asked to present the results of a landing page test where you measured the conversion rate of a sales page with an explainer video (Page B) against a text-based control (Page A). This is how most of us would typically announce the test results in the title space of a slide:

Landing Page Test Results.

That's it, that's all. This is what I call a *statement*. **The only thing a statement communicates is what the slide or visual *is*.** It doesn't communicate what the visual actually *means*, and that's the missed opportunity. This is akin to displaying a slide at the beginning of *The Avengers: Infinity War* with the title saying, "This is a movie with a lot of superheroes and a serious baddie with a nasty boxing glove." Thanks Captain Obvious, but where is the story?

If you're not making the meaning or the story of the visual immediately clear, the audience's brain is forced to divert their attention from you and focus their resources on figuring out the meaning on their own. And guess what that does: it creates extra work for them!

Now, what if we tried this title instead:

Landing Page B had an 18% higher conversion rate of 4.2%.

OK, now we're getting somewhere. **This is an *observation*, and it is an impartial, objective assessment of the data at hand.** Our observation transmits vital details about the test in almost as few words (what the winner's conversion rate is and how much higher it is than the control).

Rather than force the audience to visually hunt through the slide for this conclusion, you've already connected the dots for them so they're able to continue listening to you. But what if you had even more information about these results? Such as:

Landing Page B was a significant test winner with an 18% higher conversion rate, most likely due to the explainer video.

Alright, now this is what I call an *insight*! You've connected the data dots, plus you've demonstrated that this is a valid test result, and you're inferring the cause (without going down a jargon rabbit hole of P-values and such). That gives you enough ammunition to recommend a follow-up test scenario, such as experimenting with the placement of the explainer video.

NOTE

I use phrases like "possibly" or "most likely" depending on my confidence in the causality of my findings. It's important to be aware and transparent in your level of confidence in the data, especially if someone can challenge you on it.

Now, most of the points you're likely to present will fall in the *observation* category, and that's fine. What I want you to think about in this process is moving away from using *statements* as your titles and instead, sharing *observations* and *insights* that move your audience toward that deep, intuitive understanding. This is the depth of direction your stakeholders are craving, if you have that depth to offer.

Applying the Narrative Arc to Your Insights

Remember the narrative arc from Chapter 5 that you used to frame your whole presentation? You're going to apply a similar arc to those "baby" data stories now. I call this arc the Insight Journey, where you will lead your audience through a series of narrative points that enable them to become the hero of your data story.

These are the questions that your data story arcs should readily answer:

Exposition: What are we talking about, what do we need to know, and why is it important?

Rising action: What happened (objectively)? Why do we think it happened (subjectively)? Did anything surprise us about it (an unexpected "twist")? And what is the conflict, in terms of the problem or potential missed opportunity?

Climax: How high are the stakes if we don't resolve the conflict? How much worse can the situation get, and what will our stakeholders or customers lose or gain if no one takes action?

Falling action: What are our SMART recommendations? What should we do about it, how do we go about it, who should do it, and by when? And how will we measure success?

Resolution: What is the agreed-upon course of action?

Now, here's the thing: you may not have the whole story at your disposal yet. Locking in the data story's purpose and exploring the narrative arc are just the beginning, where the story may flesh itself out in the next step of the protocol. What's important is to get well-acquainted with these questions so that as you develop your data story further, the arc acts as a breadcrumb trail.

Where to Put Your Insights

The next order of business is determining where to place these wonderful observations and insights in your slide or visual space. The best answer I've found lies within Scott Berinato's *Good Charts*. Think of Figure 20.2 as the "anatomy" of an effective data slide: a structure that crisply communicates an assessment of data with an organized layout and clear hierarchy of visual elements.

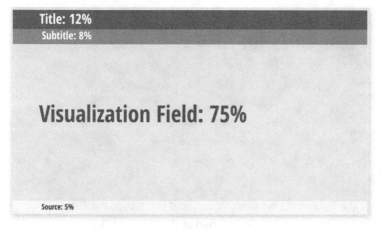

FIGURE 20.2 The anatomy of a perfect data visual
Source: Re-created with permission from *Good Charts* by Scott Berinato

This format is universally employed by the most prestigious reporting outlets, including the *Harvard Business Review*, the *Wall Street Journal*, and the *New York Times*. It consists of the following elements:

- **Title:** What the chart means
- **Subtitle:** What the chart describes
- **Visualization field:** Where the chart goes (plus annotations and callouts)
- **Data source:** The data platform, time period, and sample size (if applicable)

The Title Holds the Key

First you see the Title area, which occupies 12 percent of the graph (this is a guideline, so no need to pull out a ruler for exact measurements). Now, most presenters don't know this, but this area is the most valuable real estate on your slide. The upper-left corner is the first place your audience's eyes will look at in a visual space that isn't dense with text, and then they'll continue reading in a slightly lopsided left-to-right Z-pattern (for Western cultures)[1]—see Figure 20.3.

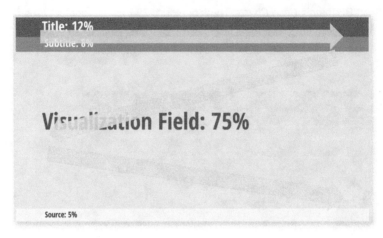

FIGURE 20.3 The reading Z-pattern

This is critical: the Title space is where you should place your invaluable observation or insight, not as tiny text stuffed at the bottom of the slide! Example: "Landing Page B conversion rate outperformed A by 18% (significant winner)." Placing your insight in the title area establishes your story as the most important element in the information hierarchy and visually reinforces what you're verbally declaring to your audience.

As for your statement about what the chart is, the perfect place for that is tucked neatly below the main title in the smaller, less prominent Subtitle section (8 percent). This enables proper reference and explanation without overpowering the more important piece, your actual story. You can write a short description using the format "Categories/Metrics, Date Range," such as "Explainer Video Test Results, May 2023."

This technique is what I came to know as a McKinsey title, and no matter the actual name, it will help you guarantee that no matter how your audience interprets your chart, your interpretation is crystal clear. This is especially important for when someone snags a slide from your deck and sends it to someone else, and you're not there to stay in charge of the narrative.

---

[1]99designs.com/blog/tips/visual-hierarchy-landing-page-designs

Now, recall the example from the prior chapter on marketing channel conversion volume, where the title of the slide is a snooze-inducing statement about what the chart is, shown in Figure 20.4.

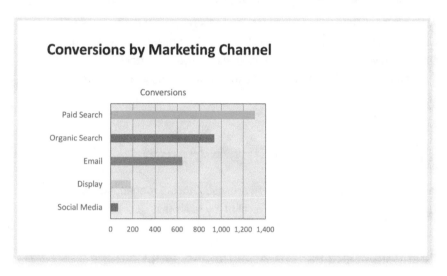

FIGURE 20.4 Original *Insight* slide from marketing example

Figure 20.5 shows how this marketing channel data story will look with the narrative in the title where it fits best.

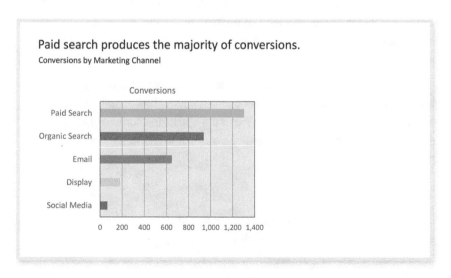

FIGURE 20.5 Marketing example slide with McKinsey title observation

This is a distinct improvement over "Conversions by Marketing Channel" simply because it connects the data dots for the audience. Now, some of your observations may need more explanation and the title runs onto two lines. This is acceptable, yet try to be as succinct as possible by omitting superfluous words.

With our initial insight, we may lean toward a recommendation to keep funneling lots of cash into our search channels since they produce so much conversion volume. However, we don't want to get too attached to this recommendation until we've completed the full protocol, and you'll see why in Chapter 21.

Visual Tools to Facilitate Insight

In addition to structural tools, there are visual tools for enabling insight. The following section explains several of my favorites.

Intentional Data Labels, Annotations, and Callouts

Whoever said that "the data should speak for itself" probably confused more than one presentation audience because data can be interpreted in as many ways as there are audience members. One of the reasons why the McKinsey title is so effective is because it doesn't rely on the data speaking for itself.

There are many ways to annotate data, from callouts that zero in on one data point to groupings of multiple data points to magnifications and expansions of smaller subsets of data. Figure 20.6 is one example of how you can annotate a line graph.

Using intentional data labels means not labeling every single data point by default, but rather, selectively choosing which points to highlight. For bar charts, you do want to label each bar to get rid of the x-axis. But for line graphs, I often see every data point labeled where they overlap and crowd each other out, as shown in Figure 20.7.

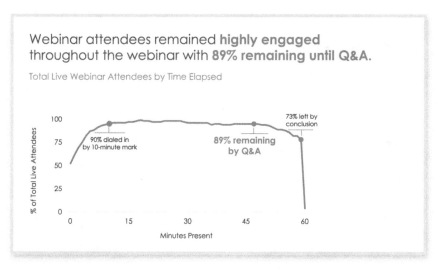

FIGURE 20.6 Examples of annotating data points for emphasis on a line chart

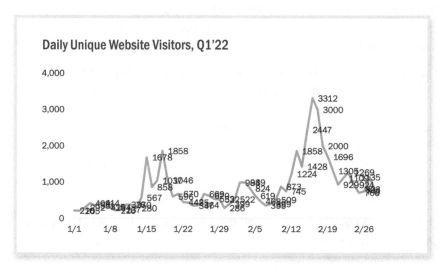

FIGURE 20.7 Overlapping data labels on a line graph

One way to eliminate "noise" that distracts from your insights is discernment around which points to call out. For lines, I label the maximum, minimum, and most recent points for context, or label only the points that I'm referring to in the moment; see Figure 20.8.

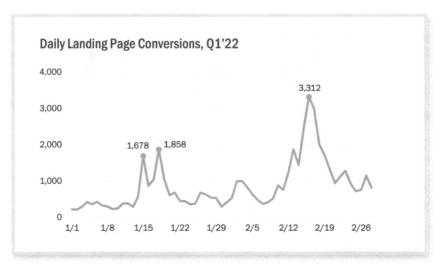

FIGURE 20.8 Line graph with specifically chosen data labels

Unlike bar graphs where you can label each bar and remove the gridlines, line graphs can support faint gridlines to help the eye have a frame of reference for unlabeled points.

Labels, annotations, and callouts are powerful tools for amplifying insight in your data visuals. The breadth of techniques for annotating data is vast and could fill an entire chapter; my suggested resource for this is the free chart annotation toolkit by Duarte (`www.duarte.com/resources/guides-tools/` `chart-annotation-toolkit`).

Multiple Chart Layout

This may sound counterintuitive to all the droning on I just did about simplicity and not shoving lots of stuff onto your slides, but there are cases where one chart isn't enough.

One example is what happens when you plot a bunch of categories in a time series or line chart. All too often, I see slides that create something I call "line spaghetti," as shown in Figure 20.9.

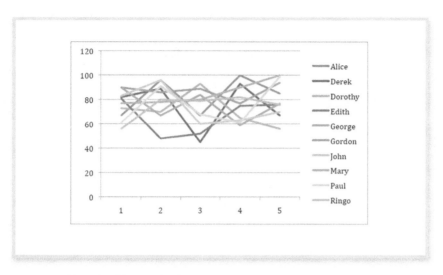

FIGURE 20.9 Example of line spaghetti

Mamma mia, that's a spicy meatball of mayhem! It's challenging to gather the observation or story you're supposed to learn from this chart, muffled from trying to speak with a mouthful of data noodles.

Now, the first solution to this predicament is asking what you're trying to communicate: do all the lines even matter to the story, or just one or two? Then show only the lines that matter. But if the goal of the visualization is to see what's happening in each trendline, the solution is a chart type called *small multiples*, which pulls apart one chart with many series or categories into separate spaces.

Figure 20.10 shows an example of a small multiples graph, where each "spaghetti strand" is neatly nestled into its own dish.

Do you see how much easier it is to pick out the unique insights in the respective trendlines? You can clearly identify the peaks and valleys of each trend without noodly entanglement.

The moral of that story is, while less is often more, sometimes *more* is more. In Chapter 21, I show you my favorite multiple-chart technique for telling a data story in a more exciting way than you're used to.

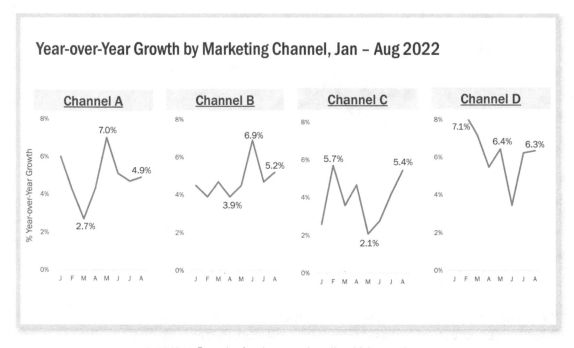

FIGURE 20.10 Example of easier-to-read small multiples graph

In short, effectively enabling insight is all about using your newfound powers of discernment and making intentional choices that reveal and magnify insights. You're doing this right when you're able to consistently stop and say "yes" to this magic question:

Does this view I've created enable that deep, intuitive, and new understanding of this thing?

Chapter Recap

- An *insight* is something that creates a deep, intuitive understanding of a thing; namely, your data.
- An *observation* explains what a visual means, and an insight explains the why, how, and what you can do about it.

- Placing the observation or insight in the slide title helps propel your narrative forward.
- Data labels and multiple chart layouts are best used intentionally to facilitate insight.

Sandbox Assignment

- Review the titles of your data story slides.
- Align the various visual elements to match the anatomy diagram.
- Modify the title to reflect an observation or insight into the data.
- Place annotations in the McKinsey title or on the slide to expedite the insight.

21 C is for CONTEXT

"Meaning is context-bound, but context is boundless."

—Jonathan Culler

This is perhaps the most fun step in the PICA Protocol process. That's because it requires putting on your detective hat and solving the true mystery within your data-banks. It's also your zone of genius as a data chef, where you roll up your sleeves and get messy with the digits. And it begins with asking a very simple question...in Dutch.

There is a wildly popular conversation starter game in the Netherlands called *Vertellis*, which translates to "tell me more." The idea is that when we're in conversation and ask questions, we often stop at the first thing people respond to and move on. But often, it's what's hiding underneath the first response that gets to the heart of the matter.

I want you to play *Vertellis* with your data stories. Even if the first insight that pops up during the protocol feels like a winner, ask your data to tell you more to reveal other interesting or actionable insights. How do we get your data to spill more beans? We go back and ask more questions!

This matters because what the CONTEXT step bids we ask ourselves is:

Q: Do I have all the information at my disposal to tell a complete picture?

Q: Am I showing all the information my stakeholders need to make a sound and informed decision?

Taking your first insight from the PURPOSE and INSIGHT steps at face value may leave a deeper story left unexamined, and that story could be even more directional in terms of strategy. If you're having trouble thinking of where to begin your context dive, here are my favorite questions to ask during the CONTEXT phase:

■ What else is my audience going to ask when they hear these insights?

■ And how may they argue against my findings?

■ Where can I go deeper with my analysis?

These are the money questions that are going to get to the heart of your audience's objections and make you their superhero since you've already anticipated their concerns.

Visual Context Tools

The following sections cover some useful angles and visual indicators to enrich your data story.

Performance Targets, Benchmarks, and Projections

If you are fortunate enough to work in an organization that proactively sets targets and benchmarks, use them to your advantage. Targets are a form of visual annotation that inspires an audience to become their own top competitor. They automatically add a story to your visual; you're not only answering the question of "What happened?" but you're also answering the inevitable, "How did we do against our expectations?"

So always, always, *always* plot targets on your data when they're available. If you don't have established targets or benchmarks for your measurement initiatives, it's time to create some. Review the last three to six months of data, account for seasonality or anomalies, and start setting some performance goals. This shows that you took the initiative to strive for continuous improvement, an invaluable trait among data practitioners.

Time Period Comparison

Looking at your results from one point in time is important, but how does the story deepen based on how it compares to the same time yesterday, last month, or last year? Comparing relevant time periods is especially important for seasonal campaigns, investigating new market trends, and examining future projections.

Knowing how a website performed this month versus last month may be critical because of a recent redesign, or this year's performance versus last year for an annual performance review. Time period comparison is especially important for time-sensitive campaign assessments such as holiday promotions, fashion seasons, and so on.

Segmentation

In many of my analyses, I've found that the devil I was seeking was truly in the data details. Aggregate numbers are a great starting point for a data story, especially if nothing is shocking, but you'll often find more interesting nuggets by drilling down into deeper data layers. Finding an unexpected nugget can also provide a story twist. Google Analytics and other platforms offer so many lenses with which to scrutinize data that I guarantee that there's something else waiting in there.

The following are some segmentation questions worth exploring when diving into your aggregate data:

- Does mobile traffic behave differently than desktop?
- What's happening on a geographic level?
- How do different demographic, psychographic, or behavioral groups interact?
- What optimization tests did we run?
- What qualitative data do we have, such as voice of customer surveys, market research, or text analytics reporting?

Make this an investigative process for collecting evidence to support, expand upon, or refute your original argument, and use it to provide an unexpected plot twist.

Additional Measures or Data Points

Sometimes, what's missing from the story is not necessarily a different segment or slice of data but, rather, a different metric or performance measure. I can't tell you how many times I've seen a data story centered around only one measure and the narrative ends there.

Our case scenario of conversions by marketing channel is a perfect example of a story not yet fully explored. While our executive stakeholders may care about the dollar signs and bottom lines, we as data explorers also care about performance; in this case, we care about conversion rate.

Conversion rate is a marker of efficiency and is an essential companion to conversion volume. So even though it may not have been asked for upfront, it's a good idea to review it anyway. Figure 21.1 shows where our story left off in the INSIGHT step.

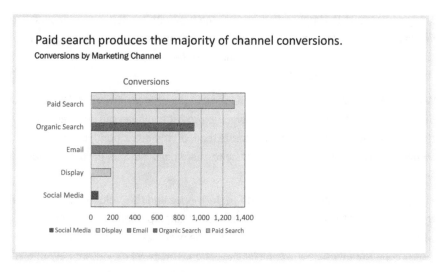

FIGURE 21.1 Original marketing example slide

Notice that there's a bit of white space left open to the right of my chart. That's not an accident; it's been kept free to continue the story. I use that space to bring in a second chart that matches the first one, as shown in Figure 21.2.

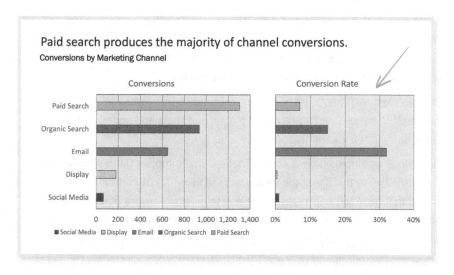

FIGURE 21.2 Addition of second chart with different measure (conversion rate)

This second chart is simply a duplicate of the first with the left category axis labels removed and the measure switched from conversion volume to conversion rate. The trick is to keep the categories *in the same order* so that each channel's measures line up!

With this augmented view, a new development in our story emerges: While Paid Search is the clear winner in conversion volume; it trails behind several other channels in the conversion rate contest! Email, on the other hand, clearly outdoes the rest in converting visitors into customers, but it is third in conversion volume.

This points us to an opportunity: high performance and low volume indicates the chance to generate sales more efficiently by scaling up quantity through whatever means makes the most sense for the organization. The conflict is what we don't potentially gain if we don't take action. This twist may ultimately inform the final steps in our insight journey, which are our recommendations.

And a surprising twist is the perfect way to tell data stories that keep an audience glued to you.

Using CONTEXT to Tell a Twist

Just because the story started out with conversion volume and pivoted with conversion rate doesn't mean we need to scrap the original story. In fact, this pivot provides the perfect unexpected twist that leverages the narrative arc, creates suspense, and amplifies audience attention.

How do we translate our story development into a visual format? In the slide in Figure 21.3, notice that I've removed the second chart and added an ellipsis (the three dots) to the end of my McKinsey title.

What does an ellipsis do in a story? That's right, it implies there's more story on the way! I like to think that the three dots stand for "to be continued"—three little words that have left billions of movie and television viewers at the edge of their seats. Figure 21.4 shows how to deliver the twist and complete the story loop.

While we started with what our stakeholders requested, we probed further and found a compelling twist that is sure to keep their attention and possibly lead to a better decision.

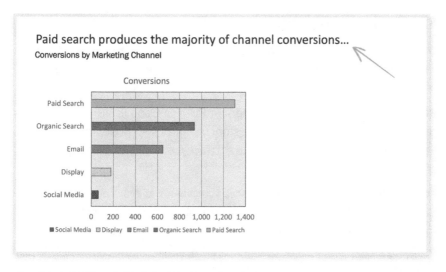

FIGURE 21.3 Addition of ellipsis in slide title to foreshadow more story

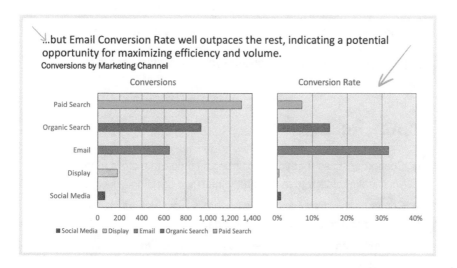

FIGURE 21.4 Completing the sentence and story loop with a second chart and ellipsis

A *slide build* **is a technique, where you open a story loop on one slide and complete it on one or more subsequent slides**. Using the slide build in conjunction with deeper context is a simple yet powerful storytelling tool at your disposal. It creates the insight element of that new and unexpected "eureka" moment and will keep executive audiences engaged, informed, and inspired.

If you're curious about the multiple chart layout I've used, this is called a side-by-side bar chart or table lens, as coined by Stephen Few.

TIP

Visit the Resource Center for a detailed tutorial on creating a table lens.

Final Thoughts on CONTEXT

This step is often an iterative process. As you saw in our example, we ended up with a completely different insight and recommendation because we dug a little deeper.

Remember, you can always go back to your PURPOSE and INSIGHT steps to refine your original choices or let the story unfold as a surprise. This process is not always linear, so don't be afraid to embrace the fluidity as part of the creative process.

The sky's the limit on the different slices you can use to evaluate your story. But be warned: this is where well-meaning analysts can get trapped in the data rabbit hole, often falling prey to "analysis paralysis" and never really finishing the story. So how do you know when that's a wrap? When you can look at the data from all angles and can say that your insights are:

- Relevant to the business objectives you're aiming to serve
- Complete and capable of robustly informing your stakeholders' decision

At this point, you can confidently conclude that the context case is closed.

Chapter Recap

- Context ensures that you're painting a complete picture of insight for your stakeholders to make a fully informed decision.
- Context can provide a story twist that is a perfect way to use the narrative arc and refine your recommendation.
- Context is an iterative process to flesh out the story with relevant data points.

Sandbox Assignment

- Review your data story's initial observations and insights.
- Ask yourself where there may be additional data you can investigate to create a fuller picture of the situation.
- Create slide builds that illustrate an unexpected twist in the story.

A is for AESTHETICS 22

One day while working as a digital analyst at my Fortune 500 financial firm, a colleague from product marketing approached me with feverish excitement.

"Lea, Lea, Lea!" he shouted while flagging me down. "We just finished launching a really cool dashboard with these awesome charts. Wanna see? You're going to *love* it!"

Oh, dear. Anytime someone tells me I'm going to love a "really cool" new data visualization or dashboard, there's a good chance I *won't* love it. This was no exception. He opened his laptop with flair, and put the dashboard on full, glorious display. I'm hoping I hid my reaction well because I was screaming on the inside.

The data structure was straightforward enough...sort of. It was a vertical column chart, but styled as skyscraper buildings and nestled in a cartoonish cityscape. Each column "building" had a different width, shape, angle, texture, and roof structure. But that's not all.

Fluffy white clouds dotted the pixelated blue-sky background while lazy pigeons perched on said fluffy clouds. I've tried to find something similar to this work of "art" in the graphic in Figure 22.1; the original was much worse.

FIGURE 22.1 Cartoonish dashboard graphic in city landscape

I cannot recall the actual data topic; however, I do recall that it had absolutely nothing to do with buildings, cities, or architecture. It was purely a visual gimmick.

This dashboard clearly suffered from a serious case of what I call *form-over-function-itis*, or FOFI for short. Telltale symptoms of FOFI include excessive excitement over a "snazzy" or "exciting" new visual, and untrained data consumers such as business-side executives are particularly susceptible.

When Dashboards Attack

Dashboards, as a communication medium, are particularly prone to this affliction. It's an example of a real-life concept pulled into the data world (similar to pie and donut charts), where you didn't have to be a car mechanic to understand the vital systems of your car and make simple executive decisions to keep it running. But somewhere along the way, that translation was confounded with FOFI, as shown in Figure 22.2.

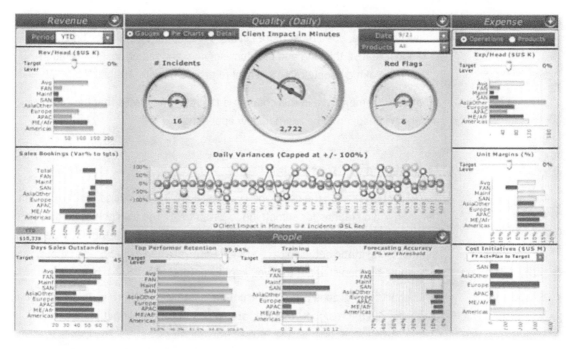

FIGURE 22.2 Example of a busy, noisy, and cluttered dashboard

In translating the concept and paradigm of a car dashboard to business data (a bit literally), dashboard engineers ran amok with brain-*un*friendly radial gauges, sardine can-packed graphs, and ancillary decorative elements like metal nuts and screws.

Even I can get hypnotized by web design trends like gradient backgrounds and iconography making their way into dashboards, until it's almost too late to realize that I can't really *see* the data. Data can indeed be beautiful, but it shouldn't be beautiful for the sole sake of beauty and at the expense of utility. And the live presentation meeting is not the place to bring incredibly artistic and complex renderings that are so bleeding edge that your audience falls off the visual cliff.

Now, that doesn't mean you should completely discard form to focus solely on function. Cole Nussbaumer Knaflic makes a sound case for appealing data design that is not *just* functional either.

"Studies have shown that more aesthetic designs are not only perceived as easier to use, but almost more readily accepted and used over time, promote creative thinking and problem-solving, and foster positive relationships, making people more tolerant of problems with designs."[1]

What you'll come to see in this chapter is that design choices that help create insight also happen to be aesthetically appealing.

Is It Signal or Just Noise?

You know how back in the days when you were driving in your car and had to flip between radio stations for something to listen to? Remember the car radio, the doohickey with spinning knobs that sound would come out of? Right. Remember that annoying static between each station until you magically hit upon that old-school hip-hop channel that you kept forgetting to save as a preset?

Well, charts and graphs can suffer from the same issue. There is an engineering measure called the *signal-to-noise ratio*, which makes a distinction between "signal" (meaning*ful* input) and "noise" (meaning*less* input).[2] The idea is that there is an ideal ratio of low enough noise to detect a signal.

Edward Tufte translated this concept to the discipline of data visualization and called it the *data-to-ink ratio*, where the meaningful chart data is the signal and the meaningless "ink" is the noise. Chart noise is equivalent to the "slide fluff" discussed in Act II, which is just as diabolically distracting to your audience.

What's data, and what's ink in a data visual, you ask? Here's a helpful breakdown:

- **Data:** The ink that encodes or annotates data (numbers, bars, lines, pies, data labels)
- **Ink:** Everything else (gridlines, borders, background bars, and so on)

Take a close look at the "ink" list: so much of the stuff that your data viz tool adds to your chart by default isn't meaningful and could possibly detract from your insight. As data visualization went digital, the concept evolved to the "data-to-pixel" ratio. Figure 22.3 shows Tufte's formula for the ratio.

---

[1] Knaflic, C. N. (2015). *Storytelling with Data: A Data Visualization Guide for Business Professionals.* Wiley.

[2] en.wikipedia.org/wiki/Signal-to-noise_ratio

$$\text{data - ink ratio} = \frac{\text{data - ink}}{\text{total ink used to create the graphic}}$$

FIGURE 22.3 Edward Tufte's data-to-ink ratio

In essence, this means that the higher the ratio, the clearer the data signal you'll transmit. Note that this is a directional concept, and I'm not suggesting you attempt to calculate this for each graph. (I know it crossed that analytical mind of yours.)

Now, this doesn't mean that all non-data ink should become disappearing ink. In the aforementioned *Show Me the Numbers*, Stephen Few describes a twofold process for finding the optimal ratio.

1. Reducing non-data ink or pixels
2. Enhancing data ink or pixels

To achieve this, I developed an easy-to-follow method that is now used by thousands of practitioners all over the world. Welcome to the cool club!

Reduce Non-Data Ink with the Chart Detox Formula

Many don't know this, but I'm a closet crunchy granola hippie who loves to do one thing every single day: detox! Charts are no exception, and learning to detox your charts and graphs of useless junk will keep your audience's attention focused on what matters most: your story.

Figure 22.4 shows where we left off with the marketing channel example.

It may not be totally obvious, but there's a lot of pixel noise in here that's "talking over" the data signal. That was my intention, so I could show you what this final step is all about. I am going to walk you through the detox step-by-step, and, in less than 10 minutes, you'll have a squeaky-clean chart!

This approach distills the proven practices behind those shared in the data viz bibles already mentioned as well as Dona M. Wong's essential *Wall Street Journal's Guide to Information Graphics*.

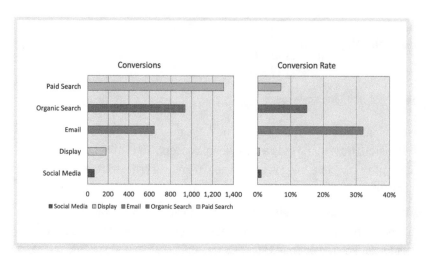

FIGURE 22.4 Pre-detox marketing channel charts

BACKGROUNDS, BORDERS, AND LEGENDS, OH MY!

Backgrounds, borders, and axis lines are the most expendable ink in your chart space. Solid, gradient, and textured background fills are especially noisy, so it's best to leave this transparent or match it to your slide's background color.

Sometimes, various chart software programs automatically apply this noise in the default design settings because, well, I'm not sure why. But notice the difference in my example after just taking a few simple steps to detox it out (Figure 22.5).

Let's break down each detox step.

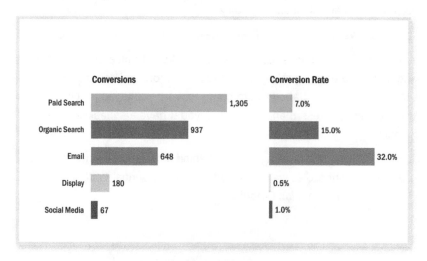

FIGURE 22.5 Post-detox marketing channel charts

Legends and Labels

Legends are tricky because no matter where they are on the outskirts of the inner plot area (as opposed to the outer chart area), they force the viewer to visually jump from the chart data to pick up a bar color to the legend to decode the color and then back and forth again. Axis lines pose the same issue in bars. So, tell those legends and lines to skedaddle!

Once you've removed your legend and axes, you must label each bar or pie segment so they don't have to visually estimate the values.

The legend issue applies to line charts as well, especially because they often have multiple series in one visual space. For lines, it's best to label the final data point with the series name on the right side. You can even match the label to the color of the line so there's no question which belongs to which, as shown in Figure 22.6.

NOTE

You don't want to eliminate so much non-data ink that your audience won't understand your chart. It's a common mistake to eliminate the axis and legend and then forget to directly label the data.

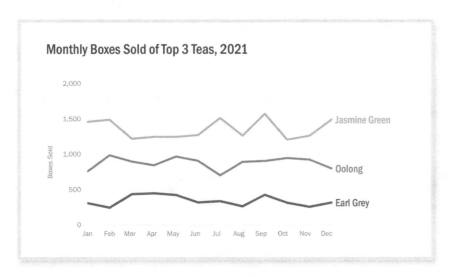

FIGURE 22.6 Clearly labeled line chart without legend

However, you never want to remove the numerical y-axis in a line chart because you'll need it as a reference to gauge the scale and because you don't want to label every data point in a line.

Bar Gap Width

In most of the bar charts I see, the gap between bars is too wide. Excel and PowerPoint both apply, by default, a scientifically informed 182 percent gap width [sarcasm]. Best practice advises to adjust the gap between bars to

50 percent of the bar width, which makes them easier to compare without invading each other's personal space.

Neutral Color

Finally, you may have noticed that my charts look like they got into a paintball fight with Rainbow Brite. Sadly, this used to be an available default formatting option in Excel! Data viz gospel advises that when you encode one measure in a graph with size or shape as the value, use just one color because the bar length already communicates the value. Scott Berinato explains in *Good Charts*:

> "Think of color in a chart as a fraction that you need to reduce. Find the lowest common denominator that still preserves the distinctions you need to convey your idea."

In other words, don't use color to distinguish data if there's already a distinguishing characteristic, such as the length of bars, size of shapes, or data labels. This is a common pitfall in candy-colored pies as well; see Figure 22.7.

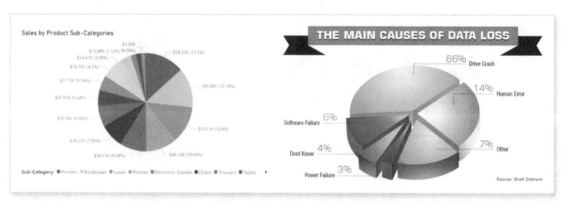

FIGURE 22.7 Irresponsibly formatted pie charts
Source: World Bank, Kroll Ontrack

This is why I earlier advised that you color all pie segments the same. If you add more *measures*, *then* use more colors. But you're not going to use a kaleidoscope of colors; instead, set both charts to uniform gray shades, like Figure 22.8.

I realize this may look weird at first; it's a bit on the gloomy side, and it can even be jarring if you're never seen data like this before. There is such a thing as too much gray and black, where the visual effect can be overly intense, as shown in Figure 22.9.

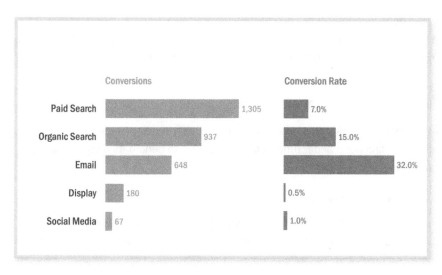

FIGURE 22.8 Example bar chart colors set to shades of gray

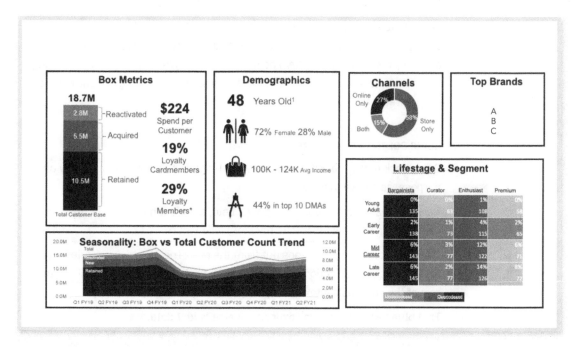

FIGURE 22.9 Slide with too much gray and black

When done with intention, you create a neutral backdrop for your data story. It sets the stage without anything taking center stage. . .yet. This enables you to move to the second part of the two-part process: data enhancement.

Enhance Your Data with Color

I've already covered the research and rationale for using color as a tool for emphasis and not a bedazzling gun. Now you get to behold its truly awesome power as a storytelling tool!

WHEN COLOR GOES WRONG

In all my years of evaluating data visualizations, color is possibly the most misused aesthetic of all. It's often what's used to meet stakeholder requests for more "exciting" and "flashy" viz.

Remember that color is best used as a tool of intention. Consider this example of a dashboard I once critiqued, shown in Figure 22.10.

Is it safe to say the effect here is a bit. . .dizzying? The problem with many charts and dashboards is that when different colors are used in such an arbitrary fashion, *none of them actually means anything.* Each color is dueling for your audience's attention, and the one who ends up losing the battle is you as the presenter.

USING COLOR TO EMPHASIZE

Going back to the marketing example, we last left it looking sad and gray on purpose, as shown in Figure 22.11.

Now, the real magic happens. I apply a bold, standout blue color to the specific data point in my chart that tells my story; see Figure 22.12.

Boom! Look how that bar pops out from the rest. The conspicuous color immediately draws your attention to that data point first, and then you'll process the rest of the chart as context.

That blue bar is your story; everything else is just data.

This is a super simple technique in PowerPoint, Excel, and Google Sheets. You're ideally emphasizing just one or two data points per slide *if* they are related to one key idea. Any more than that and you run the risk of emphasizing too many ideas at once.

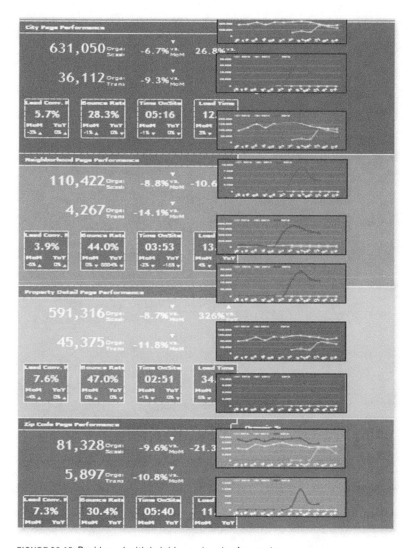

FIGURE 22.10 Dashboard with kaleidoscopic color formatting

The opportunity to leverage color doesn't end there. When I add my McKinsey title observation back to the slide, I color the part of the title text that corresponds to the accentuated data point, as shown in Figure 22.13.

Notice that I matched the color to the name of the emphasized category as well as the measure. This creates connective tissue between your data and story for your audience so that there are multiple visual cues crystallizing the insight.

TIP

Visit your Resource Center for a downloadable copy of my proprietary Chart Detox Formula for both Office and Google applications.

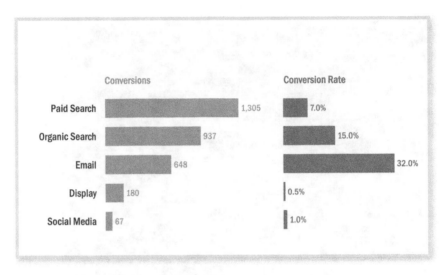

FIGURE 22.11 Bar chart color set to shades of gray

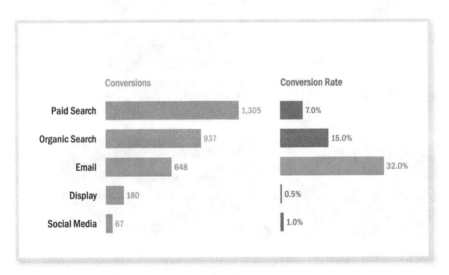

FIGURE 22.12 Data bar emphasized with blue highlight color

The exception to this is if you're consolidating your slide deck to create an offline handout. In this case, you may want to use two different colors in the same chart and match the colors of the corresponding text to create synchronicity between your data and story.

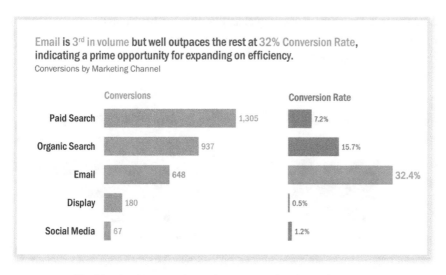

FIGURE 22.13 Matching the title text color to the corresponding data points

COLOR GUIDELINES/BEST PRACTICES

We generally know that red and green have specific meanings in Western culture—green = good versus red = bad. And yet, they are both still present in default color palettes of some data visualization tools. When these two are used haphazardly in graphs, the brain's first subconscious instinct may be to draw inaccurate conclusions about those data points.

The other downside to using red and green is that they may be confused with each other due to color vision deficiency, otherwise known as CVD or "color blindness." You may be surprised to hear how prevalent CVD is in the workforce; it affects 1 in 200 women worldwide, and 1 in 12 men![3]

The most common form of CVD is "red-green blindness," where people with certain forms (like deuteranopia) are unable to tell the difference between red and green. This means that if you use red and green in the same chart to indicate different meanings, that distinction may be completely lost on attendees who have that!

To ensure your color choices are CVD-friendly, use the COBLIS online color blindness simulator (www.color-blindness.com/coblis-color-blindness-simulator) to upload a screenshot of your slide and see if your color choices

[3]Color Blindness Awareness

pass the test. Using the marketing example, observe how indistinguishable the red bar is from the green one with a form of color blindness called *red-blind* or *protanopia* (see Figure 22.14.).

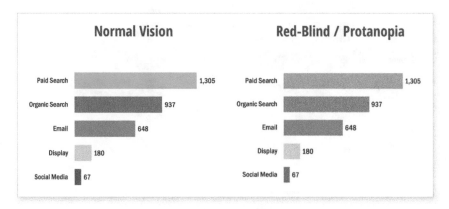

FIGURE 22.14 Color comparison with red-blind COBLIS filter

As you can see, if I were trying to create distinction with these red and green colors, anyone with this form of CVD wouldn't pick it up.

Here are some further color guidelines that have worked well for me:

- For negative indicators or areas that require attention, use a bold orange for contrast.
- Use a deep red sparingly for only the most negative indicators and avoid using green in the same visual space.

CONTEXT COLOR CUES

In the CONTEXT step of the protocol, I mentioned that I'd share additional considerations for applying color to your charts. I intentionally walked you through the rationale for color emphasis in this chapter first so that these guidelines would make the most sense.

Targets and benchmarks: Use a black dotted line to distinguish this "theoretical" data from your actual data, like the one shown in Figure 22.15.

Projections: Use dashed or dotted formatting (dash type) to continue the line of estimation. You can do this by plotting your projection line in a separate column in your data where it will take over from your "actual" line. See Figure 22.16.

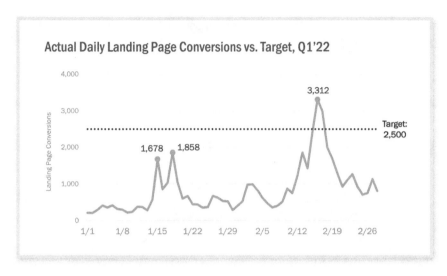

FIGURE 22.15 Performance target line in line graph

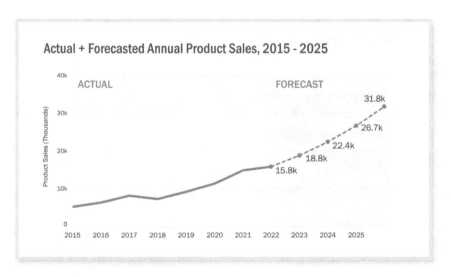

FIGURE 22.16 Target projection in line graph

You can render this by creating a second line series with an additional column of data extending through the forecast period.

Time series: If you have multiple lines in a series, I suggest coloring all but the important lines gray and emphasizing the line that matters most. Or, if a certain stretch of time is what matters, emphasize those sections and leave the rest gray. See Figure 22.17.

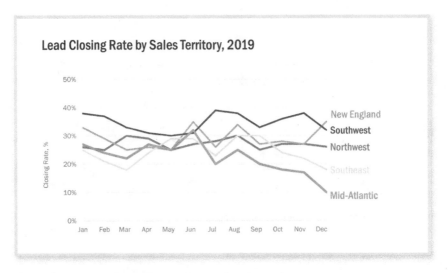

FIGURE 22.17 Highlighting one line in a multiple line time series

Time-period comparison: You want to make your current data line stand out while the "ghost" line of your past data lurks in the background. If you're using a line chart, use a bold color for the current line and a lighter shade of the same color for the past line. See Figure 22.18.

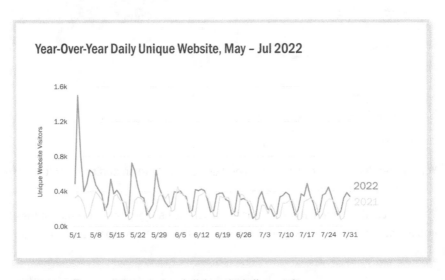

FIGURE 22.18 Time period comparison in lighter tint in line graph

Segmentation: Remember that you don't want to use different colors for categories and segments unless it's needed to create distinction. If you must use different colors to create a new lowest common denominator, use shades of the same color for related segments and be sure to label the line end points for clarity; see Figure 22.19. (This is manual in PPT/Excel and is easier done in tools like Tableau where you can easily drop a dimension as a segmentation color scheme.)

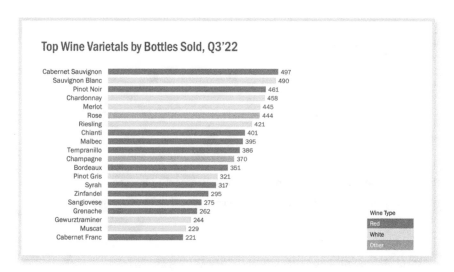

FIGURE 22.19 Bar chart showing wine varietals shaded by type

Brand colors: A question I often get is, "What if our branding guidelines use red or green?" Companies understandably want to use their brand palette to accentuate presentation elements, including in charts. However, if at some point you want to indicate positive or negative performance with these colors, you're stuck because they also represent your brand.

What I recommend to my clients is to use blue and orange for positive and negative indicators and use the brand red or green only when displaying competitive analyses where their brand is a category. See Figure 22.20 as an example.

Final Thoughts on Aesthetics

As you can see, aesthetics in data visualization is a two-pronged approach of taking away what doesn't matter and putting in what does. And that. . .is pretty much the approach you've been learning this entire time, would you say?

NOTE

The crucial question to ask each time you apply color to a visualization, be it a single data point or a color scale, is this: what does each color mean? What does the difference signify? Or am I creating random, inaccurate signals?

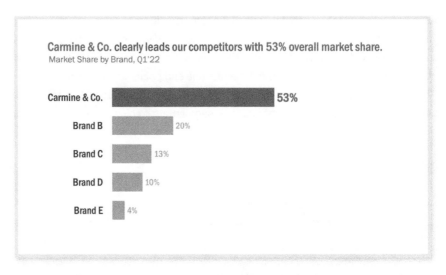

FIGURE 22.20 Bar chart with red as a brand color to distinguish from competitors

This brings the teaching portion of the PICA Protocol to a close. In Chapter 23, you get to see exactly how it plays out in real-world data scenarios.

Chapter Recap

- Data viz aesthetics are about maximizing the data-to-ink ratio through removing what isn't necessary and enhancing what matters most.
- Detoxing charts of noise is an absolute must for clear comprehension.
- Color is one of the most powerful tools for emphasizing insights.

Sandbox Assignment

- Review the aesthetic choices you've made in your sandbox chart(s).
- Practice the Chart Detox Formula (in the Resource Center) to clean them up.
- Emphasize your key data story points in the chart using carefully selected color.

Choose the Right Chart

"He chose. . .poorly."

—*The Grail Knight,* Indiana Jones and the Last Crusade

Now that you've learned about the PICA Protocol in its entirety, this chapter revisits and expands on the crux of the PURPOSE step: choosing the right chart for your data and story. Choosing well starts by understanding this: your data visualization platform does not know which chart is most appropriate for your data and purpose.

Sure, there are algorithms that help you narrow down your best options in certain tools like Tableau. But even so, you must make the final judgment call on which to choose. **Chart selection, like any other analytical skill, is cultivated through diligent learning, practice, and optimization.**

The increasing glut of chart options certainly doesn't help. Data communicators are utterly overwhelmed with the paradox of choice. I know of at least *six* charts that show composition! And yet, I believe that there are usually just one or two most appropriate choices for the type of data you're working with and for the message you're trying to convey.

The kicker to this paradox of choice is that with the proliferation of chart types, the ratio of effective charts to ineffective charts is dwindling. Not all charts are created equal when it comes to facilitating clarity and comprehension. Before you start pulling the curtain back on your Marimekko and nautilus charts during next week's executive readout, consider the effect of Figure 23.1 on an audience completely untrained in advanced chart decoding.

FIGURE 23.1 Confusing treemap and nautilus charts

Cue Zombie Defcon 4. This may not appeal to your visualization wanderlust, but here's the thing: there is a directly proportional relationship between chart complexity and audience confusion; the more complex, the more confusion.

Chart choosing is a practice of restraint and discernment, selecting a visual that is only in the highest service of informing your audience with no attachment to embellishment or grandeur.

Which Charts *Are* Safe to Use for Presentations?

In terms of what graphs to show during executive meetings, I am mainly in the camp of Nancy Duarte's perspective in *DataStory*: that most graphs are meant for data exploration by skilled data practitioners, not for executive presentation. Most charts are simply too unfamiliar and complex for a lay audience to understand in a live meeting.

Duarte recommends only three chart types for executive presentations: the bar, the pie or donut, and the line. She asserts that these three are universally understood by senior audiences, and most data will never need to be displayed with more complexity than that. I mostly agree and add that there are a few additional chart types that may be worth expanding your repertoire with.

These are the list of charts I am most comfortable using in executive presentations:

- Bar/column
- Pie/donut (with extreme caution)

- 100% stacked bar/column
- Line
- Area
- Bullet

While this list is by no means groundbreaking or innovative, that's actually the point. The magic and wonder will come from how you design, emphasize, and annotate these charts when arranging them in a narrative storyline that communicates clearly.

Choosing the Appropriate Chart for Your Data

To decide which visualization is most appropriate, I start with those first questions from our PURPOSE exploration. Here are guiding questions for choosing each of these chartss.

Q: How do I show composition or parts of a whole?

A: Either a sorted bar. . .or. . .a pie or donut. Yup, I said it. Ah, I can just hear the protests now: did someone claiming to be a data viz expert just sanction the use of the demon pie? Aren't donuts data viz heresy? Contradictory to popular opinion, they are not.

I see pie charts as similar to real pie in two ways: first, just like real pie, pie charts are desirable and comforting to an executive audience because they are familiar, and executives know what they're *supposed* to show.

But pie charts are also like real pie in that when not baked with skill and care, they can give audiences a serious case of visual indigestion; consider the pie chart in Figure 23.2.

Those sardine can segments, that cacophony of color, those creepy, spidery leader lines and labels, blech! While this is a rather extreme example, I still see confuddling pies like the one in Figure 23.3. in business presentations all the time.

First, here's where pie is going wrong: when the brain encounters a pie, which is a circle, it has difficulty visually calculating the area inside of each segment. This makes it challenging to compare the segments to each other in ranking, which. . .is the entire purpose of a pie chart. In fact, when pie segments are close in value, you can actually miscalculate the relative size if you use certain colors; consider Figure 23.4.

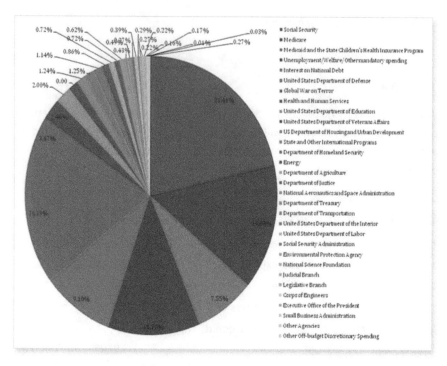

FIGURE 23.2 Deeply regrettable pie chart

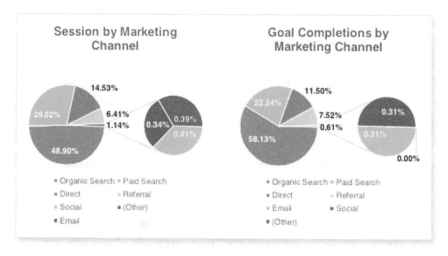

FIGURE 23.3 Example of typical business presentation pie charts

At first glance, your eye is drawn to the intense red of the Dresses category and may conclude that it is larger than the light tan Tops. But upon closer inspection, the data labels show that it's actually smaller; because the red is so intense, it can override our ability to accurately gauge its area. This treatment of pie exemplifies what happens when we choose a visual without understanding its mechanics or applying intentional design practices.

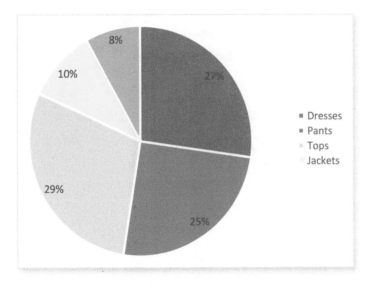

FIGURE 23.4 Confusing pie chart with misleadingly colored segments

Just like PowerPoint and presentation platforms, a pie chart is inherently neutral and can function as either a tool or a weapon. You can either use it wisely to advance knowledge or inflict brain pain. And there is a way to use it wisely. That's why my stance on pie has softened, and many data viz experts are following suit. The growing consensus is that the pie protest should not fight the use of pie but, rather, the *abuse* of it.

The most effective use of a pie is as a tool to show the contrast between one or more pieces, not how big every piece is. Composition is best answered with a sorted bar chart. Figure 23.5 shows a vast improvement.

Do you see how it's so obvious which pieces I want you to focus on? As opposed to the earlier carnival-colored example? The following are the guidelines for using pie charts correctly (and sparingly!):

- No more than two to five segments
- One or more are unmistakably larger or smaller than the others
- One segment is a different color to highlight

- The largest segment starts at the 90-degree mark and unfolds clockwise
- Direct data labels (no creepy leader lines!)
- **CRITICAL: The purpose of the pie is contrast in composition, not** *overall* **composition.**

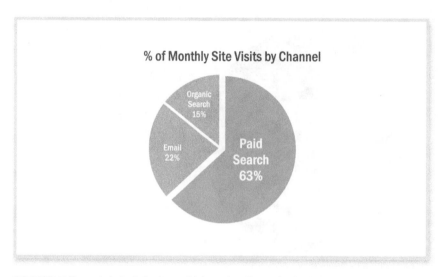

FIGURE 23.5 Properly baked pie chart with intentionally emphasized segment

The key here is to use a pie to communicate contrast and *not* **just composition.** If your storytelling purpose doesn't fit these criteria, use a bar chart instead.

Even more hated than pies are its fellow breakfast cousin, donuts. I believe this is again because most times they are not executed intentionally (3D exploded donut, anyone?). See Figure 23.6.

I've come to reframe my view of a donut as simply a pie with an annotated filling. If you keep the segment count low, you can make the most important segment even more prominent by annotating the donut hole with the value or percentage, as shown in Figure 23.7.

I hope this shows that there are cases where a pie or donut may be a more effective choice. Just remember to use them sparingly and keep practicing those principles until they're a piece of. . .pie.

Q: How do I display trended data or change over time?

A: Either a line or a vertical bar (or column) chart. Our brains have been trained to instinctively associate visual data that progresses from left to right with the passage of time.

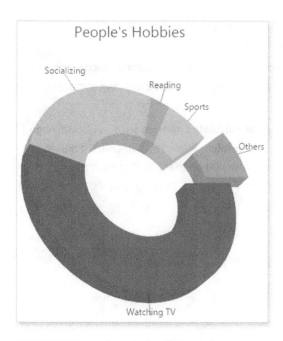

FIGURE 23.6 Dastardly exploding 3D donut chart

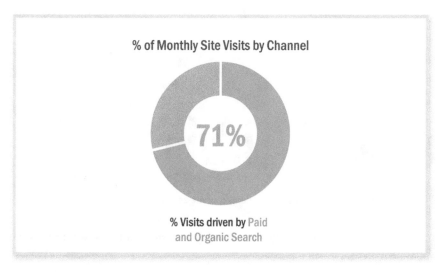

FIGURE 23.7 Correctly formatted, emphasized, and annotated donut chart

Now, is a line or column better for trending? It really is a matter of taste, but I do use these for different situations:

I use a column for volume-based metrics such as visits, conversions, and sales. The bars symbolize "buckets" that are filled with something, and comparing filled buckets is conceptually easy to grasp.

I use a line for performance-based or calculated metrics such as clickthrough rate, conversion rate, or cost per conversion. A line can symbolize a heartbeat (think of an electrocardiogram) and helps "keep the pulse" of performance. Figure 23.8 shows an example of how I used each chart type in the same view in a small multiples layout.

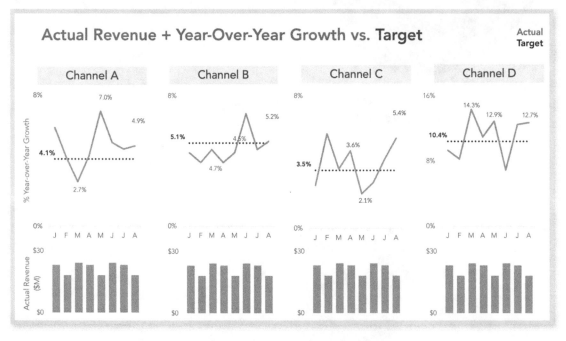

FIGURE 23.8 Vertical column versus line charts for time series

You can use color to specifically emphasize certain key points you want to draw attention to, as shown in Figure 23.9.

Q: How do I show change in composition over time?

A: 100% stacked column or area chart. 100% stacked bars encode composition within the bar while trending over time. Figure 23.10 shows an example of the composition of mobile versus desktop traffic changing over half a year.

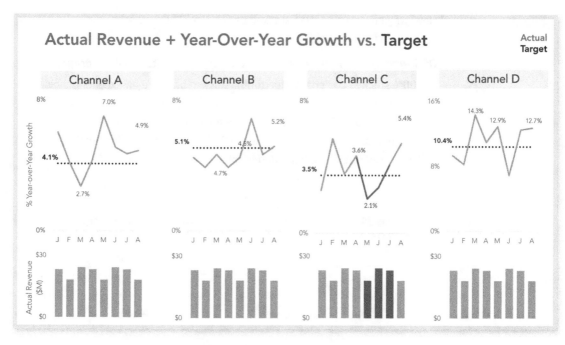

FIGURE 23.9 Combine chart space with color highlighting

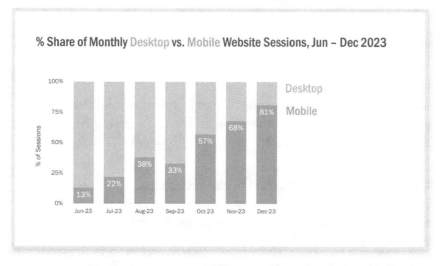

FIGURE 23.10 100% stacked bar showing an increase in mobile traffic versus desktop over time

Now, why not use a regular stacked bar chart? There are several pitfalls, which I explain in Chapter 24.

Q: How do I show survey data with different segments like demographics?

A: 100% stacked bar chart. Horizontal stacked bars are an excellent choice for visualizing all kinds of survey data, especially where you have questions with yes/no or five-step Likert scale answers broken down by different segments. In the example in Figure 23.11, I use an intentionally designed McKinsey title to transmit and emphasize my main point.

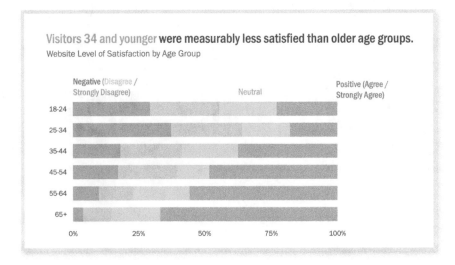

FIGURE 23.11 100% stacked bar showing survey satisfaction ratings on a Likert scale

Note that in this example, the clearly positive (agree/strongly agree) and negative (disagree/strongly disagree) values are meaningfully grouped to convey sentiment. Thanks to Stephanie Evergreen for this bit of data communication inspiration.

Note that area charts aren't subject to the same drawbacks as stacked columns and are helpful with many points of data; however, you want to make sure that the segments are different enough in size so that they don't frenetically crisscross each other.

Q: How can I show progress against a performance target or benchmark?

A: Try a bullet graph (not to be confused with bullet *points*!) The bullet graph was conceived by Stephen Few, and it aims to display category-level performance against a target. Few developed it as an improvement upon the less-than-ideal "gas gauges" and thermometer charts found on dashboards.

The bullet consists of thinner bars with individual performance target lines overlaid on each bar and shaded percentile areas or "bands," which typically encode a qualitative range. Figure 23.12 shows an example of a fully rendered bullet graph with elements explained.

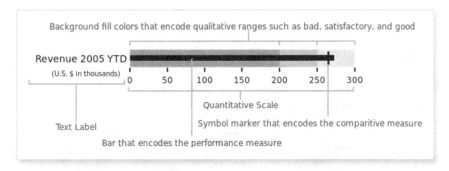

FIGURE 23.12 Bullet graph, Extemporalist, CC0, via Wikimedia Commons

I don't find the percentile ranges as commonly useful or understandable for most executive audiences, so I often omit them. Figure 23.13 shows a simplified bullet example tracking sales agent performance, where the bars represent actual closed sales against each agent's quota.

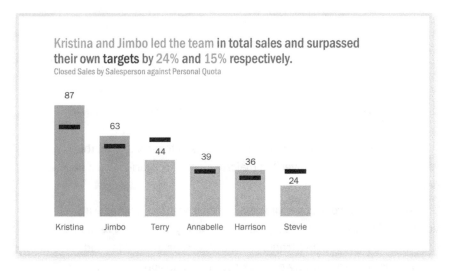

FIGURE 23.13 Simplified bullet graph showing salesperson performance versus quota

The bullet is not available out of the box in most data viz platforms, but it's now so popular that it has its own Wikipedia entry and Tableau Software has included it as a standard graph! I love any chart that overlays a goal or aspiration, because it helps "gamify" team collaboration and optimize performance.

> Visit the Resource Center for a detailed tutorial if you want to learn how to create a bullet graph in Excel or PowerPoint.

To wrap, Figure 23.14 shows a full chart-choosing guide for reference.

PICA Protocol Chart Choosing Guide

Scenario / Chart Type	Bar	Column	Pie / Donut	100% Stacked Bar	Line	Area	Bullet
Categorical Comparison	✓						
Composition (Parts of a Whole)	✓						
Contrasting one or more segments in composition			✓				
2 Categorical Comparisons	Table Lens						
Trending in Volume or Calculation		Volume			Calculation		
Trending with Composition				✓		✓	
Performance against a target							✓

FIGURE 23.14 Full chart-choosing framework for most effective presentation charts

While there are many more business questions in the world than this short list reveals, I find that these cover the majority of data scenarios you'll need to present during live meetings.

One more thing: if your stakeholder audience is well-acquainted with visualization types that aren't on this list, that's completely fine! If they're already savvy with waterfalls, heatmaps, scatterplots, Sankeys, yadda yadda yadda, absolutely continue using them if they won't risk causing confusion.

Sketch Before You Etch

As you are contemplating your chart choice, you may find it challenging to mentally picture exactly how your data is going to manifest into that structure. That's why I'm a huge fan of sketching my charts before attempting to create them in a data visualization platform like PowerPoint or Tableau.

I find that if I sketch my ideal chart first, I'm unconstrained by any technical limitations in my data, the platform, or my own charting prowess. The sky's the limit on my sketchpad, and I can mess up as many times as I need before I arrive at my desired visual. Then when I like what I see, I begin plotting the data in my tool and adjusting the visualization.

Figure 23.15 shows an example of several sketches I made for a blog post about the Bechdel Test using Stephanie Evergreen's helpful resource, *The Data Visualization Sketch Book*.

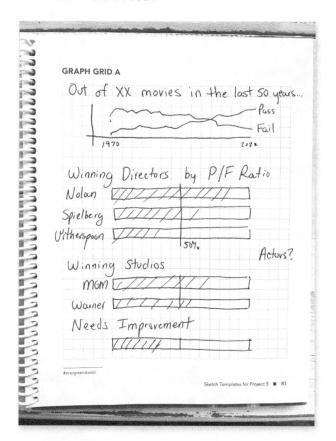

FIGURE 23.15 Sketch of data visualization and story of the Bechdel test

> **EXTRA CREDIT**
> Practice visualizing the same data in different charts for your colleagues to observe their interpretations.

While my first choice of medium for sketching is plain ol' pencil and paper for maximum creativity, there are also excellent digital drawing apps available for iPad and tablet that you can easily sketch with and share with others (my favorite is called Doodle Drawing Pad, available at `https://apps.apple.com/us/app/doodle-drawing-pad/id1503601939`).

> **Podcast Sound Byte: Scott Berinato (Ep. 035) Senior Editor, *Harvard Business Review* Author of *Good Charts* and *The Good Charts Workbook***
>
> I think one of the big mistakes a lot of people make when they make the charts is they just visualize the data. They'll have some data in a spreadsheet, they'll take this column and this row and make a line chart out of it. And that's not really what we're doing when we're creating charts.
>
> **We want to get an idea across.** That sometimes involves the data plus other things. Sometimes it involves subsets of the data and deeper calculations. There are lots of things you can do to bring an idea forward beyond just visualizing the data. So for me, a good chart is really a chart that understands its context.
>
> I'd rather see a hand-sketched chart that says exactly what it's supposed to say and is somewhat messy than a perfectly built beautiful chart that doesn't say the right thing.

In short, I recommend you move to selecting a chart type only after you've determined the purpose for your visual and that its purpose is unmistakably connected to the purpose of your presentation.

Nail this decision, and the rest is gravy.

Chapter Recap

- Choosing the most appropriate visualization for your data is a critical juncture in the data storytelling process.
- Just because a chart type exists doesn't mean it's an effective choice.

Sandbox Assignment

- Evaluate the purpose of your selected sandbox example using the questions in this chapter.
- Consider the type of chart or data visual you would use to fulfill its purpose.
- Remember to ask the question, "What am I trying to answer with this chart?"

Avoid the Most Common Visualization

24 Violations

"Rules are for fools to follow and for wise men to be guided by."

—*Winston Churchill*

You've already learned how to avoid several data viz no-nos in the PICA Protocol; however, there are still a few more to consider. These chart types and practices are considered violations of how the brain most effectively receives information, and they are more common than you think.

I'm going to ease you into the violation section with perhaps the one you'll feel the most uncomfortable with. Why? To rip off the Band-Aid! Once you move through this one, it's relatively painless from here.

Viz Violation: Dual-Axis Charts with Different Scales

The dual-axis chart consists of two different chart types overlaid in the same plot space using two different scales (usually a bar and a line). This is known as a *combo chart* in Excel and PowerPoint. Figure 24.1 shows an example.

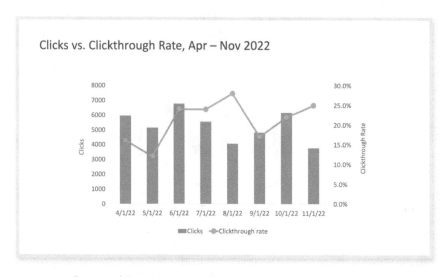

FIGURE 24.1 Example of dual-axis bar and line graph with different scales

I'm quite familiar with the appeal of this viz; in my agency days, I used dual-axis bar/line charts like it was my job. Because ... it *was* my job. Stakeholders wanted more, more, more, and these charts enabled me to squeeze as much data as possible into an itty-bitty living space, especially on dashboards. I'll show you why that's really a drawback, not a benefit.

Our eyes and brains are wired to draw conclusions and create meaning around the intersection of data points (or the lack of intersection, if it deviates from the other points). This visual mechanism is the basis for understanding charts like scatterplots, where the proximity of points and clusters indicate something meaningful.

The problem is that in a dual-axis chart, two sets of data are plopped into the same space with two different chart types for no other reason than sharing the same time frame. When the data points on different scales intersect, it can imply correlation or causation when there is none. In other words, it may inadvertently signal to the viewer's brain that something meaningful or notable happened because of the intersection. See Figure 24.2.

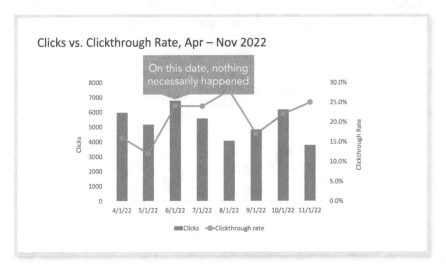

FIGURE 24.2 Callout denoting intersection that potentially implies inaccurate correlation

The intersections we see are meaningless, but your audience's eyes will zoom in on them like a homing beacon. So, the chart is secretly saying the same thing as my sign: that on this intersection (or lack thereof), nothing *necessarily* happened.

If you won't take my word for it, you can ask a man named Tyler Vigen, a statistician and author of a blog and book called *Spurious Correlations*; spurious means "false or misleading."[1] Tyler first analyzed hundreds of the most random publicly available data points, like the divorce rate in Maine and per capita consumption of chicken. Then he painstakingly plotted their trendlines on different-scaled dual-axis charts for the sole purpose of showing how closely correlated they appear to be. The trendline similarity is eerie and yet hilariously preposterous, as you can see in Figure 24.3.

---

[1]Vigen, Tyler. Spurious Correlations. www.tylervigen.com/spurious-correlations

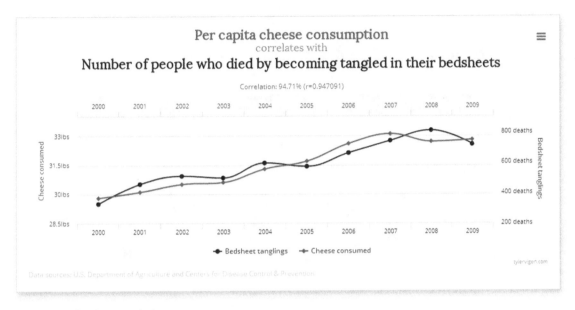

FIGURE 24.3 Spurious correlations
Source: Tyler Vigen, Spurious Correlations

The convincing correlation between the amount of cheese consumption and the likelihood of dying by bedsheet entanglement was almost enough to convince me to go Paleo. . .almost. Tyler's work shows how suggestible the brain is to correlation through spatial intersection and alignment. As data communicators, we must be wary of the unintentional connections and assumptions our visuals create for the audience.

Yet another pitfall of dual-axis charts is that your audience's brains must work to determine which data set belongs to which axis. Those are precious seconds lost where they're audibly tuning you out.

Finally, bar/line combination charts are particularly tricky because bars are most accurately interpreted when they are visually uninterrupted. Figure 24.4 shows an example where the second series lines and labels interfere with the bars.

Now, I know what you're thinking. . .

But, but, don't take my dual axes away!

Yes, this one is hard. Now that I've made my case for ditching dual-axis disasters, I'll address what's likely bubbling up for you right now.

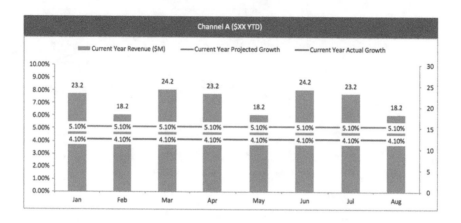

FIGURE 24.4 Example of dual axis bar and line chart where lines visually interfere with bars

The first question I get is this: but what if the metrics *are* related? For example, what if I'm comparing a bar chart showing display ad impressions and a line showing ad clickthrough rate (CTR), isn't that OK? The answer is no, no-kay.

If the metrics are related, you have a better chance that the trends will appear more correlated, but you still run the risk that the audience will create meaning around intersections and must figure out which side belongs to what and may inaccurately interpret any intersections as meaningful.

The next question I get after that is usually this: what about dual-axis charts on the same scale, will that work? Yes, if you're using lines. That will work. Because then, you're not plotting two data sets on two different axes. You're plotting two data series on the same axis, which is essentially a single-axis line chart.

I get the most resistance to this violation because of its widespread popularity. I suspect this is equal parts cultural (the organization or client has come to accept and expect them, despite their flaws) and habitual (trying to save as much space as possible.)

The habit is what I'd like for you to examine by asking yourself this question: why are you trying to save space on your slide? Is it possibly to cram in too much stuff? If you begin to think about your chart choices in relation to white space, you'll realize that the solution often goes right back to simplicity.

The Solution: The Table Lens

One of my favorite visualizations for presentations is called a *table lens*, or *side-by-side bar chart*. It's the multiple chart layout that I used to pivot the story during the CONTEXT step of the marketing channel example.

The power of the table lens lies in its simplicity: it's nothing more than multiple bar charts with the same set of categories in the same order. It essentially creates a visual "table" with a list of categories on the left and "columns" of bar data to the right.

The table lens is another gift from Stephen Few, which he describes this way in *Now You See It*:

"A table lens provides a simple way to look for correlations among several variables all at once. It uses horizontal bars to encode values, arranged like a table, with a separate column for each variable, and a separate row for each item that has been measured."

Figure 24.5 shows an example of a table lens displaying four measures for the same list of categories.

Notice how quickly you're able to assess these categories across two measures without having to wade through intersections between their values. The key is that you're able to read across the "cells" of the invisible table without visual interference.

The greatest number of measures I would use in a table lens is five; any more than that and you run the risk of losing the audience in confusion because that's too much information at once. Make sure there's a good reason to do so. **When presenting live, I animate in each chart one at a time to ensure I'm walking the audience through at a manageable pace.**

It's possible to create a sort of vertical table lens for time-series charts. In this case, simply separate the charts into different stacked spaces, as in Figure 24.6.

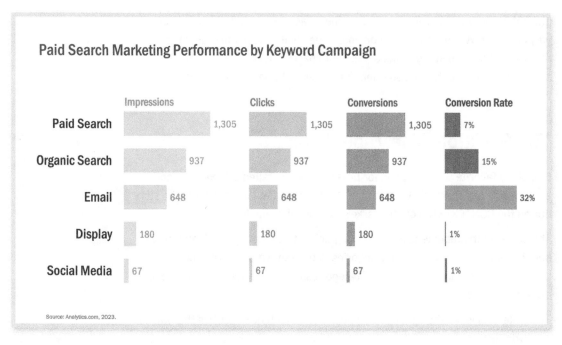

FIGURE 24.5 Example of a four-column table lens
Source: Adapted from Analytics.com, 2023

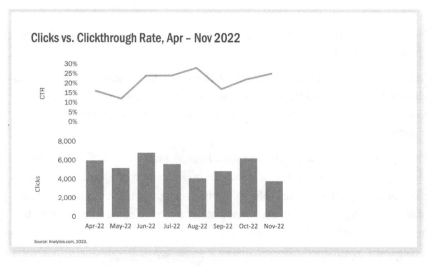

FIGURE 24.6 Vertical table lens with stacked time series line and column charts
Source: Adapted from Analytics.com, 2023

Viz Violation: Tables

Tables are a wonderfully useful form of data organization. . .when you're leisurely perusing your E*TRADE portfolio over a morning latte. Unfortunately, tables are one of the least effective data visualizations to clearly transmit information during a live presentation.

Remember that your job as a data presenter is to make your audience do less mental work. Tables are the visualization equivalent of The Wall of bullet points, where you are overwhelming the audience with all the numbers at once, rather than spotlighting specific data points. Figure 24.7 illustrates this.

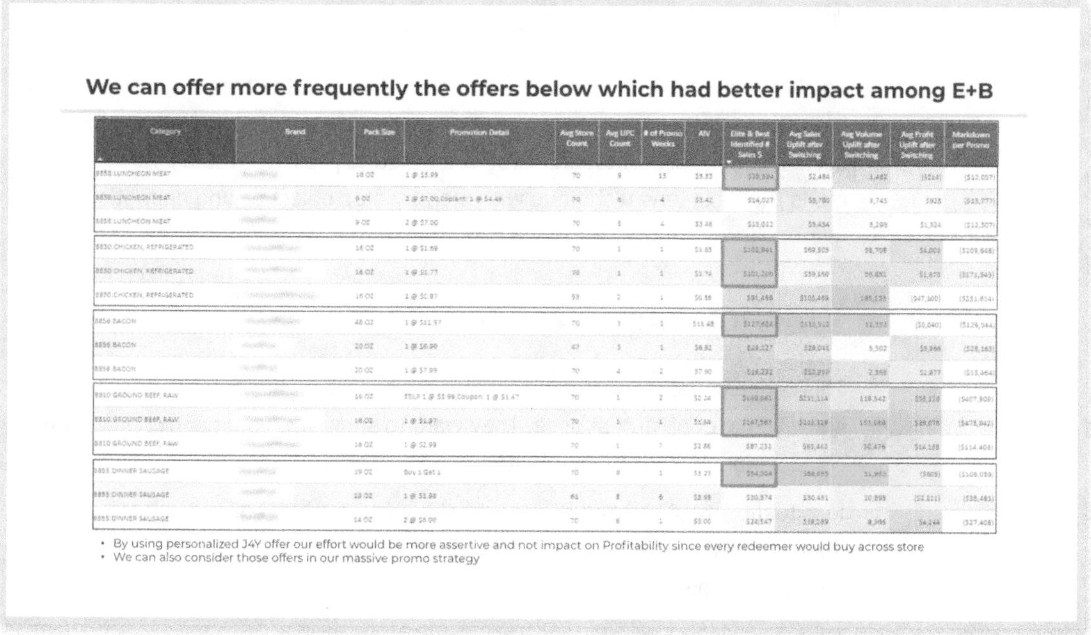

FIGURE 24.7 Example of ineffective table for presentation

Tables also create a ton of work for the audience because there are no visual cues to quickly compare the figures to each other; digits are hard to compare. Combine that with how many measures are often jammed into one table, and now their brains are melting down with many more chunks of data than they're equipped to handle. They also demolish the single idea per slide philosophy just by their nature!

Now, there are stakeholders who insist upon seeing tables during meetings. These folks are particularly prevalent in finance departments. In this case, use your best judgment because the ultimate goal of presenting data is to meet the needs of your audience.

If they feel the need to call a meeting for you to observe them absorbing the contents of a table by themselves, then that is what they need. But if you're finding that you're presenting table data and wondering why your stakeholders are bored, distracted, and secretly browsing their Reddit feeds, it's a sign that something isn't working.

The Solution: A Table...Lens!

You have several options here. First, make sure that the truly *key* performance indicators are front and center, with no more than three in the introduction section of your presentation. If you are asked to present a table live, I recommend the table lens technique with step-by-step object pacing animation.

Viz Violation: Stacked Bars

This is one of the most ambitious charts in the viz stable because they want to show you a lot of stuff at once. They want to show you volume, trending, and composition all in one view. Quite a workhorse!

In actuality, most stacked bar charts show *too* much at once, much more information than our brains are equipped to handle. Figure 24.8 is a perfect example.

As important as I imagine the data in this chart was, it was likely more effective at strapping the audience's brains into a Six Flags roller coaster.

Numerous challenges are found here: first, different length bars showing volume confound the relative composition within the bar. Then, the inconsistent baselines of most segments make it impossible to accurately compare the segments across categories or time. This can mislead you in determining how segments are shifting. With this bar chart, how easy is it to answer these questions:

- Is the overall share of AF-Zip Code increasing or decreasing over time?
- Was the AF Market NEW share larger or smaller in May versus June 2014?
- Is AF Amenity bigger in share than AF-County in August 2015?

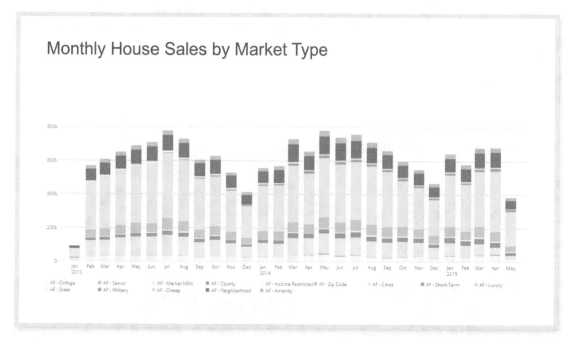

FIGURE 24.8 Example of ineffective stacked bar chart

The only segments whose trends are more easily understood are the top and bottom because they each have a consistent baseline. The potential for misuse of this chart is high, and that's why determining the purpose of your visual is exceptionally important when choosing a stacked bar. **Pause and ask yourself: what question am I answering with this chart?** The answer will determine your choice.

The Solution: A 100% Stacked Bar Chart

For me, when the question I'm answering is how the composition of something changes across categories or time periods, I turn to a 100% stacked bar chart. I choose it only when the desired story is about a change in composition in specific segments, *not* the overall volume of each bar and segment in each time period.

Just choosing a 100% stacked bar won't solve your comprehension issue, however; as evidenced in Figure 24.9, you can still create an ineffective view with certain aesthetic choices such as loud and conflicting colors and dual axes with different scales.

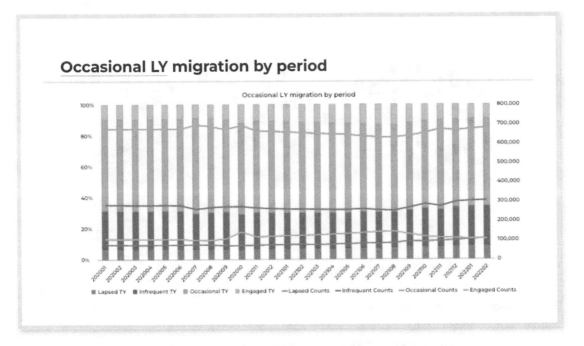

FIGURE 24.9 Example of poorly formatted 100% stacked bar chart

Here are guidelines for effective 100% stacked bar charts:

- Use 100 percent vertical bars to illustrate the change in the composition of categories over time.
- Plot no more than five segments in a bar.
- Make the most important segments the bottom and the top of the bars.

- Color all segments different shades of gray to "mute" the story.
- Use color to accentuate only the most important segment or two (see Figure 24.10).

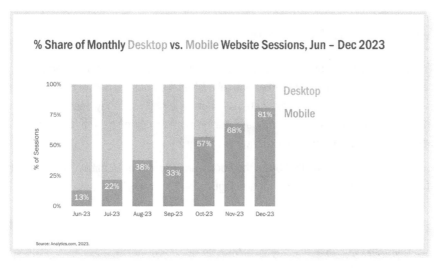

FIGURE 24.10 100% stacked bar showing increase in mobile traffic versus desktop over time
Source: Adapted from Analytics.com, 2023

- Add a complementary side-by-side volume bar to add context if necessary (see Figure 24.11).

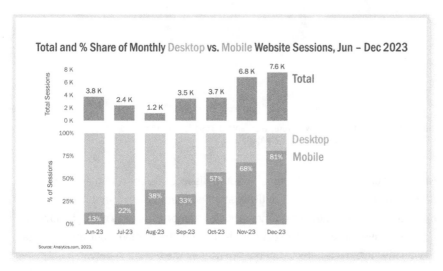

FIGURE 24.11 Prior 100% stacked column with total session table lens
Source: Adapted from Analytics.com, 2023

- Use 100 percent horizontal stacked bars to illustrate the composition of segments within categories, such as with qualitative survey results on a Likert scale. Remember *not* to use horizontal bars for a time series.

Viz Violation: Clustered Bars

This popular chart type is a perfect example of when a chart is conceived with certain intentions, but executed effectively. Clustered bars group two or more segment bars in clumps across categories or time periods. They answer two questions: how do x, y, and z compare during the same time period (or category), and how do x, y, and z change over time?

But just like regular stacked bars, they don't answer either question very well at the same time. Consider the image in Figure 24.12.

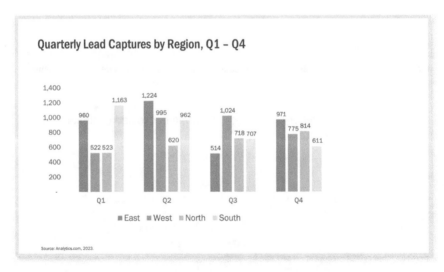

FIGURE 24.12 Clustered bar with four segments across four time periods
Source: Adapted from Analytics.com, 2023

Now, your brain might instantly attempt to dissect this chart to make sense of it. And as you're doing that, you've likely stopped reading. Translation: mucho distracto. Comparing the first time period's categories is easy enough; however, once you have more than two categories in each time period, your audience has to visually "trip over" interstitial bars to assess the trends in between each time period.

The Solution: It Depends

Once again, we must consider the question we're asking when using this chart. Is the question how do your categories compare to each other, or how are they changing over time? Remember, *what is the story here?*

One solution is to use color to focus the audience on the most important segment or time period. In Figure 24.13, I use color to highlight a particular category and its growth.

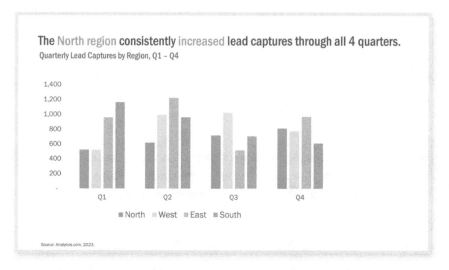

FIGURE 24.13 Improved clustered bar with emphasized data story point and rearranged segments
Source: Adapted from Analytics.com, 2023

This overcomes the shortcomings of the cluster by making it easy to spot my story.

If you're plotting a time series, a more straightforward solution is a line graph. This allows you to demonstrate trends across the series without tripping over the bars standing in the way, as shown in Figure 24.14.

One final alternative for a clustered bar is a slope graph if you're comparing multiple categories over two time periods with a single measure. You'll learn about that advanced chart in Chapter 25.

To close, the last thing you want to do with this or any of these precarious chart types is to confuse your audience when they are intended to inform them. That would be a *real* cluster.

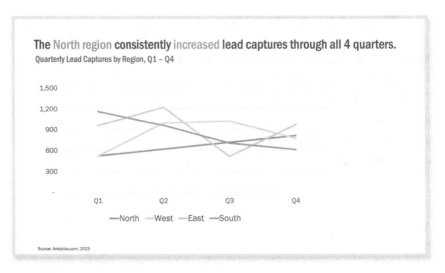

FIGURE 24.14 Alternative line graph to clustered bar
Source: Adapted from Analytics.com, 2023

Now, those are violations regarding the type of chart you'd choose. There are also a couple of potential pitfalls with the way practitioners frame their insight titles on chart slides. The following sections cover the most common issues.

Viz Violation: Vague and Subjective Insight Titles

Decision-makers want one thing and one thing only: the whole truth, nothing but, and they want it fast. As you've learned, your insight title is instrumental in facilitating that fast, accurate, and deep intuitive understanding. Consider whether the slide in Figure 24.15 achieves that goal.

Paid search is. . .better? What does better mean exactly? How much better? By what measurement? These are all questions an audience member could ask upon seeing this. I often observe "mushy" and subjective language in titles to describe the chart's story.

Your best bet is to use objective language to answer the "What happened?" question. Rather than subjective terms like "better" or "worse," I'll use terms like these:

■ Higher versus lower
■ Faster versus slower
■ More versus less

- Outperformed versus underperformed
- Exceeded or outpaced versus fell behind

Also, I try to add the value of the metric I'm referencing in the insight title so that it takes even more analysis work off my stakeholders' mental plate, as shown in Figure 24.16.

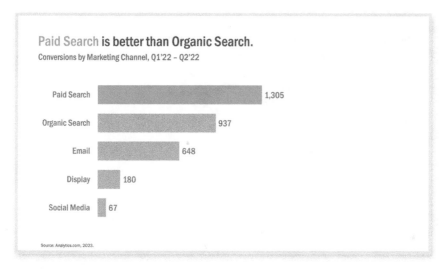

FIGURE 24.15 Bar chart with vague insight title
Source: Adapted from Analytics.com, 2023

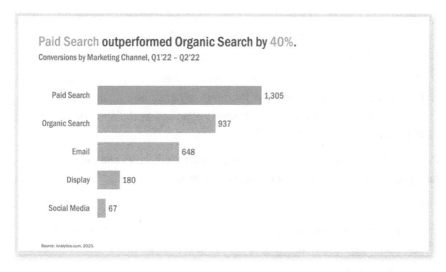

FIGURE 24.16 Clearer insight title
Source: Adapted from Analytics.com, 2023

Viz Violation: Mismatched Title to Chart

The ideal reason we visually display data in meetings is to immediately corroborate our verbal story, which builds trust with our decision-makers. Consider the slide in Figure 24.17 and guess why it might not fill that order.

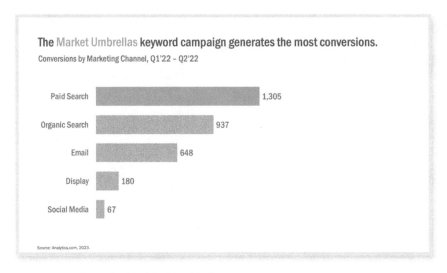

FIGURE 24.17 Mismatched insight title with chart
Source: Adapted from Analytics.com, 2023

Did you notice how the Market Umbrellas campaign referenced in the title isn't found in the chart data? This could confuse the audience because they're seeking to confirm your story.

I call this the "talk track" blunder. You know how when you're streaming a show on Netflix and after an internet blip, the speaking track doesn't quite line up with the video? Have you tried to continue paying attention as if it's not happening? Well, I've never been able to do it.

Even the slightest visual mismatch creates total distraction and disconnection, taking you out of the present viewing experience.

These are the two ways I see this happen the most:

- Referencing data in the title that isn't shown in the chart or visual
- Using vague and mysterious language in the title that doesn't make the visual any clearer

Next-Level Charts to (Carefully) Consider

"The effectiveness of data visualization can be gauged by its simplicity, relevancy, and its ability to hold the user's hand during their data discovery journey."

—Jagat Saikia

As I mentioned at the beginning of this act, a snazzy new chart type can feel like a shiny holiday present to a data practitioner. The new shapes, the colors, the lines, yeehaw! And as you're learning, the downsides are that many charts don't communicate data well and most executive decision-makers don't understand unfamiliar charts.

The upside is that there are several unconventional chart types that are well-suited to facilitate accurate comprehension. . .once your stakeholders become familiarized with them. I highly advise against walking into a meeting and displaying these charts cold without preparing to do a step-by-step walkthrough (preferably using the Object or Shape Pacing methods).

The following sections introduce my favorite off-the-beaten-path chart types that you won't find in most data visualization tools.

The Target Variance Bar Chart

I have a groovy kind of love for this visualization. There may be scenarios where you have categorical or time-based results with individual performance benchmarks, such as salesperson-level sales quotas or profitability by quarter. Consider the example in Figure 25.1 before I break down the mechanics.

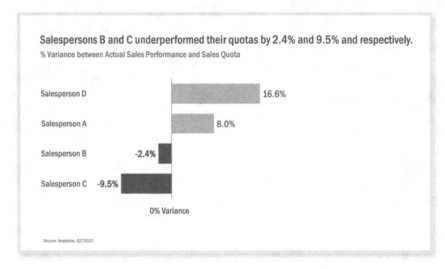

FIGURE 25.1 Target variance bar chart showing deviation of salesperson performance from quota
Source: Adapted from Analytics Q3' 2022

Notice that the bar lengths encode a percentage, not a quantity. This percentage represents the delta between a measure's target and actual performance. The zero y-axis represents the target itself as a baseline, with performance landing above or below it.

That target might be the same or different for all bars; **the key is that the bar length displays the percentage difference between each category's actual performance and its respective target.**

In the example in Figure 25.1, every salesperson has a different sales quota, and the zero axis represents the different targets for each. Success means that the bar is either at or above the zero axis. This means that even though Salespersons A and D may have had higher quotas, the story that matters here is that they not only met their quota, but they also well exceeded it. This is in contrast with B and C, who fell short of their targets.

This chart is a cousin of the waterfall chart, except it doesn't "spill" the excess amount into the next bar. Each bar is a discrete calculation, but the common baseline makes it possible to compare performance between the bars in a single view.

In another case, let's say you need to show company profitability on a quarterly basis against a static annual target. A time-series variance chart could look like Figure 25.2.

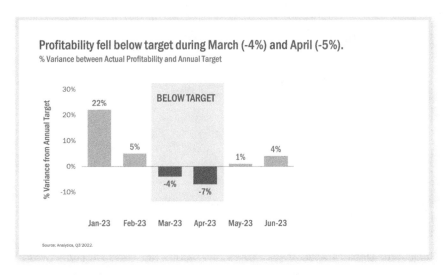

FIGURE 25.2 Target variance column chart showing deviation of performance from an annual target over time
Source: Adapted from Analytics Q3' 2022

In this case, the value of the target remains consistent throughout the year. However, the chart still works if you had different profitability targets each month, quarter, and so on. Because this chart is a bar by nature, it requires less handholding for an unfamiliar audience than, say, an alluvial or Sankey. However, it's still not entirely straightforward. **The key to explaining it is that the zero axis represents the target, no matter what the value of the target is.**

The Slope Graph

I believe slope graphs are one of the best-kept secrets of the data visualization world. They almost feel too simple, and yet, we now know that simplicity is the key to communicating data quickly, clearly, and accurately.

A slope graph is a line chart that plots measures of categories on two vertical axes. The lines connecting the points on the axes create a slope that allows the viewer to clearly see the difference or change. See Figure 25.3.

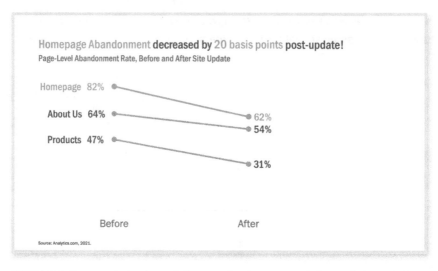

Homepage Abandonment **decreased by** 20 basis points **post-update!**
Page-Level Abandonment Rate, Before and After Site Update

Homepage 82%

About Us 64% — 62%
54%

Products 47% — 31%

Before   After

Source: Analytics.com, 2021.

FIGURE 25.3 Slope graph showing website page abandonment rate before and after redesign
Source: Adapted from Analytics.com, 2021

Think of the slope as a "zoomed-in" view of a regular line chart with only two points. Measuring change between two points in time is the most common usage, but the structure may be used to measure the difference between other variables such as demographic segments or survey answers.

The reason why you would choose a slope graph is that you want to not only quickly compare the difference between two points for each category, but you also want to compare each category to each other. It's an excellent alternative to a clustered bar chart with two groups of multiple bars.

Here are some scenarios where you can use slope graphs to visualize change:

NOTE

This chart works best with fewer than ten categories and with one or two categories where the change really stands out.

- Comparing the abandonment rate of website pages before and after a redesign
- Comparing year-over-year or month-over-month change in marketing channel conversion
- Comparing Yes or No answers by survey respondent segment

At time of writing, I haven't found any widely available data visualization tool offering slope graphs except for a PowerPoint plugin tool called Vizzlo (`vizzlo .com`). For now, you need to create them with some legwork and creativity in Excel or Tableau. I put an additional spotlight on the slope graph in Chapter 27.

The Dumbbell Dot Plot

This chart is one I hope goes mainstream as it is so effective at communicating specific information. A dot plot displays a list of categories and places the value of a measure as a circle (or a large dot) on a line. The measure of each category in the chart is represented by the relative position of each category's dot on their respective lines.

Figure 25.4 shows an example of a dot plot displaying the rankings of a mobile app in different Apple App Store categories.

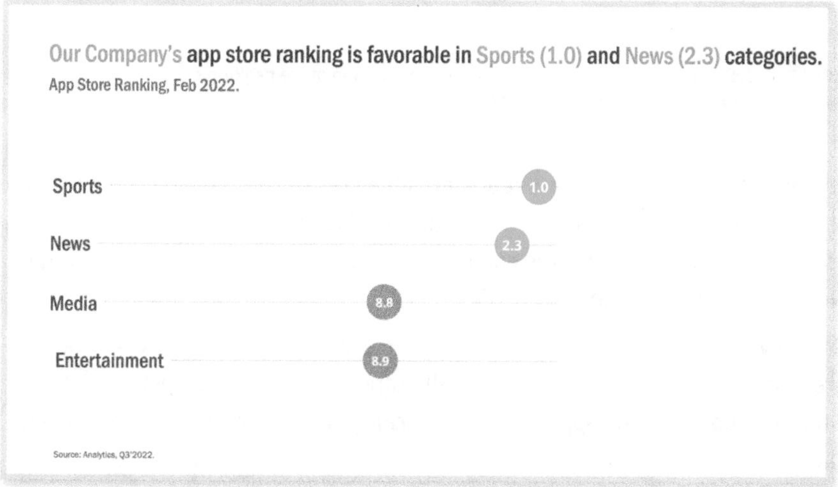

Our Company's **app store ranking is favorable in** Sports (1.0) **and** News (2.3) **categories.**
App Store Ranking, Feb 2022.

Sports	1.0
News	2.3
Media	8.8
Entertainment	8.9

Source: Analytics, Q3'2022.

FIGURE 25.4 Dot plot depicting a company's app store ranking
Source: Adapted from Analytics Q3' 2022

You can see how the chart structure is similar to a bar chart. The distance from the zero axis to the middle of the dot serves in lieu of the length of a bar. So, it is yet another alternative to bar charts if you choose to expand your repertoire.

While this is already a data story worth celebrating, I've left space open to the left of the dots as a space to bring in an even more exciting story. This chart really shines when you add a second dot on each category's line, which results in a visual "dumbbell" effect. In the graph in Figure 25.5, I added a second set of dots indicating what the rankings might be for a competitor.

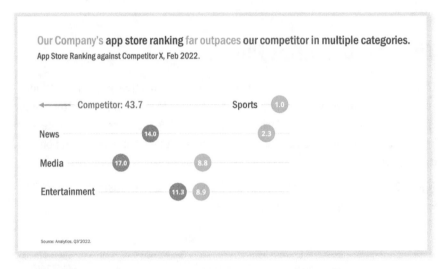

FIGURE 25.5 Dumbbell dot plot depicting a competitive app store ranking comparison
Source: Adapted from Analytics Q3' 2022

The distance between the dots represents the spread between the company app and the competitor app within each category. This view is even more compelling as a success story because the competitor's rank in Sports is so much lower, it would skew the graph to include it!

See how easy this is to understand once I've explained it? This makes for a great story that the company app is well outperforming the competitor and in which categories. If the app were underperforming, you could easily see which categories need attention.

How to Use These Charts

These are the best ways to use these unorthodox charts:

- To show the percentage distance between categorical performance and its target, use a target variance bar.

- To show one instance of a measure for many categories, then the single dot plot works great (instead of a single bar).
- To show two instances of the same measure, such as pre/post analysis or comparing two segments, then the dumbbell dot plot or the slope graph will work for that (instead of a clustered bar).

While the process for creating these charts is too detailed for the scope of this book, I have linked to several of my own and others' tutorials in the Resource Center.

Now, remember how I said that these are effective chart options, but only when your audience is aware of how they work? That means you'll need to train your audience in reading them as if you're demonstrating a new reporting platform.

And guess what? The Shape Pacing technique I described earlier is the perfect way to walk your audience through charts like these, step-by-step! Animated shapes are the ideal way to reveal portions of a new chart to both orient them with its structure and create suspense for what you'll reveal next.

> **EXTRA CREDIT**
> Read Stephanie Evergreen's *Effective Data Visualization* (SAGE, 2019) for an excellent primer on more advanced chart types and ways to visualize survey data.

Chapter Recap

- The target variance bar, slope graph, and dumbbell dot plot charts can communicate more advanced insights in a crisp, clear way while injecting visual variety into your presentations.
- When presenting advanced charts, use the Shape Pacing method to walk your audience through them step-by-step for total comprehension.

> **Sandbox Assignment**
> - Go to the Resource Center to read tutorials and download templates to practice creating these advanced charts.

26 Create Ethical Data Visualizations

"In God we trust. All others bring data."

—W. Edwards Deming

By now, you're seeing how incredibly powerful data is as a vehicle of persuasion and that it can unintentionally mislead the audience. But what about *intentionally* misleading the audience, or, at least, manipulating the narrative to fulfill an agenda?

Of course, we as bright-eyed data professionals have a strong moral compass and always want to find and tell the truth in the data. But that doesn't always mean that what we present is free from external—or internal—influences.

I used to jump into judgment on any misshaping of a data story, but softened my view that the line is not always so clearly drawn. Once again, I'll quote Scott Berinato from *Good Charts* when he describes a scenario of a data designer asked by a superior to manipulate a data view to support a specific position on a decision.

What I love about Scott's perspective here is that rather than jumping to judgment of either the designer or the superior, he shows the nuance of the situation and how common it is to fall into.

"Would that a clear line existed between visual persuasion and visual dishonesty. Even if it were a fine line, at least we could see it and stay on the ethical side of it. But in fact, and of course, no such line exists. Instead we have to negotiate a blurred and shifting borderland between truthfulness and unfair manipulation."

Berinato goes on to explain the two sides of this coin: aspects of visual persuasion (emphasis, isolation, adding or removing reference points) on one side and deception (falsification, exaggeration, omission, and equivocation) on the other.[1] He makes the point that these are obvious in some cases but that others are not so apparent.

Let's explore some of the most common ethical gray areas tripping up practitioners today.

---

[1] Berinato, Scott. *Good Charts.*

Truncating the Measure Axis

This is a common practice in all walks of the data visualization field. Data designers at times feel at liberty—or are asked—to simply "zoom in" on an area of a graph that eliminates data altogether. **Data viz canon asserts that under no circumstances should a bar chart's measure axis ever be truncated.**

This is because the brain requires the full length of each bar to comprehend them accurately and truncating them artificially inflates the differences between the bars.

Fox News is notorious for manipulating bar and line charts by truncating the measure axis, which is likely to contort the narrative. For a few shining examples of completely fudged viz (not to mention voluminous chart junk and cognitive load), visit www.politico.com/blogs/media/2014/04/fox-news-corrects-obamacare-chart-186120, flowingdata.com/2011/12/12/fox-news-still-makes-awesome-charts and, oh my goodness, flowingdata.com/2009/11/26/fox-news-makes-the-best-pie-chart-ever. (Thanks to Nathan Yau of Flowing Data for spotting these beauties!)

In fact, entire blog posts have been dedicated to the deeply spotted history of data visualization manipulation of Fox News, so consume any charts it publishes with a wary eye.

Truncation happens even when the intentions aren't nefarious, but perhaps one is simply uninformed about the risks. I'll play a game to explain: look at the real-life example of a column time series showing annual widget sales in Figure 26.1 and immediately call to mind the first observation or conclusion you make.

If you were this company's stakeholder, your first impression may have been that you did gangbusters in 2016 with an apparent 50 percent year-over-year increase, woo-hoo! Send everyone home for the afternoon.

But upon closer inspection of the data labels, you notice that the 2015 value is only roughly 15 percent less than 2016! This means the design set the y-axis much higher than 0. Naughty, naughty! Figure 26.2 shows this same data with the y-axis properly restored to zero.

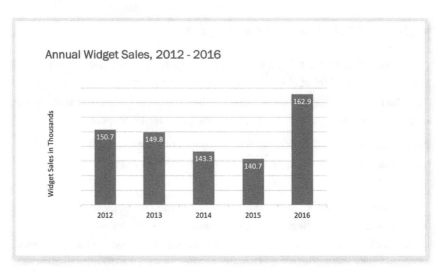

FIGURE 26.1 Vertical column time series showing annual widget sales

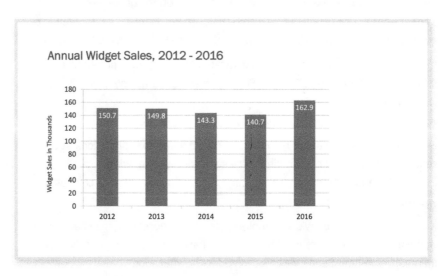

FIGURE 26.2 Vertical column with y-axis corrected back to zero

So now we're clear: never, ever truncate a chart axis, right? Not so fast. There is an exception to this rule where the lines get blurred (in line *charts*, that is!)

Exception: Truncating Line Chart Axes

It turns out, the zero-axis mandate is not a hard-and-fast rule with line charts. This is because rather than comparing lengths of data points, you're comparing the slope of the angle between data points. Truncating the axis is actually permitted here; however, it's vital to understand the rationale for *why* you would do that and communicate as such.

A performance metric may have a narrowly limited range, but small changes may profoundly impact the bottom line. Consider a company like eBay, which reportedly makes extremely minute moves in changing website functionality because the financial impact from changes in customer satisfaction could be massive. The scale of that performance might be too great to appreciate with a full zero axis.

I explain this using a real-life metric like body temperature. Let's say I used a fitness tracking ring to monitor my body temperature for two years. If I plotted the data on a zero axis, the results may look like Figure 26.3.

NOTE

You can truncate a line axis to demonstrate small changes that translate to a big impact, *not* to create an interpretation that wouldn't hold up if the whole view was shown.

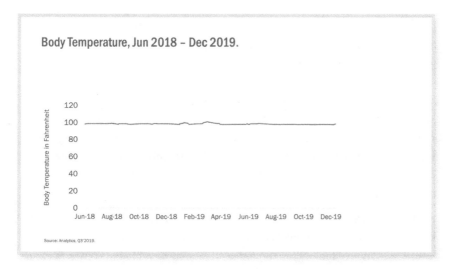

FIGURE 26.3 Vertical column with y-axis corrected back to zero
Source: Adapted from Analytics Q3' 2019

While this chart's scale is accurately rendered, it may also be the least interesting data story of all time. Body temperature has a finite scope of change, and veering just a few degrees away from the healthy average could be life-threatening. Now, if I zoom in on the line to where I'm leaving plenty of room above and below for the range of motion like so, you can see the story better (see Figure 26.4).

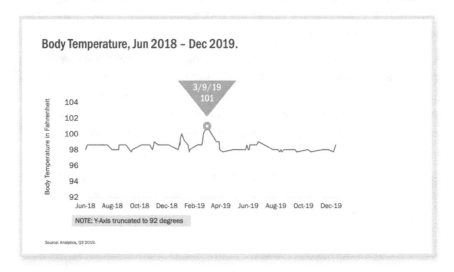

FIGURE 26.4 Body temperature line graph with truncated y-axis
Source: Adapted from Analytics Q3' 2019

Now the plot thickens, where I clearly experienced an immune event in January and March (it was a rough winter). That story doesn't jump out nearly as prominently without truncating the axis. **Note that I inserted a small flag disclosing how I've manipulated the view**; I do this with full transparency and openly explain my reasons for doing so to my viewers. Disclosure is key to data communication integrity.

This scenario translates to business data when you have a measure that has a large scale, and minor changes can translate to big money or other matters. A small shift in profitability for companies like eBay or Alphabet comes to mind.

The other truncation to be wary of is excluding periods of time or data, or "zooming in," that shift the story. For example, if I showed truncated data that focused only upon the winter months, I could make a misleading statement about my health, like in Figure 26.5.

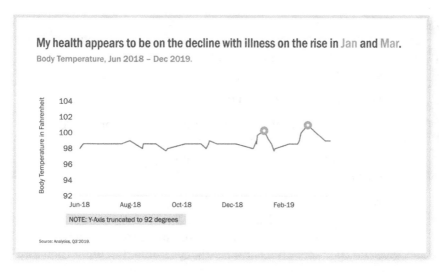

FIGURE 26.5 Body temperature line graph with truncated data set
Source: Adapted from Analytics Q3' 2019

My headline and chart treatment might lead you to extrapolate and believe that my health is indeed worsening over time. But as you've already seen in the earlier slides, those were blips on the radar of a longer time period, in which I spent mostly well and am on the up and up.

Data visualization ethics are compromised when the intention behind zooming, truncating, and manipulating a data view is aimed to either conform to a desired story or avoid confirming a new story. The ethical data designer is once again always asking themselves, *"Why am I doing it this way?"*

Another area of ethics is confidence; decision-makers want to feel certain they can put their trust (and their money) in your capable hands. But alas, data is quite imperfect, and misleading the audience about your confidence is simply not the way to go.

> **Podcast Sound Byte: Alberto Cairo (Ep. 049) Knight Chair, University of Miami, and author of *The Truthful Art, The Functional Art* and *How Charts Lie***
>
> Here's what I mean when I say in my book "A chart shows only what it shows and nothing else." So you want to understand a chart. You cannot assume that you can understand a chart just

by taking a quick look at it. You really need to pay attention to it, and you really need to ask yourself, what is this chart showing? What is this chart not showing?

Moreover, what am I seeing in this chart?

This really applies to any chart or graphic that is intended to depict or to convey data. In the world of journalism and the world of graphic design, this is a kind of binary thinking that is also very simple.

We all need to make an effort to help people understand that no data is 100 percent certain. There is always a level of uncertainty around it. When someone asks to "show me the facts" or "give me the facts," they should always imply that what they really mean is give them your most confident interpretation of those facts.

Most likely, your most confident interpretation of those facts is not 100 percent certain. It never is. The ethical thing to do is to say "I feel very confident that this is the explanation. There is another possible explanation that I am less confident about, and we should explore that further."

That's the ethical thing to do.

As you're beginning to see, the hard shell of right-and-wrong dogma begins to fall away to reveal a softer, more nuanced decision-making path for you as a communicator of data.

Check Your Own Bias

In Act I, I discussed overcoming confirmation bias, that tricky character influencing how your audience takes in and reacts to your information. We all harbor that stowaway, and as a data communicator, it's important to ensure that we're checking our own confirmation bias at the conference room door.

Here are the questions I ask myself when I'm presenting a slice or view of information with a persuasive angle:

- Did I bring a beginner's mind to this analysis?
- Did I seek out specific data to confirm a preconceived story in my mind?
- Is there an agenda or attachment to an outcome influencing this view?
- Could I defend this view in a court of law during cross-examination?
- Will I be able to sleep at night if my audience acts on this?

If you can answer all these questions with confident ease, then there's a good chance your story has integrity, and you'll stay out of data jail. And believe me, data jail is no place for a great practitioner. The food is terrible!

Chapter Recap

- Data visualization is often manipulated, intentionally and unintentionally.
- As a data communicator, it's critical to be mindful of your influence on the data story.
- It is advised to never truncate the measure axis of bar charts.
- You may truncate a line chart's measure axis to zoom in on minor changes that have major impact, as long as you disclose doing so and why.

Sandbox Assignment

- Review your content and visualizations for any potentially manipulated or misleading views.
- If you're choosing to change the view, such as zooming in, ask yourself what that is in service to and whether it serves the integrity of the story.

Build the Story: The PICA Protocol in Action

27

"Data visualization is powerful. Still, data storytelling is the thing driving decision-makers."

—Monika Piekarska

Here's where you get to see the entire prescription in sequence so you can apply it to your own scenarios. I'll synthesize the PICA Protocol with the storytelling narrative arc from Act I and the slide design techniques from Act II.

You're also going to see the big picture of how each baby story arc unfolds and how each of them fit into the greater parent story arc. Since solving data challenges is like solving a mystery, we're going to don our gumshoe hats and get on these cases!

Case Example #1: The Conversion Rate Caper

Recall once more the marketing channel conversion example from the PICA Protocol chapters. This section explains how this case example could unfold in a real presentation, with each step explained.

Purpose

The purpose of this data story is to answer the stakeholder question of what marketing channels drive the most conversions, or sales in this case. I'll use a horizontal bar chart to represent the marketing channels as categories and rank them descending by conversion volume.

Insight

What happened? Paid search generated the largest share of conversions, followed by organic search, email, display ads, and social media.

What surprised us? Nothing initially; it's common for paid search to be a high-volume contributor of conversions.

Why did it happen? Paid search is the channel where adjusting the flow is the easiest, as our other marketing channels are either longer-term strategies or still getting up to speed with implementation and testing.

Recommendations? So far, it appears we should stay the course with our current marketing mix.

Stakes if no action? Not sure yet because our initial action appears to be to continue as before.

Not the most exciting story so far, I know, but that's because I haven't fully explored it using the next step. Here's where it gets interesting.

Context

We realized that looking at only conversion volume tells an incomplete story. When we pair conversions with conversion rate, we see that email is our most efficient marketing channel for converting customers, yet it's third in volume. We'll use a table lens to walk the audience through these two insights in succession.

This changes the story, so we update our insight journey.

What happened? Paid search generated the largest share of conversions, followed by organic search, email, display ads, and social media.

What surprised us? When we brought in conversion rate, email was our most efficient channel; however, it is only third in terms of conversion volume.

Why did it happen? When we dug into both channels, we found that paid search conversion rate declined by 12 percent during third quarter. We also learned that while our email click-to-open rate is well above our benchmark, our open rate is falling below target. This would explain the surprising shift in these channels.

What are the stakes? These trends will continue if we don't take action. Based on our best calculations of average order value, if we do nothing, we could continue to decline in conversion rate. Let's calculate what that would be.

What do we recommend?

- Review the least efficient ads and keywords of our paid search campaign to identify areas of improvement.
- Further analyze email campaigns for the last six months to identify our most effective subject lines and develop a new test plan.
- Research enhanced testing capabilities with our email platform.

Aesthetics

In addition to clean side-by-side bar charts, we will use our blue highlight color to first draw attention to Paid Search, but then change to highlight Email on the build slide.

Now I'm going to show you how this story sequence could play out on a series of presentation slides, complete with your live narration.

Exposition

"You asked us to take the temperature on which marketing channels produce the most conversions. We took a look and paid search is still in the lead with 42 percent of conversion volume.

"However, when we dug a bit deeper, we noticed something interesting. . ." [pause for dramatic effect]. See Figure 27.1.

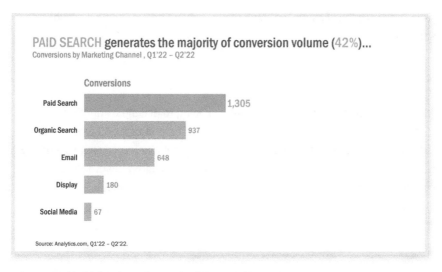

FIGURE 27.1 Marketing channel example slide: exposition
Source: Adapted from Analytics.com Q1'22- Q2'22

Rising Action

"We saw that email was our most efficient channel in driving sales, with a whopping conversion of 32%, and a threefold increase above paid search!" See Figure 27.2.

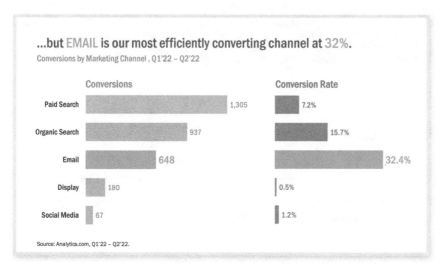

FIGURE 27.2 Marketing channel example slide: rising action
Source: Adapted from Analytics.com Q1'22- Q2'22

"Now, here are the reasons we think this is happening. . ." [explain reasons and show data].

Climax

"It appears that the paid search situation is going to decline by another 10 percent in the next three months. If we leave paid search and email where they are, by our best estimates it's possible we could be leaving approximately 6,200 sales on the table, which, using our average order value of $47, is a potential loss of over $291,000" [let that land with a brief pause]. See Figure 27.3.

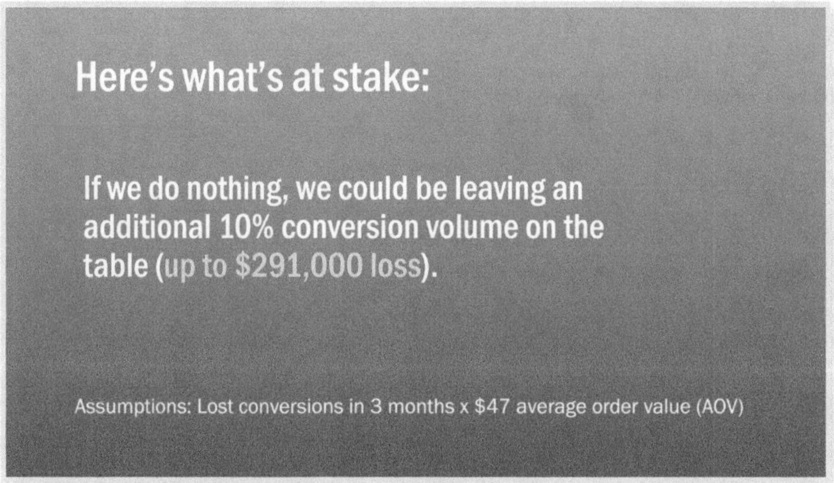

FIGURE 27.3 Marketing channel example slide: the stakes

Falling Action

"The good news is, we have several recommended plans of action to turn the tide on this trend and maximize our channels" [read your SMART recommendations]. Ideally, you're animating each of these table rows one step at a time with Object or Shape Pacing. See Figure 27.4.

Here's our recommended SMART solution:

	Specific	Measurable	Assigned	Relevant	Time-Bound
1	Review least efficient keywords of paid search campaign	Clicks, CTR, Conversion Rate	Search & Business Intelligence Teams	Declining paid search conversion rate	3 weeks
2	Analyze email campaign subject lines for the last 6 months	Open Rate, Conversions, Conversion Rate	Email Team	Declining email conversion volume	2 weeks
3	Approve email platform testing capabilities upgrade	Open Rate, Conversions, Conversion Rate	CMO	Declining email conversion volume	End of month

FIGURE 27.4 Marketing channel example slide: falling action (recommendation plan)

Resolution

"Alright everyone, let's talk about our game plan" [make your recommendations extra SMART].

That's the story! Do you see how this sequence verbally and visually takes the audience through a true narrative and visual journey, and not just a bunch of random charts? Remember, the goal of this approach is that by the time you reach your recommendations, your decision-makers are practically a yes!

Let's go through another example that will feature one of our not-so-common advanced chart types to illustrate a journey through a common data scenario.

Case Example #2: The Roguish Redesign

In this scene, your company redesigned the entire website layout template after months of planning and testing. The team eagerly awaits initial results of how the redesign impacted visitor behavior before and after implementation.

Purpose

You have been charged with presenting the results of a website redesign on page engagement and abandonment. You choose a slope graph with each line representing a web page to display the before and after performance results using the measure of single-visit abandonment.

Insight

What happened? The site redesign appeared to successfully reduce abandonment rate across the board for the main navigation pages.

What surprised us? The Contact Us page deviated from these results, where abandonment dramatically increased post-redesign.

Why did it happen? One possible reason is that the site redesign template didn't consider the layout shift in the submission form on the Contact Us page, which got pushed further down the page.

What are the stakes? This increase in abandonment could translate to losing an estimated 50 sales inquiries per month and $150,000 in potential sales within the next two to three months.

What do we recommend? Collaborating with the user experience (UX) team to test and improve the form layout and usability.

Context

Analyzing the voice of customer survey data shows a marked decrease in the satisfaction score of Contact Us visitors, which commentary further supports.

Aesthetics

Paint all the slope chart lines gray in the first slide and keep Contact Us hidden at first. Then reveal the build with Contact Us and emphasize it with a deep red color to show that this area needs immediate attention.

Since you're using a slope graph in this example, you'll need to train the audience in how to understand it. You can take more time during the exposition phase walking the audience through chart structure and then revealing the story piece-by-piece.

And now, for the presentation game-day script.

Exposition

"As you know, we completely rebranded and refreshed our website last quarter with many usability and design enhancements. We were asked to analyze how the update impacted the abandonment rate of primary navigation pages. Here are the pages we looked at. . ." [show blank slide with just the list of pages *except* for Contact Us]; see Figure 27.5.

FIGURE 27.5 Website redesign slope example: exposition 1
Source: Adapted from Analytics.com, 2021

Rising Action

"As you'll see in this visual, this order represents the pre-refresh abandonment rate of our primary pages, with the home page understandably first" [animate in the pre-update data points, data labels, and left axis and data labels]; see Figure 27.6.

[Reveal right side of slope graph and imagine you're a zoo tour guide leading them through an exhibit.] "Now, here on the right, we have the abandonment rates after the site was relaunched. We were pleased to see that abandonment decreased across all our main navigation pages by at least 10 basis points. . ." [reveal full lines and right side of the graph]; see Figure 27.7.

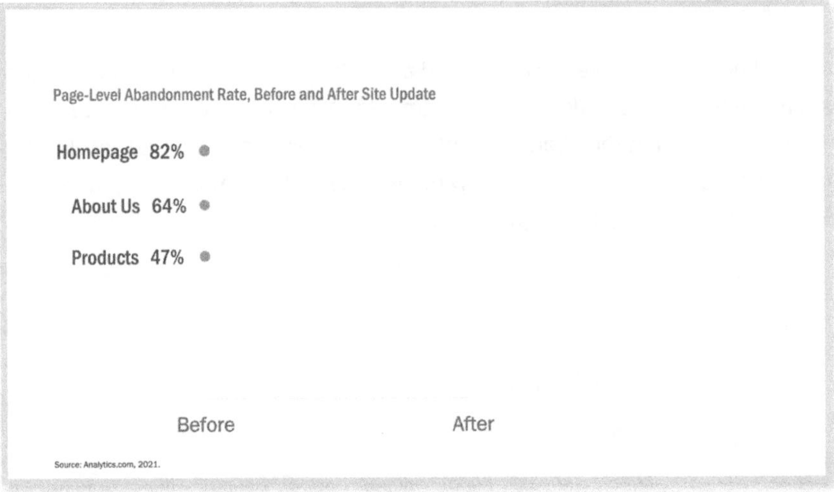

Page-Level Abandonment Rate, Before and After Site Update
Homepage 82%
About Us 64%
Products 47%
Before
After
Source: Analytics.com, 2021.

FIGURE 27.6 Website redesign slope example: rising action 1
Source: Adapted from Analytics.com, 2021

Page-Level Abandonment Rate, Before and After Site Update
Homepage 82%
About Us 64%
Products 47%
62%
54%
31%
Before
After
Source: Analytics.com, 2021.

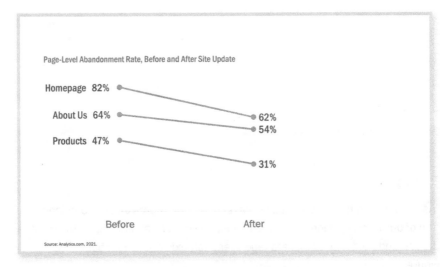

FIGURE 27.7 Website redesign slope example: rising action 2
Source: Adapted from Analytics.com, 2021

"We were especially happy to see how much abandonment on the home page dropped, from 82 percent to 62 percent! We credit the improved layout above the fold based on our survey feedback" [highlight the home page line and labels in blue to emphasize]; see Figure 27.8.

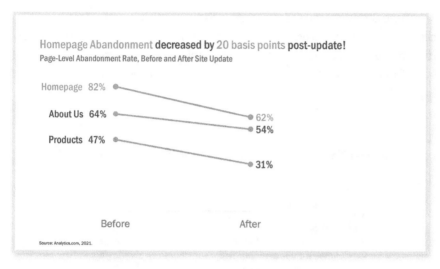

FIGURE 27.8 Website redesign slope example: rising action 3
Source: Adapted from Analytics.com, 2021

"It was great to see every primary page improve. . .except for one. One of our pages actually *increased* in abandonment after the update. Can anyone guess what that is?" [Pause and wait, which creates anticipation and participation.]

"It's the Contact Us page! We saw a 27 percent increase in abandonment after the update. Upon closer look, we noticed that the site update drastically impacted the layout and visibility of the contact form, possibly driving down form completion" [reveal the next slide with this twist]; see Figure 27.9.

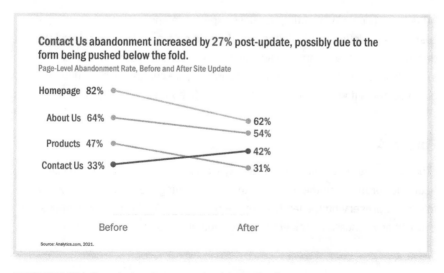

FIGURE 27.9 Website redesign slope example: rising action 4
Source: Adapted from Analytics.com, 2021

"When we checked our voice of customer data, we saw a marked decrease in customer satisfaction scores for those who encountered the Contact Us page or came to the site to contact us. Here are several pieces of commentary that stood out. . ." [show pertinent comments and animate them in one at a time]; see Figure 27.10.

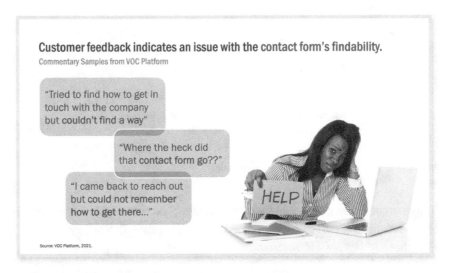

FIGURE 27.10 Website redesign slope example: climax (stakes)
Source: Wordley Calvo Stock / Adobe Stock

Climax

"This issue is clearly affecting our user experience and potentially costing us customers. It definitely won't improve if we do nothing. We've calculated that this increase in abandonment can translate to losing an estimated 50 sales inquiries per month If we don't take action now, we could lose $150,000 in potential sales if we let this go for another 2–3 months." See Figure 27.11.

Falling Action

"That's why we recommend immediately working with the UX team to run a heuristics protocol on the page and then test moving the form back above the fold while preserving the features of the refresh" [reveal recommendations and address any concerns or objections your audience has]; see Figure 27.12.

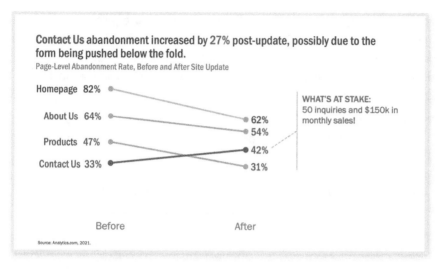

FIGURE 27.11 Website redesign slope example: climax (stakes)
Source: Adapted from Analytics.com, 2021

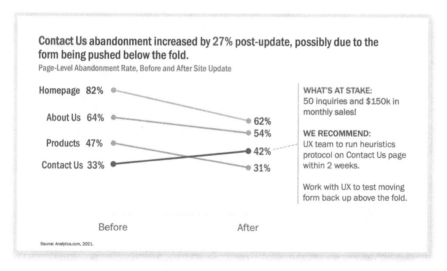

FIGURE 27.12 Website redesign slope example: falling action (recommendation plan)
Source: Adapted from Analytics.com, 2021

Resolution

"Alright everyone, what are we doing, how do we do it, who's going to do it, and by when?" And your story is a wrap.

These stories were told using cinematic storytelling techniques including suspense and climax, while visual tools used gradual reveals and color emphasis. In Act IV, I further explore strategies for building suspense.

I hope you're beginning to see how all aspects of this process coalesce here in the PICA Protocol and how you can apply it to any data scenario you can possibly dream of. While the PICA Protocol can feel like a lot of new steps to remember, just try to implement what stands out to you first, master that, and keep building on using the full toolbox.

As a bonus, Figure 27.13 shows how you can reformat this story into a single view that would be more email or print-friendly for an offline audience handout.

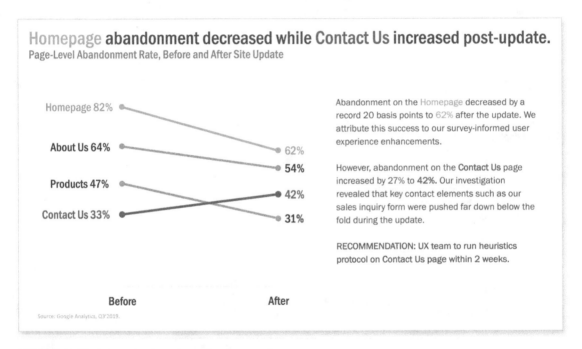

FIGURE 27.13 Single-page handout view of the slope graph
Source: Adapted from Google analytics Q3' 2019

You should now see that the PICA Protocol can be consistently applied across multiple data types, scenarios, and chart types. Implementing a new paradigm like this always has bumps in the beginning, but with diligent practice, it will lead you to smooth sailing through your data presentations.

Sandbox Assignment

■ Take your completed PICA Protocol prescription and build your slides to tell the story in the most powerful way possible.

Act III Intermission

You've now experienced the intersection between the data planning and story principles of Act I and the simple and intentional design techniques of Act II. You'll use this paradigm to visually communicate each of the insights in your presentation, remembering that they should all be able to hook onto the overarching throughline and purpose of the presentation.

You're at the three-quarters mark, rounding the corner into our final phase on effective public speaking and communication.

Let's review the flow of steps of how to visualize your data stories once more.

- Identify your visual's PURPOSE. Use keywords in the exploratory conversation to confirm its reason for existence and choose the most appropriate chart.
- Surface the INSIGHT. Use the insight journey questions with slide builds that foster anticipation, and take your audience on an adventure, starting from what happened through to your solution.
- Use CONTEXT to strengthen and deepen the storyline. Investigate your story using segmentation, timeframe, benchmarks, and other contextual inputs to provide the most complete picture for decision-making.
- Apply data visualization AESTHETIC principles to your charts by reducing what doesn't matter and emphasizing what does.
- Use the Chart Choosing Guide (Figure 23.14) to determine the optimal visual for your data and message.
- Stay mindful of data visualization violations and ethical dilemmas.

Act IV: Deliver

Public Speaking, Preparation, and Communication Mastery

Why Does Delivery Even Matter?

28

"People will forget what you said, people will forget what you did, but people will never forget how you made them feel."

—Maya Angelou

Remember that cautionary tale from the beginning of the book, about my colleague who struck out big time with our executives during a major media presentation? One of the reasons it was so painful to witness was not just from empathizing with my own challenging experiences, but because I knew just how talented and capable my colleague was at his job.

Unfortunately, this seemed lost on the people calling the shots on our projects and our careers. To them, he possibly appeared unprepared and unconfident in his material, and their discomfort was visible. I wish it had been the last time I'd observed something like that, but it wasn't.

Throughout these last two decades of delivering and attending presentations, I have watched some presenters successfully win the audience over with their confidence, poise, and attunement to their needs. And I've seen other presenters create wildly uncomfortable tension and discord when they arrive nervous, unprepared, and defensive to audience commentary.

Presentation delivery mastery will separate those who carve the career trajectory of their dreams and those who will remain on the hamster wheel of data squirreldom.

But what does delivery mastery entail exactly? There are many directions to pursue in public speaking, so I've worked to give you the simplest, most practical blueprint without going to unreasonable measures.

I've identified several key areas that notably influence the outcomes of data presentations:

- You (your practices, patterns, and mindsets)
- Your audience (their beliefs, biases, and behaviors)

This act isn't like the others. You're going spelunking into the cavernous depths of what makes you tick and ticked off in the conference room.

Chapter Recap

- How you deliver your insights is crucial to winning the trust of your decision-makers.
- There are two key areas to master: yourself and your audience.

Practice Like the Pros

29

"By failing to prepare, you are preparing to fail."

—Benjamin Franklin

There are umpteen reasons why we want to hit the ball out of the office park with our presentation audience. We want to inform them, delight them, and create an impact. But from my research and experience, the greatest drive to do this well is something that drives most of our human behavior: **fear**.

There is an urban legend in the presentation sphere that the foremost fear of humans is public speaking, ranked higher than *death*. However imprecise or implausible this statement is, I believe there is a smoking gun here.

While there are numerous contributing factors to why we get thrown off our game, there's one that I'd like to focus upon first. I believe it's the number-one cause of presentation meltdowns; can you guess what that is?

It's. . .nerves! Nervous stress is the great conference room equalizer; those shaky hands, sweaty palms, sudden dry throat, and strangled voice are dead giveaways that we aren't confident in delivering our material.

And while we may be supremely confident in our numbers, remembering everything we want to say about them and staying cool in front of a stone-faced group of very important people is an entirely different animal.

The Cure for Presentation Nerves

What's a jittery presenter to do? The answer is quite simple, yet many find themselves completely blocked from hearing it. You may have heard the famous musical theater adage, and it absolutely applies here:

Practice, practice, practice!

Yes, yes, yes! Practice and preparation are the master keys of delivery mastery. I believe that if you practice every presentation three times, you will be infinitely more confident during showtime. That's because practice uses the maintenance rehearsal principle I mentioned with regard to recapping information. The act of practice is recapping your presentation to your own brain!

The third time's the charm for me because, at that point, I begin to integrate my material in a way that I can speak through it with confidence and ease. When I look back at my most nerve-wracking presentations, the common thread was my unpreparedness.

If you aren't available to practice three times, make an effort to practice at least once more than you practice already. And for many of us. . .*that's just one time*.

If a presenter loses track of their thoughts due to lack of preparation, they're not the only one who suffers. This creates palpable tension and a disconnect from the audience, who can visibly detect the speaker struggling to find their footing.

Now, I'm not suggesting that you memorize your readouts like you would for a TED Talk. I'm suggesting that you take your slides and talk through each one as if you were presenting live. **The first time you speak through your deck should not be the live presentation.** If there's one thing I've learned the hard way, quickly glancing through your deck 10 minutes before the meeting is *not* sufficient practice.

Luckily, I have a hack for you. Remember how I had you speak through your talking points and place them in the PowerPoint speaker notes box in Act I? That counts as one practice round! Of course, I recommend going through it again at least once or twice before showtime. But at least you're not going in completely ice cold.

Now, you might be feeling resistance to my plea for practice. The first complaint I usually hear from my students is that they don't have time to prepare. When this presentation was due yesterday and we're still finalizing the figures, how can we be expected to stop what we're doing and practice?

I'm quite familiar with this objection and without a mindset shift, it's going to be your archnemesis. The following sections outline the steps I've taken to adequately prepare.

Make Presentation Practice Non-Negotiable

Humans are suffering from a pervasive scarcity mindset around time. The busyness trap does have a vice grip on our schedules; I would argue, though, that this grip is part reality, part perception. I'm going to dispense a dose of tough love once again.

We make time for the things that matter to us.

For most of us, practice simply isn't a non-negotiable step in our presentation process yet, which makes it unlikely to happen. But it can be likely if we get creative. Here's the mindset I used to help me indoctrinate practice as a habit:

When we give presentations, we are required to bring certain components as the "price of entry" to show up to the conference room and start speaking. Those components are typically yourself and your presentation deck (and often, your computer). The presentation can't happen without those things, right?

What if another price of entry was that you could not enter that room without having practiced your presentation three times? Imagine being asked by a mystical gatekeeper at the door saying, "Did you practice thy session thrice?" And if the answer were nay, you'd be turned away. As in, *come back when you're ready.*

I'm sure both you—and your awaiting stakeholders—would not be too thrilled at your inability to present. If the stakes were that high, you would find a way to make practice a necessary part of the process. So, the first thing that needs to shift is your perception of *how important practice is.*

Once you make this shift, you'll see how time magically shifts as well. Each of our days is compiled of our ingrained habits, behaviors, and obligations that appear non-negotiable. That includes everything from attending endless meetings, checking email, brushing our teeth, brewing coffee, biting our nails, catching up on social media, and so on.

Some of these activities are essential to continuing business and life. But some are more flexible than we realize, and some are not essential at all. These habitual minutes add up, and yet, we while them away in ways we don't see because they are *unconscious* fixtures of our daily life. I call this the "time scarcity trap."

When you begin to look at your day with a conscious eye, you start to see pockets of time reveal themselves.

- If you eat lunch, you have time to practice.
- If you skip to the coffee shop for a 30-minute double venti macchiato break, you have time to practice.
- If you catch yourself mindlessly scrolling your Facebook wall or Instagram feed in the afternoon, you have time to practice.
- If your schedule is routinely snapped up by random last-minute-yet-not-necessary work meetings, you have time to practice.
- If you own a TV and it's plugged in, you have time to practice.

Are you getting it yet?

The solution to the time scarcity trap is reevaluating your day and seeing that there is more time available than you realize. Ideally, you'll maintain a proper work–life balance and not use personal or family time to rehearse. But sometimes, the sacrifices I made were worth striding into my meeting with ease if there was simply no other time available. Now let's talk about making the time available for practice.

- **Pencil it in:** The most effective strategy I have for guaranteeing practice time is scheduling it. I block off time on my calendar a day or two before the session. Then it's no longer at risk of being hijacked by marauding meetings or encroaching coworkers. The time simply becomes unavailable, and other people's needs magically adjust to accommodate.

    Better yet, book a conference room for your practice run to test the technical stack. Better *better* yet, invite colleagues or teammates who may attend the meeting for more realistic practice and feedback.

- **Roll back the tape:** I discovered another excellent trick for practicing my talks entirely by accident. To prepare for my first conference keynote speech, I decided to record myself so I could listen to it during my commute instead of awkwardly reciting it out loud in public. Since it was my own voice, listening counted as a form of practice, and I found myself integrating the content into my brain much faster.

    The bonus benefit was that I could evaluate my speaking ability from a third-person perspective, and I was shocked by what I heard—more on that in Chapter 30.

When Practice Makes Perfect

There are several reasons why Carmine Gallo cites the Macworld iPhone announcement as the best presentation of all time. Yes, Steve Jobs expertly wove in cinematic storytelling techniques and psychological triggers like a dramatic setup and surprising twists. But the true magic isn't what happened on the stage that day; it's what happened for months *beforehand*.

A former Apple employee reported that Jobs rehearsed his keynote for weeks in advance, spending entire days prepping on stage.[1] By showtime, his delivery was so impeccable that it felt like a part of him. When you know your material so well that your deck becomes an extension of you and not a script, that's what I call *integration*.

Now, most of us don't have the luxury of prepping a single presentation for months and are not delivering it in a dramatic high-stakes environment like Macworld. But that doesn't mean we wouldn't massively benefit from assimilating practice into our routine.

When we learn to treat preparation as an immovable object in the process, real magic happens with our confidence in the conference room.

It just takes. . .practice.

Chapter Recap

- Presentation nerves are the number-one reason why we lose our confidence, and this can create trust issues with the audience.
- Lack of preparation is the number-one reason we get swallowed by presentation nerves.
- Presenters often overlook practice and preparation because they don't consider them required steps in the process.
- Preparation is a habit that requires advanced planning and effort.

---

[1] www.theguardian.com/technology/2006/jan/05/newmedia.media1

Refine Your Speech Patterns

30

"It usually takes me more than three weeks to prepare a good impromptu speech."
—*Mark Twain*

One of the most common misconceptions is the myth of the "natural" speaker, meaning that all successful speakers possess an innate talent for perfect rhetoric, oratory skills, and stage presence. This couldn't be further from the truth.

The truth is, there are no "natural speakers." There are only natural-*sounding* speakers.

Prosody is a fancy word for the cadence (vocal pitch) and inflection (emphasis) of our speech. It wields influence upon the interpretation our audience makes of our insights, trustworthiness, and credibility. I'll prove it with the help of an example from an American English pronunciation expert named Rachel Smith. Read the following sentence out loud in the most monotone, robotic voice possible:

I didn't say he stole the money.

Now read these next lines out loud and emphasize the highlighted word. As you do so, notice your interpretation each time:

I didn't say he stole the money.

I ***didn't*** say he stole the money.

I didn't ***say*** he stole the money.

I didn't say ***he*** stole the money.

I didn't say he ***stole*** the money.

I didn't say he stole ***the*** money.

I didn't say he stole the ***money***.

It's the same sentence, yet you likely took away seven different interpretations of it simply based on the inflection point. That's how important it is to examine our speech patterns when becoming a voice of influence. Beyond inflection, there are several common patterns to be aware of.

Remember **how you recorded your presentation to practice?** You can also use it to diagnose interfering speech patterns. This was the unexpected benefit I experienced when I recorded my first keynote. I suggest you listen to the recording three separate times to identify these irritating "earwigs," discussed next.

Hyperspeed

The first delivery critique I ever received, delivered by my high school public speaking teacher, was that I talked *way* too fast. This is the most prevalent issue I hear with the untrained speakers I work with, especially in younger generations.

Since most of us have never listened to ourselves speak, we have no idea that we're rattling-off-facts-and-figures-a-mile-a-minute because we-just-wanna-get-the-heck-out-of-there! That's understandable, considering how uncomfortable these meetings can feel. Having faith in ourselves is a big first step in overcoming the nerves that feed hyperspeed, but refining the pattern is also important.

The solution: slow it down. Like, Barry White slow. Listen to three minutes of your recording and observe your speed. If you find it hard to follow you or you're feeling agitated, it's time to slow down. Write down several speedy sentences and practice repeating them slower and slower.

Take care to enunciate each word. Slow down until you sound a bit *too* slow, and then gradually speed things up to a pace that feels a bit slower than where you started. The more you practice, the more confident and relaxed you'll become.

Filler Words

Our modern language is rife with meaningless words like *um, ah, well, oh, so,* and *you know.* These are called *filler words,* and because they have no substance or meaning, they create noise. While a moderate number of filler words in our speech is natural, if the ratio of noise (filler words) to "signal" (real words) gets too high, you're in trouble.

Excessive filler words are like audible slide fluff; they add to the cognitive load of our listening audience, which makes them work to parse out meaningful content. They also expose our nervousness. Examining this and finding the right ratio is key to progressing as a speaker.

The solution: embrace the pause. Just like filler words are like slide fluff, pauses in speech are like the white space of a slide. Intentional pauses allow the audience's brain to breathe and focus on your information. Here's what to do:

Listen to that recording again, and this time, count the number of filler words you say in three minutes of speech. Restate those sentences and omit as many filler words as you can. Continue this practice of creating awareness and removing them. And keep an eye on your filler word frequency while you are engaging in conversations with people throughout your day.

Now, we often use filler words to delay responding to an audience question that's stumped us. I suggest a new practice: respond with, "What an insightful question, let me think for a moment. . ." and then take an intentional pause for two to four seconds. This is an act of strategy and compassion toward yourself; we tend to give ourselves much less time to respond to a question than we'd give others.

Pausing has several benefits.

- You'll appear more thoughtful to the audience.
- You create anticipation (which snaps them to attention).
- They may give your answer more weight when you arrive at it.
- It buys you time to think and prevent interruptions because the audience will be anticipating your answer.

Uptalk and Vocal Fry

There's this thing people do when they end every sentence by trailing their voice upward? As if they're asking a question even though it's a statement? This is called *uptalk*, and it's a prevalent yet irritating speech pattern? (If those question marks threw you off there, that is the exact effect uptalk has on listeners.)

Uptalk, also known as *upspeak* and *high rising terminal* (HRT), is the pattern of ending statements with an upward inflection, indicating a question. It's deadly in corporate meetings because it causes confusion about whether the speaker is asking a question or making a statement.

A survey conducted by Pearson of 700 corporate supervisors reported that 85 percent of respondents found uptalk to indicate insecurity and emotional weakness, while 57 percent said that it could potentially hurt an employee's chances at a promotion or raise.[1] I can't imagine anyone would want an uncon-scious speech pattern factoring into their annual performance review or bonus!

Uptalk is frequently paired with another pattern called *vocal fry*, which is when we speak from our lowest register (a range of vocal tones). What the heck did I just say there? Take a moment and say "I went to the store" out loud but say it in the lowest voice you can. It will likely sound like your words are scraping through gravel, with a fast, popping sound that can be unpleasant to an audience's ears.

While uptalk and vocal fry are by no means wrong, it's worth reviewing and refining your speech for a smoother audience listening experience.

The solution: practice putting closure in your speech and speaking in a normal range. Whip out that recording one more time and listen for uptalk and vocal fry, especially together. Repeat those sentences until you have them in a mid-range register and properly ending downward.

Now, one reason we use uptalk is that we're afraid we'll be interrupted. This can be managed with conscious communication skills. If I am repeatedly interrupted or cut off, I gently raise my hand and say in a calm voice, "If I may continue," or, "Almost finished, thank you!" in a patient and friendly tone.

> **TIP**
>
> **EXTRA CREDIT**
> Search YouTube for a video called *What Is Vocal Fry & Is It Bad For You?* by Seeker to understand the downsides of these patterns.

Get "Fun-Comfortable" with This Process

You may feel resistance during the recording and examination process for a common reason. In the beginning, I felt nauseous hearing myself talk; listening to my own voice used to be like hearing dragon talons dragged down a chalkboard.

I pushed through this discomfort in the early days of my podcast when I had to edit it myself and even had to confront this when extracting podcast sound bytes for this book! My advice is to push through that discomfort and examine what is bothersome about your speech.

Do you sound too high-pitched? Watch some YouTube videos on expanding your lower vocal registers.

---

[1] www.dailymail.co.uk/sciencetech/article-2538554/Want-promotion-Dont-speak-like-AUSSIE-Rising-pitch-end-sentences-make-sound-insecure.html

Do you stumble over your words? Practice those words over and over until they come out silky smooth.

Get comfortable with being uncomfortable and focus on where you need to grow. I promise it won't kill you, and it *will* make you stronger on stage.

Enlist Some AI Assistance

Recording yourself and examining your speech is invaluable yet challenging for many. But you don't have to do it on your own. This is where technology shines! There are fabulous mobile apps that can act as speaking and accountability coaches using the power of artificial intelligence.

My app of choice is Speeko. Speeko (www.speeko.co) reminds me every day to practice vocal tune-ups and can help you detect hyperspeed, filler words, and uptalk! It makes this otherwise uncomfortable process easy and even fun, and it has dramatically improved my speech without hiring a five-figure speaking coach.

Becoming a natural-sounding speaker is a process of practice until mastery, just like any other physical, verbal, or technical skill. While some of us may possess an innate ability to speak, it does not mean that those without that innate ability can't groom themselves to be powerful and effective speakers.

They most certainly can.

Chapter Recap

- Speech patterns such as hyperspeed, filler words, uptalk, and vocal fry are worth identifying and refining.
- Nerves create vocal and facial tension, which is alleviated through conditioning.

Master Your Mind and Body

31

"If you think you're too small to be anything, you have never been in the dark with a mosquito."

—*Betty Reese*

I hope you now understand that preparation is a game-changer in defusing that sweaty-palm bomb waiting to go off the moment you lose your train of thought while presenting. Yet even the most prepared presenter can lose their cool during a meeting for a seemingly endless array of worries or "thought forms", such as these:

- I'm terrified before even going in the room!
- Ack, I can't remember what comes next!
- I'm an imposter, and they'll realize I'm a fraud!
- They're asking me difficult questions!
- They don't get me! They don't get what I do!
- Why are they looking at me like that?
- Why isn't my clicker working?

Experiencing just one of these thoughts can scramble your egg yolk; imagine the compound effect of multiple, and you have a frantic frittata in your brain. Thankfully, there are strategies to prevent this death spiral. I'm going to unpack some of these pests and empower you with a new mental survival kit.

I'm Terrified Before Even Going in There!

This is a big one, yet are several solutions to this problem.

Solution: A Pre-presentation Ritual or Routine

If you aren't already familiar with the term *state mastery*, now is the time. *State mastery* is the act of pursuing practices that enable you to master your emotional "state" during stressful moments.

One of the most helpful things I learned from watching the world's great speakers was building a ritual and then doing it every single time before I speak. During my workshops, I ask participants what they do to relax when they're stressed out.

The range of answers impressively clusters around exercise, meditation, reading, music, breathwork, and even hanging with a pet. Many of those are my go-to tools for getting grounded before the big day. Now they can be yours.

Solution: Exercise

As far as health benefits go, exercise hardly needs an introduction. However, it's particularly beneficial for priming the body and mind for speaking. Exercise increases blood flow to the brain, improves cognitive function, and releases endorphins, which relieve stress. And it helps melt the congealed blob we become by sitting at our desks all day.

Exercise can also be a good luck charm. My dear friend and digital marketing expert Eric Feinberg told me that before every conference keynote, he does exactly 22 pushups. No more, no less. It's Eric's ritual, and his commitment to it ensures that he generates the exact amount of energy and blood flow he needs to bring down the house without breaking a sweat.

If I'm speaking at a conference, I do 10 minutes of vigorous movement and yoga in my hotel room before heading down to the stage. You can try jumping on the treadmill in your company gym or taking a brisk walk around the office park.

I find that a jolt of exercise helps me start the meeting with higher energy, remember my speaking points better, and field questions with greater ease.

Just be sure not to overexert yourself to the point where you're breathless and sweating through your shirt or you might worry your audience.

Solution: Meditation

The scientific evidence is mounting on how even a few minutes of meditation activates the parasympathetic nervous system, or the side of our nervous system that keeps you cool. I use an app called Calm (www.calm.com) that has countless meditations ranging from two minutes to several hours long.

Everyone can find two extra minutes somewhere, and the rewards you'll reap in your state of calm will be noticeable. Other great apps to try are Shine (www.theshineapp.com), Insight Timer (insighttimer.com), and Aura (www.aurahealth.io).

Solution: Breathwork

Remember breathing? That bodily function where air enters your lungs and keeps you alive? The function that inconveniently appears to cease when you're asked a question that you totally don't have the answer to?

When we experience anxiety, our biology triggers a survival mechanism to take shorter, shallower breaths or even hold breath in.[1] Here's the thing: our breath is just about the only thing we have control over in life. And feeling any sort of control over a provocative situation alleviates anxiety fast.

Simply being aware of your breath is a powerful regulation tool on its own. When I notice I'm off-center, I use a breathwork technique called the "Box Breath," used in high-stress occupations like the military. It was popularized by former Navy SEAL Commander Mark Divine to regulate the nervous system and improve concentration.[2] The basic idea is that you inhale for four counts, hold for four, exhale for four, and hold out for four. It works fast!

You can also try pressing on an acupressure point called the *inner frontier gate*, which is about two fingers down your wrist from your palm. Gently massaging this point supposedly brings your autonomic nervous system back into balance, the way those cruise ship bracelets help with seasickness.

---

[1] www.healthline.com/health/shortness-of-breath-anxiety
[2] www.medicalnewstoday.com/articles/321805

Now, about these techniques: whether you believe that acupressure or breath-work or rituals work, what *will* work is the conscious action you take to notice your state and regain your composure. Belief is a powerful ally in emotional agility, and if you believe you are taking an action to regain control, there's a good chance you will gain control.

Why Are They Looking at Me Like That?

Visual cues that you or your information isn't landing with your audience are utterly unnerving. That scrunched-up brow and downturned mouth may feel worse than if your stakeholders are verbally questioning your analysis.

I know those befuddled or checked-out expressions seem to send home a painful message: you are confusing me! You are boring! I hate your presentation! While they are unlikely true, those messages can dismantle the confidence of even the most advanced practitioner.

When you observe an audience member with a negative-looking expression, you have several options:

- **Imagine a different possible story.** That frowny face may speak to you of disagreement and frustration, but it's also possible that *it's just their face*. Take note of their expressions throughout meetings when you're not presenting. You may find that pensive is their default setting.

- **Get more information.** If you've just dropped a bomb that the stakeholder's beloved ad campaign drastically underperformed expectations, allow for a moment of silence to pass so they can process the information and then ask the room how the news lands for them. You'll likely find out that they need clarification, *not* that they hate you or think you're confusing.

- **Let it go.** Accept that your information is not going to make everyone happy or satisfied. The audience is responsible for sharing their thoughts and feelings, but they are sometimes too shy to speak up. Make sure they have ample opportunity to express themselves, and then leave the rest up to them.

■ **Find friendly faces.** I use this strategy to overcome the stone-face effect, especially if the audience is unfamiliar. I locate three friendly, approachable-looking faces in the real or virtual room early in the session. I try to space them out around the room and make direct eye contact with them, which also gives the impression that you're addressing the entire audience. Look for the head-nodders for the confidence boost you need to stay in flow.

I Can't Remember What Comes Next!

Even when you've prepared for your presentation, it's still possible to blank out on the next content. That's why I'm a proponent of using the Presenter View of your presentation tool whenever possible.

Presenter View is the crystal ball and teleportation device through your deck, enabling you with a vastly greater degree of navigational control as a speaker.

I'm No Expert/They're Going to See I'm a Fraud!

I saved this gem for last because it is one of the most difficult obstacles to overcome. Every single practitioner and presenter I've ever spoken with has at some point done battle with a sinister villain that lives within: **Imposter Syndrome**.

Imposter Syndrome is a simmering cauldron of critical self-talk and the arch-nemesis of a presenter's confidence. My Imposter Syndrome reared its diabolical head while I was preparing for my first industry conference keynote in 2014. I had been invited to speak at a software provider summit after dreaming of stepping on stage for years. I couldn't believe I finally had the chance to share my knowledge about information communication at a real live conference!

But I soon realized how bold and risky it was for me, a conference newbie, to present about presenting. No pressure, right? I imagined all kinds of horrifying scenarios: being booed, the audience throwing conveniently stowed rotten heirloom tomatoes, or a giant cane pulling me off stage. Why? Because

I believed I didn't deserve to be up there. Who was I to tell anyone anything? Didn't they already know all of this?

It turns out, I was not alone. These thought forms are called *limiting beliefs*, and they plague practitioners and presenters from all walks of corporate life. These are the most common limiting beliefs that I encounter:

- "I'm not a good speaker."
- "Everyone already knows this."
- "I have nothing unique to offer."
- "They're going to realize I'm not that smart."
- Or in my case, "I'm a nobody."

Later I realized that these beliefs are myths, and left unbusted, they will stunt the confidence and full potential of perfectly capable presenters.

Solution: Affirmation Mantras

An *affirmation* is the act of confirming something that we want to believe, most often a positive statement. A *mantra* is a word or phrase repeated to aid concentration during meditation. These two combine forces where you repeat positive statements to shift a limiting belief into an optimistic outlook.

Affirmation mantras are an easy yet mighty way to send those beliefs packing. They empower you to become your own fierce cheerleader *from the inside*. These are the mantras that helped me:

- "I have something valuable the audience needs."
- "I was asked to present because I am an expert in this matter."
- "No one else has the unique perspective I bring to the table."
- "I am here to serve, and the audience wants to see me win at that."

Every time I felt my imposter creeping up on me, I stopped and repeated my mantras until it was showtime. I wrote them on sticky notes and stuck them to my mirror. This reminded me to recite them each day until I could speak with full conviction.

My effort paid off: I delivered my insights to the best of my abilities, and the audience responded favorably; the talk became one of this company's top-rated summit sessions ever! I could see that I had valuable information for the audience and transmitted it in a way that inspired them to care.

Believe That Nerves Are OK

I will offer one last nugget: give yourself permission to be nervous. Nerves are a healthy stress adaptation that shows you care about how your insights and ideas will help your audience succeed.

Whenever I'm feeling nervous and it's not from lack of preparation, **I channel it into enthusiasm and excitement for serving my audience**. I'll even speak aloud how I'm feeling with, "Ooh, I'm feeling so nervous because I can't wait to see how my audience is going to use the new tools I'm about to share!"

Channeling nerves this way demonstrates passion. When you believe in the work that you do and how your insights will serve, that belief comes through in your tone and body language. Passion draws the audience in and opens their eyes to the landscape of your world. Carmine Gallo says:

"People cannot inspire others unless and until they are inspired themselves. Science shows that passion is contagious, literally. You cannot inspire others unless you are inspired yourself."[3]

It may take time, but you can overcome your limiting beliefs with affirmation work and striking the match of your passion's flame. Thanks to affirmations, I came to believe that I deserved to be up on that stage and the stage responded in kind.

Your nerves don't have to be your downfall; harness them as a tool for exploring yourself and as an ally for fueling your passion.

Sound Body, Sound Mind

Yet another crucial area of speaking is how we involve our body. The following sections include some quick tips for mastering nonverbal cues, gestures, and movement for a more masterful speaking experience.

---

[3]Carmine Gallo, Talk Like TED: The 9 Public-Speaking Secrets of the World's Top Minds

Say Cheese!

Smiling is a natural reflexive facial response to something that feels good. Because data presentations can feel nerve-wracking, tense, and downright distressing, smiles can be elusive creatures.

Research suggests that people can "hear" you smile, even if they can't see you.[4] In a study conducted by the University of Portsmouth, Dr. Amy Drahota discovered that listeners not only can hear when a speaker is smiling, but they can even distinguish between different *types* of smiles![5] So go ahead and flash those pearly whites whether in person or on screen; you and your audience will feel better for it.

Mind Your Hands

Have you ever seen a presenter speak while keeping their arms glued to their sides and feet cemented to the stage? Even though we typically use hand gestures by nature in day-to-day conversation, presentation nerves often cut the connection to our extremities. This is because an activated sympathetic nervous system can cause us to dissociate (or "detach") from our body, where we speak only from our head in a strained and robotic manner.

Hands are a visual extension of our words, used to emphasize or reinforce what we're saying; gestures send subconscious signals to the audience that you are confident, passionate, and engaging with them.

So, if something gets you excited or fired up, relax and show it! Wave your hands to demonstrate just how grand something is or how minute. Gesture toward your slides to show the audience exactly where they should look. Movement also draws the audience's attention, which helps them keep their eyes on you and not secretly on their inbox.

Watch Your Posture

Remember how annoying it was to hear your mom (or doting parent) harp on your slouching and insist that you sit up straight? Well, thank her now because

---

[4]www.discovermagazine.com/mind/you-can-hear-a-smile-when-you-do-youll-smile-back

[5]www.sciencedirect.com/science/article/abs/pii/S0167639307001732?via%3Dihub

she must have been preparing you for a career in public speaking! Here's what to become aware of:

- **Stand or sit up straight.** A straight posture is a quiet signal of confidence for anyone trying to inhabit a role in the spotlight.

- **Don't stand still.** In my early pro speaking days, I was so nervous that I would cement my feet behind the podium and impersonate a talking tree. Now I make sure to cover the entire stage, pausing on one side for a few minutes and then gradually crossing over. This ensures the audience feels fully addressed without distracting them with excessive movement.

- **Face the audience.** One of my biggest in-person pet peeves is when the presenter mostly talks to the projection screen instead of the audience. This muffles the voice and forces the audience to gaze at your back.

- **Don't fidget.** Toe-tapping, pencil-chewing, and leg wiggling are clear indicators of ungrounded nerves and are perceptible to the audience.

Effective presentation delivery is about more than just saying the words and showing the slides. Learn to become aware of and master your fears and engage your body, and you'll begin to embody the calm and confident speaker that you—and your audience—desires for you to be.

Chapter Recap

- Rituals and grounding practices help you master your state before going in.
- Affirmation mantras can be an antidote to Imposter Syndrome.
- Manageable nerves are normal and a healthy sign that you care about your audience.
- Being mindful of hand gestures, posture, and facial expressions are key to leveraging the power of body language while speaking.

Master Your Audience and Overcome Challenging Communication

32

"The art of communication is the language of leadership."

—James Humes

"How can we be confident in these spend and efficiency projections?"

"Why do these ads (that we do not control) look like that?"

"How do these results compare to Q3-2016 (or some other random date very far back)?"

"Can't we just skip to the X,Y,Z sections?"

"How do we stack up to our industry benchmark?"

Any of these questions sound familiar? I'm often asked why our decision-makers say the darndest things during presentations—asking impossible questions, repeatedly interrupting, and even undermining our authority on the subject. It can make presenting data feel pretty darn unfulfilling.

No matter how skillful we are at analyzing, designing, or speaking, true mastery of the presentation experience comes from how we handle the dialogue inspired—or incited—by our insights. Our first instinct may be to fire back clever and searing retorts at the peanut gallery, but that never leads to anywhere productive.

That's why this chapter's going to feel a little different from the rest; it isn't going to teach you how to gain the upper hand on an antagonistic audience member. You'll learn what's at the root of confrontational commentary so that you can do two things during challenging moments:

- Cultivate compassion and empathy
- Deftly maneuver the conversation and come out a winner

I begin by shelving preconceived notions about why audiences challenge us.

It's All About Needs

This may be incredibly hard to believe, but the confrontational behavior you observe may have nothing to do with you. It's unlikely that your stakeholders want to take you down or make you a department laughingstock; it's more likely that either:

- Their needs are not getting met or won't get met
- They *believe* their needs are not getting met or won't get met

These are two different situations; however, the outcome is the same because in both cases, they *perceive* their needs are not met. And everything in every aspect of human relational life boils down to needs. Everything. That's why the key to conquering challenging conversations is communicating in a way that gets to the heart of and acknowledges what they need.

Answering Challenging Questions

One of the most wonderful tools I've been blessed to receive in this life is a toolset called nonviolent communication, or NVC for short. NVC was created by conflict-resolution expert Marshall Rosenberg.[1] I can honestly attest that its principles have changed my presentation outcomes as well as every relational aspect of my life. Its cornerstones include compassion, curiosity, and empathy and is emphatic on meeting the needs of others.

One of the core tenets of NVC is learning to "see" others and understand their needs, not just to visually see their physical presence but to understand them from the inside. NVC champions radical compassion toward any mindset or behavior, no matter how infuriating. It doesn't promote coddling or not holding someone accountable but leads with empathy and understanding.

If you take one thing from this entire Act, it would be to do this whenever someone poses a challenging question or disagreeable comment:

Always acknowledge them first. It doesn't matter how annoying, crazy, or just plain wrong someone's expression is to you. It's valid to them, and when you share that perspective, you "see" them.

---

[1] Rosenberg, Marshall. *Non-Violent Communication.* PuddleDancer Press, 2015. ISBN # 978-1892005281

By acknowledging their expression, you are making their feelings, concerns, doubts, and fears feel safe. Acknowledgment isn't pandering, sucking up, or indulging your audience's less-than-desirable behavior. It is a positive response that facilitates a calm, productive discussion. And it is *not* happening enough during meetings.

Whenever someone asks me a question, even a challenging or disagreeable one, I always acknowledge it first with:

- "Thank you for asking! Happy to answer. . ."
- "Well, that one makes me think! Let's see. . ."
- "What an insightful question. I hadn't thought of it that way!"

All I'm doing here is making my first response agreeable, which only leads to good things.

The second step is validation. One of the most potent phrases in the English language is, "I get it." These three magic words demonstrate your understanding and compassion for someone's experience. Other iterations are "I can see why you'd be interested in that," or even a simple "That makes sense." This lowers the wall of resistance in others and makes them receptive to what you have to say next.

Next, I respond using a mini-decision tree model with these criteria:

- If I know the answer
- If I don't know the answer
- If I know that what they're saying is incorrect

If I know the answer, I acknowledge them first and then deliver the answer in the friendliest way possible, evaluating whether they're on board. I answer as simply as possible because perhaps the way I explained something the first time didn't land with them.

The trickier moments as a speaker come when you don't know the answer. Here is the most calming piece of wisdom I can offer if you're feeling like you're being boiled in a lobster pot:

Success is not knowing all the answers: it's how you handle yourself *when you don't.*

You are not Siri or Alexa or ChatGPT. You are a human being and perfectly entitled not to have an answer ready if it wasn't previously expressed. The trick here is to own that with complete confidence and not in a groveling, apologetic manner that indicates failure.

Here are some common challenging questions I've received as a presenter and heard from my students as well, paired with answers I've generally found successful:

Q: "What is the average [metric where you don't know the average]?"

A: "Thank you for asking (acknowledge)! I can see why you'd be interested in that (validate). I don't have that answer available at this moment, but I'm happy to follow up with you offline."

I do three important things here: I acknowledge them for asking, validate their question, and then disclose not knowing the answer in a matter-of-fact manner. I do this with confidence and without shame.

But there's an extra piece here: **I offered a chance to extend the conversation with them privately.** This allows me to build rapport with them outside of a potentially tense group dynamic, a key relationship-building strategy. I don't fear the opportunity to talk to them outside the meeting; I *welcome* it.

Here is another common, related question to the previous:

Q: Why isn't the [something is barely related to the meeting topic] working?

A: "Wow, what an insightful question (acknowledge)! I appreciate your concern (validate). I wonder if it might take us off-topic, and I want to make sure we get through the rest of our insights. I can stay behind to discuss, or I'm happy to take it offline with you."

This answer is similar, but it also delicately proposes that their question may not serve the greater audience. I invoke the earlier wisdom of Kevin Hillstrom in the appendix: go down the rabbit hole if it serves the wider audience or ask the group to weigh in if it doesn't, especially if time is running out.

Last, here's a comment that ties into the third branch of our decision tree model:

Q: "I think you missed something. . ." *or* **"That doesn't seem correct. . ."**

This prompts a two-part answer:

A: "Thank you for pointing that out! I hadn't thought of it that way."

(Now, either their comment makes sense to you or it doesn't, so respond accordingly and with patient, compassionate acknowledgment.) Continuing on:

"I'm curious about this perspective, as it doesn't quite line up with what we've seen. Can you tell me more about that?"

Notice I didn't rebut their viewpoint but, rather, inquired more deeply into it with curiosity.

Curiosity, as you've seen since Act I, is a powerful force in conscious communication. It casts aside the ego, lays down the sword, and makes us receptive to alternative ideas and perspectives. Rebuttal closes the field of communication, while curiosity *opens* it.

I realize those answers can feel risky to deliver to an executive or client. If so, consider enlisting a senior team member to step in if the meeting is in danger of derailment.

Becoming more elastic around why certain people do and say certain things is not only the key to business meeting serenity, but pretty much the key to all relationship serenity. What you choose to do with that space in the moment is a pivotal decision. In the timeless words of Indiana Jones's Grail Knight, *choose wisely.*

Chapter Recap

- Difficult and challenging remarks are often a product of unmet needs, which can be served with simple explanations and compassionate curiosity.
- It's not whether you know all the answers; it's how you handle things when you don't.
- "Tell me more" (curiosity) is a powerful phrase for getting under the hood of what your audience is trying to express.

Beast Mode Techniques for Maximum Audience Engagement

33

"The size of your audience doesn't matter. What's important is that your audience is listening."

—Randy Pausch

Several years ago, I was pinged by my fellow analytics expert and dear friend Tim Wilson (aka Gilligan on Data aka The Grumpy Cat of Analytics) to do something I'd never done before: to co-present a session at a popular analytics conference. I tend to be a lone rider on stage, so this was a stretch mission for me. Since we were sharing a time slot, it meant I had to drastically cut content from my signature keynote.

The issue was, I didn't cut deep enough and realized this *during* the session. There was no clock in the room, and my screen was too far away to keep the time.

Suddenly, Tim called out to inform me that we had gone over our time limit—like, not a little, but *way* over time. I nearly froze in shock; this had never happened to me before. I apologized to the audience and sped through my remaining content. Luckily, the audience was quite forgiving and responded warmly to our closing.

Nevertheless, I left feeling down on myself; as a professional speaker, it's a big no-no to run over. I deeply respect my audience's time and the conference organizer's agenda. But there was a silver lining peeking its way out of my raincloud: I didn't notice I was over time because no one had got up and left.

The next day, I conducted a post-mortem on my talk. Playing back the mental tape, I made two observations.

First, I needed to prepare more effectively to streamline my content and keep a clock nearby when there wasn't one available. I did not want to earn a reputation for blowing past my time slot. But the second learning hit home in a big way.

My audience had lost track of time and didn't get up to leave.

For most conference sessions I've attended, a certain percentage of the audience typically "defects" in the last 10 minutes or so. If the presentation is especially boring, sometimes you'll see an exodus as early as halfway through.

Audience movement is an excellent gauge of a presenter's ability to hold attention. If I see a lot of movement in the middle of my session, I know that something isn't working. I now believe I know what it is.

When we think of social gatherings like parties, weddings, and concerts, notice that they center around one thing: entertainment. Not unlike books, movies, and songs, which are all forms of entertainment, agreed?

As I went deeper into my presentation journey, I pondered: the corporate meeting is one of few social gatherings with no entertainment of any kind. Could this provide a clue as to why we despise meetings so much?

What would happen if we incorporated some elements of cinematic entertainment in our meetings? Could that potentially lead to longer attention spans and better engagement?

I went on to study various cinematic storytelling techniques to learn what keeps audiences on the edge of their seats. Curious about what I found? Read on and you'll see!

Two Questions Your Audience Is Silently Asking You

Psst. . .I have a secret. All the information in this book will benefit you not only in the conference room but on the conference stage as well. There is something I notice in most conference sessions I attend: the content is usually quality, and the topics are relevant to the audience. There's a lot of brainpower on those stages!

And yet, I find myself walking away, time and time again, without a clear understanding of what I was supposed to walk away with. I feel unchanged and uninspired. Here's the thing:

The more and more presentations we sit through and aren't moved or changed or inspired by them, the more of our life we never get back.

That's not how we want our audience to feel about our sessions, right? During my presentation journey, I identified three important questions our audience is silently asking us when they show up to the room.

If you answer these questions for your audience, I guarantee you will be blown away by their response. Let's dive in!

Audience Question #1: Why Am I Here?

As in, why should I come to your session, especially if I have a choice between you and someone else? Conferences are busy, distracting places and often have simultaneous session tracks, so why should I choose you? Why is your session the best investment of my time?

Often, a well-meaning and knowledgeable presenter gets up on stage and projects slides, yet their content doesn't speak *to* the audience. They transmit information, not facilitate transformation. Answering this question well separates *talkers* from *speakers*.

Just as companies and products survive by having a crisp and clear unique value proposition, so does your session. Crystallize it before you deliver. Because the last question you want to hear an audience member ask someone else at your session is, "Why am I here?"

Audience Question #2: What Can I Do Differently Starting Tomorrow?

It sure is nice to hear that someone thought your session was "great" or "amazing." But for me, as a presenter, I want to know that I hit my mark. I want to know *how* my presentation will help them in the future. That's why I pack my sessions with practical tools that people can get started with right away, because I often find most conference sessions don't leave me with anything to do.

So whenever someone tells me they enjoyed the session, I reply with a gracious thank-you and one or more probing questions like these:

- "What's the one thing you're going to do differently starting tomorrow?"
- "What's your biggest takeaway?"
- "What's something that you learned that you didn't know before?"

Doing this has several benefits: first, you show you genuinely care that they got value from your talk. Next, it helps you understand what insight, tool, practice, resource, or mindset made a lasting impression.

Make your presentation goal that they have something to try right away. The trick is learning how to present it in a way that they're going to remember and integrate into their work. Focus on these two inquiries, and your next session will undoubtedly rank as memorable, actionable, and inspirational.

How to Invoke Suspense

There is a powerful and underutilized cinematic technique that is also incredibly simple. But you must have the courage to try it.

I'm going to use it on you right now.

Would you like to know what it is?

I'll bet you do. . .

[Waits, leans forward, which prompts you to lean forward.]

It's. . .making you wait! Was that a weird and tense reading moment or what? And it's exactly how I planned it, by invoking suspense! Suspense is a fundamental storytelling device; whether it's the beginning of the next episode in a high-octane television series like *24* or the simple turn of a page in a children's bedtime story, we are a species who loves to hate to wait. Yet, it's sorely missing from business presentations.

Invoking suspense by making an audience wait to hear what you say next is extremely effective for two reasons.

- For those who are listening, waiting triggers suspense, which activates the brain.
- For those who *aren't* listening, the momentary pause alerts their brain to pay attention and then triggers suspense.

In an article by Kim Eckart of the University of Washington, she explains how anticipation works to activate the brain through an executive function called *selective attention*.

"Selective attention — the ability to focus on a specific thought or task at the expense of others — is an executive function skill related directly to anticipation, because it involves knowing what to expect of an event, however small, and how to respond to it."[1]

This means that anticipation grabs attention so that an audience can prepare a response, which diverts them from anything else in that moment (selective attention).

If you're curious, that little waiting game was inspired by my friend Nir Eyal, neuroscience expert and bestselling author of *Hooked* and *Indistractable*. I once watched him use this exact technique to great effect at a digital marketing conference, and I never forgot the audience's heightened attention.

Podcast Sound Byte: Nir Eyal (Ep. 047) Neuroscience Expert and Bestselling Author of *Hooked* and *Indistractable*

On his signature "Make Them Wait" technique:

"The idea I was trying to impart when I "made them wait" during my session was around variable rewards. Variable rewards are this very old concept that comes from operant conditioning. In the 1950s, the psychologist B.F. Skinner took pigeons and he put them in a little box called the Skinner Box and he gave the pigeons this little disc to pick up.

"And every time they picked up the disc, they would get a little reward, a little food pellet. And at first, he could train these pigeons to peck at the disc as long as the pigeons were hungry. But then, he ran out of these food pellets, so he started to give them to the pigeons intermittently.

"One time, the pigeon would get the food pellet. The next time, they wouldn't. What he found was that when he gave pellets on a variable schedule of reinforcement, the rate of response where these pigeons pecked at the disc increased when there was a variable reward as opposed to a fixed schedule of reinforcement.

---

[1] www.washington.edu/news/2018/12/12/attention-please-anticipation-of-touch-takes-focus-executive-skills

"I wanted to demonstrate to folks how to create desire. The way I did this was to ask this question: "Would you like to know how to manufacture desire?"

"And then I went silent and felt the tension build in the room. It's only 10 seconds, but it feels like I'm silent for 5 minutes. Everybody is sitting there staring at you. What is he going to say next? Why isn't he talking? Did he forget his lines? What's the answer?

"And it turns out that the waiting is the answer. The crowd has now received a variable reward. There's uncertainty and mystery in that long pause.

"And yes, they are holding on to every word you're saying."

So the question is, how can you leverage the cinematic power of suspense in your business readouts? If you can't wait, read on!

Three Ways to Make Them Wait

Suspense is an extremely effective tool for keeping an audience's attention engaged, and there are several options to use it in even the most mundane work meetings.

#1: Before a Big Reveal

As you read earlier, one of my favorite techniques is to split one of my baby data stories over multiple slides. I'll set the stage by showing a data point with an expected result that isn't shocking and then reveal a more surprising insight.

I might say something like, "When we initially looked at our paid search campaign, we weren't surprised; everything looked fine and as expected. But when we looked a little deeper at our outdoor furniture campaign, we found something that surprised us."

And then. . .I make them wait for a long beat. One that will feel almost too long, which will snap them back to attention.

Then I advance to the next slide and reveal that the landing page is losing 80 percent of our visitors and needs immediate remediation. Now, no one misses that point because they were side-shopping at Zappos instead of listening to me!

#2: After a Big Reveal

The second technique I use is to make them wait right after a big reveal. I learned this from *Good Charts*. In it, Scott Berinato says to use this in a situation where you might have an important insight that you want to land hard with your audience, like a proverbial piano falling from the sky.

In the paid search example, it would go like this:

- I still set the stage the same way with "When we looked a little deeper at our outdoor furniture campaign, we found something that surprised us."
- This time, I foreshadow that the situation is dire, with something like, "We learned something that we believe is critical for us to address."
- I click to advance to the next slide immediately and announce that "We found that 80 percent of our landing page visitors abandoned the page right away."
- **Now I take a dramatic pause.** Boom! That is a big problem, and the pause afterward allows the gravity of the information to sink in the way I desire.

#3: Play "Guess the Outcome"

The third way I make my audience wait is to have them guess at a particular result or outcome before I reveal the answer. This is a fantastic tool if you are in the landing page or conversion rate optimization fields and you're running lots of tests.

What you can say is, "OK, here were our two best contenders. Who would like to take a guess at which one was the winner?" or "Show of hands for A as the winner? B?"

This strategy leverages gamification to increase attention; the audience will love their playful involvement because play activates the brain's signaling systems and elevates the nervous system (in a good way).[2] You relish the pause and ask, "Everyone ready for the answer?"

---

[2]Wang S, Aamodt S. Play, stress, and the learning brain. *Cerebrum*. 2012;2012:12.

You then reveal the answer slide and triumphantly announce the winner! The audience's attention is now your invisible trophy for such stellar storytelling.

As you can see, there's a lot more to data storytelling than even the actual story and the data. Doing this right is truly an art and a science, but it's not hard. You just have to know the techniques and put them into practice.

So, how do you know you're doing this right?

When your audience loses track of time. That's how you'll know.

Chapter Recap

- There are two questions to ask before every presentation that will ensure its success.
- Invoking suspense by making your audience wait is a powerful tool for snapping the audience to attention.

Send an Effective Presentation Handout

34

"Communication is about getting others to adopt your point of view. . .if all you want to do is create a file of fact or figures, then cancel the meeting and send in a report."

—Seth Godin

At some point during my keynotes and workshops, there is a 100 percent probability someone asks this question: "With so many more slides, how do we handle creating printable presentation handouts?"

This is an understandable dilemma considering having learned the "slid-ea" philosophy, which can significantly expand the number of slides in their decks. Presentation handouts or leave-behinds are a globally required artifact of business presentations. They serve to inform an offline audience who either wants a reference of the meeting or wasn't present for it.

With larger decks, however, the dilemma inevitably becomes how such a document will communicate without you, the narrator. My answer to this question is best illustrated through this real-life fable.

Never Goad a Godin

When you're a marketer *and* a presentation enthusiast, watching marketing deity Seth Godin[1] present to an intimate audience of 100 is as close to a professional religious experience as you can get. I was gifted such a privilege many years ago while attending a digital marketing forum. Unsurprisingly, Godin the Great stole the show with his musings on the death of mass marketing and the birth of the individualized tribe. As the iridescent gold dust settled from his talk, I was shocked when they opened it for Q&A. I could not think of an elevated enough question to ask Seth. But *someone* did.

A young gentleman in the front excitedly raised his hand and asked, "Will you send us your presentation slides?" Cue exasperated gasps, crashing plates, and cars screeching to a halt. Well, I might be overdramatizing a bit. It was awkward, though.

I observed Mr. Godin's inscrutable expression. The audience member may as well have asked him to please pass the jelly. It was not an unusual question; it's been asked in every meeting, conference presentation, workshop, and webinar I've ever attended.

Yet I knew his question had broken the First Rule of Slide Club: **you don't ask Seth Godin to send you his slides.** Seth's response was so spot-on that it became a teachable moment for all in attendance. He said something to the effect of, "I don't send people my slides. I designed them so that without me, you wouldn't understand what they're saying."

Boom.

That's why whenever I'm asked the handout question, my answer is always the same: I don't email my live slides. **This is because I believe that the presentation handout is at the root cause of the presentation zombie apocalypse.**

Why Sending Your Slides Doesn't Work

We already know that we never learned how to design live presentation slides. But I believe that handout question comes up so often because most of us learned to create live presentation slides *with the handout in mind.*

---

[1]Seth Godin. (2023, April 17). In *Wikipedia*. https://en.wikipedia.org/wiki/Seth_Godin

When we create one document to serve both our live attendees and our email recipients, we underserve both audiences. A simple and well-designed live presentation deck effectively guides the audience through the narrative. But simple and well-designed live slides are not explanatory enough for a self-driven reader.

On the flip side, you now see that overcrowded, text-heavy slides designed as a handout will lose the audience's attention and undermine their live experience. That is why I try to avoid distributing my original live presentation slides after the session.

If you must choose to invest your effort into the live deck or the handout, choose the live deck. I believe the squeeze with the most juice is the live presentation because that is where you truly get to shine as a partner with your teams and clients. Unfortunately, we as an overworked corporate collective have succumbed to presenting and emailing text-heavy presentation slides as standard practice.

Today, we talk through reports instead of delivering presentations.

This middle-of-the-road report is what Nancy Duarte has dubbed the "slideument" (a creepy cross between slides and a document). As Godin explains in *Presentation Zen*,

> "Slides are slides. Documents are documents. They aren't the same thing. . .the slideument isn't effective, and it isn't efficient, and it isn't pretty. Attempting to have slides serve as both projected visuals and as stand-alone handouts makes for bad visuals and bad documentation."[2]

And as Nancy Duarte agrees in *slide:ology*: "The audience will either read your slides or listen to you. They will not do both. So ask yourself this: is it more effective if they listen, or more effective if they read?" I'm bringing in the heavy artillery on this point for a reason: out of all the unproductive habits I'm asking you to reconsider, this one is maybe the biggest.

So what's my solution to this quandary? **You create two documents: one tailored for the live show and one for the no-shows.**

The Double Document Doctrine

When I share this answer with workshop participants, it garners me Guinness Book–long eye-rolls. I believe it's because this conjures visions of creating two

---

[2]Reynolds, Garr. *Presentation Zen*. New Riders, 2019. ISBN # 978-0135800911

documents entirely from scratch amid being buried in mountains of number-crunching and wackadoodle deadlines. Not to worry; that is *not* what I'm suggesting.

I devised a technique for creating both documents from the same live presentation document. In fact, this method leverages a step I had you complete during the **Conceptualize** phase!

Remember how I had you speak through your talking points way back in Act I? Or even record and transcribe them? Well, not only did those become your Presenter View prompts during the presentation, but your notes will also now become your handout narrator! This is one example of how there is no wasted work in my process; I craft my live story in the very beginning, which becomes the offline story for those who couldn't be there.

This method requires some advance planning and carving out just 30–45 minutes of your time to create both deliverables well.

The Practical Presentation Handout Solution

Remember that reading is an entirely different consumption environment for your audience, where they can be presented with more information at once because they aren't also trying to listen to you speak. This is important: this procedure leverages the Notes View of PowerPoint or Google Slides. *Do not* use the Handouts view. The Handouts view is ironically horrible for handouts.

Here's the method. . .

Adjust the handout layout using the Notes Master view. In this view, you can change the default font family, color, and size, as well as add necessary information elements such as page numbers (recommended). You can also adjust the size of the slide on the Notes Pages and change the page orientation. See Figure 34.1.

Here is where you can add your company logo to every slide to comply with corporate information distribution policies. Here, and only here (*not* on your live slides, if you please).

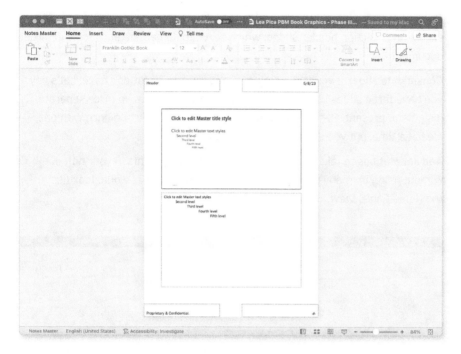

FIGURE 34.1 Notes Master view in PowerPoint for Mac

However, the Notes Master is quite unlike the Slide Master in that you have limited formatting flexibility outside of what I've listed. Although you can add shapes and lines or remove the slide border in the Notes Master, the changes will not show on your Notes pages. A bit of false advertising, but you can always add those elements to the individual Notes pages.

Next, we're going to transform your individual slides into handout pages. Click Close Master, go to the first slide, and then choose View ➢ Notes Page.

For every slide, rewrite and format the notes you wrote using bold, numbered lists, and bullet points (they are acceptable here). Make it read like a well-organized narrative for the audience's benefit. Remember, you won't be present to guide them, so write your notes in a professional yet conversational manner.

Add certain slides for follow-up questions or requested data that weren't available during the live meeting.

Remove certain slides if a separately printed page doesn't provide value. The exception is section header slides, which serve to demarcate each topic in larger documents.

Consolidate slides if you feel a single idea is too sparse for one page. Let's say you have three slides using the same chart because you have three separate insights to present. Remember, you want to pace your live audience with one idea at a time, but you don't need to do that here.

Add annotations to take them through corresponding points in your notes without using up many pages. Figure 34.2 shows what that would look like in the Notes Pages view.

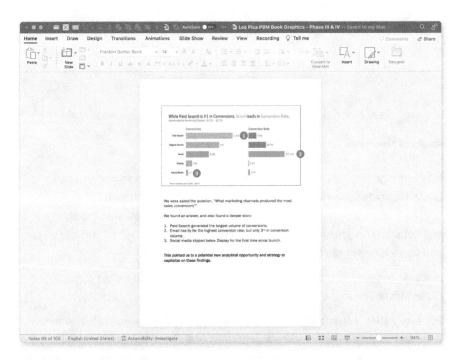

FIGURE 34.2 Notes Pages view of a consolidated handout slide in PowerPoint for Mac

Note that all the additional images and annotations you add to the Notes Page *can be seen only in Notes view* (they won't display during presentation mode).

When you're finished, convert the deck into a printable PDF and you're done! It may take a few tries to nail the final product, but once you get the hang of it, you'll never sweat the handout step again.

Final Thoughts on Presentation Handouts

I hope this chapter provided just one solution to this age-old dilemma. I'm by no means saying it's the best or only way; this process is not set-it-and-forget-it and it does require some extra elbow grease.

But it is a practical method that takes advantage of the built-in steps in my presentation process. I've also used this approach to create conference presentation handouts for session attendees to great effect.

Considering how pervasive this dilemma is for practitioners and professional speakers, **doing this right is worth the time it takes**.

Chapter Recap

- The presentation handout is often the focus of creating live presentation decks and is possibly at the root of the present-pocalypse.
- You can create an effective handout by creating an offline document using the Notes View of your live presentation slides and speaking notes.

TIP

Visit the Resource Center for a step-by-step tutorial and a downloadable handout template.

Act IV Intermission

You're nearing the end of your training journey, my apprentice. Before our time together is complete, let's review how you can learn to **Deliver** with absolute mastery:

- Master the two key areas of presentation delivery.
    - **Master you** by preparing and rehearsing, managing your nerves, and refining your speaking skills and body language.
    - **Master your audience** by learning conscious communication skills.
    - **Prepare a separate handout** perfectly tailored to an offline reading environment.
- Take the rest of the day off for a tremendous job making it this far. . .starting at 5 p.m.!

This Is the End. . .and Just the Beginning

As we bring our journey together to a curtain close, you may have mixed feelings right now. Perhaps you're buzzing with excitement over your rockin' new toolset. Or perhaps you're feeling overwhelmed, frustrated, or doubtful about how you're going to put all of this into practice.

I find that my course and workshop students experience a mix of both. But I observe they also experience immense relief. Something along the lines of, "I knew this whole time that something wasn't right, but I had no idea what it was."

I liken this reaction to receiving a long-awaited diagnosis of a chronic illness. Imagine finally discovering the answers to an affliction that has caused years of pain and suffering. Aside from feeling relief, you've gained a treatment plan because you now understand the root cause.

And, as with learning the diagnosis, the first questions usually asked are, "Can I really resolve this? Will things actually get better?" I believe the answer is yes!

When I stepped on that very first tech conference stage many years ago, facing down an audience of hundreds of industry practitioners, experts, and even my former boss, I was wracked with fear and doubt. Every limiting belief I had threatened to swallow me whole. Yet, I marched toward my deepest fears armed with passion, skills, and a faith that I had the power to facilitate a transformation for the audience.

I could have never anticipated the amazing places that bold step would lead me to. Now, that step has led me to you. I have no doubt that the transformations I've witnessed in the practitioners and leaders I've trained are possible for you too.

You now hold my formula for _presenting beyond measure_. Find and illuminate the story of your customers, your stakeholders, your leadership, and you. Let the emotional power of those stories fuel your insights, and there is no limit to where you'll go.

It's my deepest belief that if we as a global data community are all empowered with the skills of human-centered presentation and data storytelling, meeting productivity and the progress of organizations will make a quantum leap forward.

The encouraging part is that none of these practices are terribly complex or difficult. They're quite simple. But they do require diligence to learn, practice, and master.

So where do you go from here? Well, you certainly have a lot of shiny new tools in your toolbelt. Let's step through it one more time:

- **Phase I: Conceptualize** your presentation content by assessing audience needs, selecting the right insights, and organizing it into a cohesive framework.
- **Phase II: Design Slides** using simple and intentional design techniques.
- **Phase III: Visualize Data** with storytelling mechanics and visualization design best practices.
- **Phase IV: Deliver** your information with confidence, ease, and the agility to navigate challenging environments.

Make Small Moves

Remember that it's taken months, years, or even decades to adopt the presentation habits you've acquired in the workforce. So be patient with yourself in untangling this wiring and laying down pathways for more productive practices. Do this right now:

Pull out a notebook or piece of paper and write down three things you plan on doing differently tomorrow.

Whether it's the Boxes framework, using color to emphasize data, or obliterating uptalk, think of whatever stood out most. Now make those three things your main target practices for the next presentation. After that, target three more things for the next one if you feel like you're getting the hang of the first three.

Give yourself the latitude to make gradual changes over time, mastering each new technique or principle as you go. This will also help ease your audience into what could be a dramatically different way of seeing your insights.

Take the Next Step

There is a big difference between reading about data storytelling and decisively implementing data storytelling. Remember that reading is at the bottom of the cone of learning, so here's how we can work together to go to the next level:

- **Practitioners:** Visit my comprehensive Resource Center for this book (https://LeaPica.com/pbm-resource-center) where you'll find an opportunity to upgrade learning experience with the online course version of this book (`https://LeaPica.com/bootcamp`) and coaching options.

- **Leaders:** If you manage a team of practitioners, are responsible for learning and development, or lead teams at a marketing or analytics agency and you are ready to ramp up the storytelling firepower of your staff with live training, reach out at `https://LeaPica.com/Workshops` to collaborate.

- **Speakers:** If you work as a consultant or service provider in the data and digital marketing field and want to gain greater exposure and opportunities as a conference speaker, drop me a note at `https://LeaPica.com/Contact` for private coaching.

Learn Through Teaching

According to the cone of learning, the second most active step in retaining what you've learned is by teaching it to others. Share these principles with your colleagues, help your boss with their next presentation, or host a lunch-and-learn meeting to cement them in your mind and your practice.

Plus, this gives you a chance to demonstrate your new presentation prowess and establish yourself as the resident data storytelling expert!

Parting Thoughts

Coming into the field of data, we as practitioners were never given the tools to succeed at presenting data effectively. That doesn't mean those tools can't help you make a massive impact starting today.

Remember this: when you're in the 11th hour of that next campaign readout and you feel like it's all going to hell in a handbasket, I want you to write this across your heart:

You **are your presentation, not your PowerPoint.**

You are the most important ingredient to your audience's success. You are the reason they are in that room, in the flesh, or on their screen. So, create a presentation that meets their needs and showcases what you are capable of, and well-deserved glory is yours.

I'll leave you with a little bit of wisdom from the late, great Aldous Huxley that has served me well:

"Facts do not cease to exist just because they are ignored."

While that may be true, I think getting ignored sucks. It is my sincerest hope that this book has planted new seeds of thought and action in your mind that will help you prevent bad things from happening to your good data.

You work so hard to locate and distill your valuable insights. It's time to stand up and pave the way for your hard work to work harder for your customers, your stakeholders, your clients, your organization, and, most of all, for you.

Congratulations for taking this bold step forward in service as a star storyteller.

And always remember: viz responsibly, my friend.

Namaste,

Lea

Did You Enjoy This Book?

Congratulations on completing your journey through this book! I truly hope you'll put all this new information to good use.

If you can spare a minute, it would mean the world to me if you would review the book online. Honest reviews help other readers like you find the right book for their needs.

A million thanks in advance! Please visit:

https://LeaPica.com/BookReview

And please send any comments, edits, questions, or feedback to:

https://LeaPica.com/Contact

In deep gratitude,

Lea

Resources

Data Presentation Process Documents

Here is a list of each of the sandbox worksheets and reference books mentioned throughout each phase of the presentation process that you can also find in the online Resource Center.

Phase I: Conceptualize

- ❏ Stakeholder Savvy Quadrant
- ❏ Throughline Generator
- ❏ Data Story Narrative Arc
- ❏ SMART Recommendations
- ❏ Presenting by Boxes Framework

Phase II: Design Slides

- ❏ Typography Cheat Sheet
- ❏ Imagery Sources
- ❏ Slide Doctor Exercise

Phase III: Visualize Data (PICA Protocol)

- ❏ PICA Protocol Worksheet
- ❏ Office Chart Detox Checklists
- ❏ Google Slides/Sheets Chart Detox Checklists
- ❏ Lea's Chart Chooser

Phase IV: Deliver

- ❏ Nerves Journaling
- ❏ Technical Pre-Flight Checklists
- ❏ Meeting Kickoff Superhero Script

Recommended Reading, Resources, and Experts

This is a comprehensive list of recommended data storytelling books and authors, compiled into one convenient library list and organized by topic.

Data Storytelling

- Scott Berinato: *Good Charts* and *The Good Charts Workbook*
- Cole Nussbaumer Knaflic: *Storytelling with Data* and *Let's Practice Storytelling with Data!*
- Janine Kurnoff & Lee Lazarus: *Everyday Business Storytelling*
- Brent Dykes: *Effective Data Storytelling*
- Nancy Duarte: *DataStory*
- Chris & Zach Gemignani: *Data Fluency*
- Chip & Dan Heath: *Made to Stick*

Presentation

- Garr Reynolds: *Presentation Zen* and *Presentation Zen: Design*
- Nancy Duarte: *Resonate* and *slide:ology*
- Cole Nussbaumer Knaflic: *Storytelling with You*
- Jonathan Schwabish: *Better Presentations*
- John C. Medina: *Brain Rules*
- Sarah Hyndman: *Why Fonts Matter*

Data Visualization

- Stephen Few: *Show Me the Numbers* and *Now You See It*
- Dona M. Wong: *The WSJ Guide to Information Graphics*

- Edward Tufte: *The Visual Display of Quantitative Information*
- Alberto Cairo: *How Charts Lie* and *The Truthful Art*
- Jonathan Schwabish: *Better Data Visualizations*
- Kristin Solsuski: *Data Visualization Made Simple*
- Stephanie Evergreen: *Effective Data Visualization*
- Nathan Yau: *Visualize This*
- Andy Kriebel & Eva Murray: *Makeover Monday*
- Steve Wexler: *The Big Picture*

Delivery

- Chris Anderson: *TED Talks*
- Dale Carnegie: *The Quick and Easy Guide to Effective Speaking*
- Dale Carnegie: *Stand and Deliver*
- Carmine Gallo: *Talk Like TED*

Dashboards

- Stephen Few: *Information Dashboard Design*
- Andy Cotgreave, Jeffrey Shaffer, & Steve Wexler: *The Big Book of Dashboards*
- Depict Data Studio (blog of Ann K. Emery)

Closing Credits

I humbly submit my declaration of eternal gratitude to all those who helped me manifest this creation.

To **Gavin**, my cherished son, the existence of whom I owe this entire beautiful experience of pursuing my life's passion and service to this community. Thank you for being my spiritual teacher and force for positive change in my life.

To **Mom** and **Dad**, my biggest cheerleaders. Thank you for every class, lesson, camp, and encouragement you provided to help give me the skills and resolve to make this book happen.

To **Shai**, my partner-in-time, without whom this book would have never come to life. Your unwavering devotion and support throughout all my fears, doubts, and limiting beliefs are the reason I could bring my work to the world in a bigger way.

To **Skyla** and **Noah**, my beloved spirit children who brought so much levity and laughter when I was pulling my hair out during editing.

To **Krissy**, my best friend, cat meme soul sister, and light along the dark path to authorship. Thank you for the repeated kicks in the pants to give this project the time and attention it desperately needed.

To **Jim**, **Kezia**, and the whole team at Wiley for boosting this literary effort through the finish line after years of delays and imposter syndrome!

To **Tim Wilson** and **Jim Sterne**, you know what you did (see dedication).

To **Seth Godin**, **Garr Reynolds**, **Nancy Duarte**, **Stephen Few**, and all aforementioned data storytelling luminaries for igniting the gift of story in so many of us, and whose work was the torch that shone a light on the seemingly perilous path of presenting.

To **Ann K. Emery, Jonathan Schwabish, Cole Nussbaumer Knaflic, Brent Dykes**, and **Kristen Solsuski** for your inspirational leadership in the field of visual data communication and entrepreneurship.

To **Rand Fishkin**, the most approachable and supportive industry celebrity I've ever met and for your radical acceptance and advocacy of all those who wish to be exactly who they are.

To **Larry Freed, Eric Head,** and **Eric Feinberg** for taking a chance on a wet-behind-the-ears mid-level analyst with big data dreams and inviting her to a formative conference speaking experience.

To **Marilee Yorchak, DeAnna Morrison,** and **Adrienne Segundo,** fabulous femmes of the Digital Analytics Association. Your staunch support through the years was and is a gift!

To **"Dr. Joe" Perez,** one of the most excitably passionate and talented data storytelling speakers I've met and a staunch supporter of my mission.

To **Jeff Sauer,** analytics industry titan and the most caring business accountability I could have asked for when I was just starting out.

To **Moe Kiss,** for our conversation halfway around the world from my home that somehow made me feel completely at home. Watching your meteoric rise has been one of the great joys of my career. Go on, girl!

To **Branko Kral,** for your unexpected professional and personal friendship. Your zest for life and commitment to excellence is a huge source of inspiration.

To **Kevin Ertell,** whose unforgettable keynote at the Foresee Summit planted the seed of inspiration that I could get up there too and share my passion with the world.

To **Jessica Koster,** for being to this day the most benevolent and badass boss lady I've had the privilege of working for. May all employees bloom under the care of someone like you!

To **Krista Seiden, Kate Strachnyi, Michelle Kiss, Alli Torban, Christina Stathopolous, Valerie Kroll, Mico Yuk,** and all the other rockstar Women in Analytics who are paving the way for talented femme fatales to take their rightful place in the field of tech and data.

To **Ian McCammon,** analytics practitioner extraordinaire, whose generous donation of time helped make this book all it could to be in the highest service.

To **Emily, Hal, Bianca, Holly, Francine, Michael, Chas, Hussein,** and everyone at the Scribe Tribe who never stopped believing I could do this book.

To my **invaluable podcast guests,** for taking the time from busy schedules to share your boundless wealth of wisdom with my eager and passionate listener community.

To my **cherished workshop clients**, for the dedication you show toward equipping your teams with the tools and mindsets they need to realize their destiny as unstoppable strategic partners and agents of change.

To my **tenacious conference event organizers**, who are often the greatest unsung heroes of creating these transformative learning and networking experiences.

Finally, to all the **incredibly talented and passionate data and marketing practitioners** who've inspired this fantastical journey and continue to support my work. You are my greatest teachers, and I bow to your brilliance.

Profound thanks to you all.

About the Author

Lea Pica is a data analyst turned data storytelling advocate, creator of the PICA Protocol, workshop facilitator, and international speaker who teaches thousands of data and marketing practitioners around the world how to present data and inspire action. Her mission is to transform presentation snoozefests into vehicles for change using the synergistic power of neuroscience, storytelling, emotion, persuasion, visualization, design, and effective communication.

Lea is a seasoned data analytics practitioner and digital marketer with more than 13 years of experience building search and analytics practices for agencies, publishers, and top retail and finance companies. She facilitates team workshops for both Fortune 500 brands and marketing and analytics agencies and hosts the industry-acclaimed Present Beyond Measure Show podcast.

She is a frequent keynote speaker at global live and virtual marketing and analytics conferences such as Digital Summit, MeasureSummit, and ConversionXL Live. When not nerding out on data storytelling, she enjoys cooking Paleo, yoga and meditation, and dominating at karaoke and laser tag on family game nights.

Index